4-3-64
6-24-64

POET IN EXILE: EZRA POUND

POET
IN EXILE

EZRA POUND

by

NOEL STOCK

BARNES & NOBLE, INC. · NEW YORK
Publishers · Booksellers · Founded 1873

First published
in the United States
1964
BARNES & NOBLE, INC.
105 Fifth Avenue, New York 3

for
W . F .

Printed in Great Britain

1260047
Contents

Acknowledgements

MY thanks are due to Mr Ezra Pound, his daughter Mary de Rache-wiltz, and Mrs Dorothy Pound, for allowing me access to the Pound papers and library at Brunnenburg; to that patient and indefatigable bibliographer, Mr Donald Gallup, for his expert help, precise and to the point; to Patricia Hutchins, for putting her knowledge of Ezra Pound's London years at my disposal; and to Mr Wally Martin, for information on the life and times of A. R. Orage. If Professor Hugh Kenner's early book *The Poetry of Ezra Pound* now seems inadequate, it is only fair to record here that in the years after the Second World War, when Ezra Pound's contribution to English Letters was almost completely overshadowed by politics, it was this work which pointed the way back to the Poundian texts. My thanks are due to the Trustees of the Bollingen Foundation for awarding me a Fellowship for 1961. I also wish to acknowledge that parts of this book have appeared in the following publications: *Modern Age* (Chicago), *The Texas Quarterly* (University of Texas), *Quadrant* (Sydney), and *X Quarterly* and *Agenda* (both of London).

For permission to quote from the published work of Ezra Pound I am indebted to the following:

For the U.K. and Commonwealth: the Committee for Ezra Pound (A. V. Moore, Redcot, Stockens Green, Knebworth, Herts.).

For Europe: the Princess de Rachewiltz (Brunnenburg, Tirolo, Merano, Italy).

For U.S.A. and Canada: New Directions, New York.

Uncollected early poem from the Hamilton College Literary Magazine and the Rimbaud translation: the Committee for Ezra Pound (H. P. Gleason, Boston).

Poems from the *Classic Anthology as Defined by Confucius*: (World rights except Commonwealth excluding Canada), reprinted by permission of the publishers, Harvard University Press, Cambridge, Mass., Copyright 1954, by the President and Fellows of Harvard College.

The publishers of the published writings of Ezra Pound quoted in this book are given in the bibliography on pages 261–2.

Preface

HALF a century after he first became known to the literary
public in London, the intellectual centre of the English-
speaking world, Ezra Pound is one of the best known and yet
least known of modern poets. He is read not as an important
figure in our literature, which he is, but in terms of theatrical
images. Some at least of the impetus for this state of affairs has
come from Pound himself—not Ezra Pound the poet whose work
is the main subject of this book, but Pound in the role of 'the
man who gets things done'. There followed a whole industry of
commentators ready to extend this image and turn him into a
one-man show in which he plays both the leading part and supporting roles, rings up the curtain, and even sells the programmes.
One of the few critics to concentrate on the work rather than the
actor was T. S. Eliot, who deftly pointed to some of Pound's
main weaknesses at a time when he might have benefited from
such criticism; but of later critics scarcely any seem to have taken
any real notice of what Eliot has said about his fellow-American
in a series of essays and lectures beginning with *Ezra Pound: His
Metric and Poetry* in 1917.

Much that has been written about Pound, in the way of final
judgement, has been based upon the study of part of his work
only. It is not necessary for the critic to read carefully every word
that Pound has written, but anyone wishing to make a large judgement must know how his work fits together; how his method
of thought affects his thinking on history, how his thinking on
history has affected the *Cantos*, and so forth. What Pound means
by a particular sentence sometimes depends upon our understanding one or more of his main aims. But much criticism pretending
to depth and finality stems from a haphazard reading of only
part of his work, including an excellent and entertaining but
sometimes very misleading selection of his letters, which is then
interpreted by way of assumptions based on the theatrical public
image.

The aim of this book is not to explain Pound's work but if possible to cut through the tangle of opinions, favourable or unfavourable prejudices and the various irrelevancies stemming from Pound and others, which prevent many a reader of goodwill from getting at the best of his work. This study began, in a sense, about sixteen years ago, when a friend put into my hands some lecture notes used at Melbourne University in which I saw some of Pound's poetry for the first time. Interest aroused led gradually to the reading of all the published work that I could lay hands on, collected and uncollected, and finally in 1959 to a long examination of Mr Pound's own books, magazines, papers and letters stored at Brunnenburg in Northern Italy. As a result I have been able to use in the following pages a great deal of material that is completely new or little known even among serious students of modern poetry. I have not, however, used such material for its own sake, or simply because it is new, but in order to supply fresh reinforcement for something already visible in the main current of Pound's work.

The disease of modern criticism (or criticism crossed with biography) which this study is designed to counteract may be illustrated by the following example. Almost every person who reads Pound is influenced, in varying degree, by the mental picture of a gay, bohemian American who strode purposefully across the London scene some forty or fifty years ago doing single-handed battle with England and English literature. This picture has some basis in reality, but if it is not balanced by other factors it twists the reader's view of an important phase in the history of English poetry. The truth is that after his arrival there in 1908 Pound enjoyed London immensely. It was absolutely a new world for him. He learnt there many essential things which he could not have learnt anywhere else at the time, for London, for good or for bad, was the intellectual capital; and even after he became involved in various literary and artistic 'revolutions' Pound was an accepted rebel who worked inside the system, not as a complete outsider. In April 1915, after *Imagisme*, after a year or more of *Vorticism*, after the first issue of *Blast*, the *Times Literary Supplement* was only one of a number of periodicals which praised Pound's *Cathay* for reasons which were quite sound even if not exhaustive. And for several years after this Pound continued to work against the prevailing system, but from the inside, as one who was interested in the past, present, and future of English literature. There is no doubt whatever that English literature in 1915 was in a sad state, but if Pound failed to become an arbiter of opinion it was not entirely because London was too stolid to appreciate his brilliance and what he had to offer, but partly at least because of something in his own character—a lack of prudence and humility—which threw up a barrier between him and his objective. In other words it is only by a careful understanding of biography that we have any chance, now, of eliminating the biographical confusion which overlays his essential work.

A similar misunderstanding has caused many people to misread various aspects of the *Cantos*. Some, for example, while they have not approved of many of Pound's opinions, have looked upon him as a victim of American society. They have seen his behaviour during the 1920's and 1930's as illustrating the hopeless struggle of the artist against the horrors of modern industrialism; or they have seen his 'bitterness' as stemming from America's refusal to recognize one of her greatest writers. And this of course is true, up to a point. The American education system, which failed to make use of Pound's talents, was, I have no doubt, very imperfect; but we must also recognize that Pound's temperament and character were against him. Had he gone about it properly he might have made himself an honourable literary career in the United States, or even in England. But he refused promising offers from both quarters. During the 1930's, to mention but one instance, he was offered a teaching job which he declined because he did not want to be tied down to literature. He wanted to be free to teach economics and his Social Credit theories, to expound the Autobiography of President Martin Van Buren, and to draw lessons from Chinese history, Canon Law, and Confucius. Let us by all means admit the faults of America, but by themselves they do not explain Pound's attitude to his country. Much of the strife in Pound's career has sprung from a revolutionary and anti-conservative element in his make-up which may be traced to the Enlightenment and nineteenth-century liberalism and science.

In an article published in 1912 we find examples of a 'mechanistic' and 'naturalistic' attitude to thought. He speaks of 'dynamic particles' of knowledge in such a way as to show that he is already beginning to endow the concrete world with some of the properties of thought which exist only in man as an intelligent and logical being. Man's thought may be limited but nevertheless it sets him apart and even his greatest leaps and intuitions start from, and in the end return to, his habit of logical thought.

Pound, as a child of the Enlightenment and the nineteenth century, with visions of the perfectibility of man always before him, in one form or another, even where his reason told him otherwise, failed to see that most of the knowledge we gather in a lifetime is for negative use rather than positive. He saw knowledge of the world, of man's soul, as part of a process of liberation; he did not see, or did not want to see, that most of this, if wisely used, is to enable us to know where our knowledge ends and to make more effective use of what we are competent to handle. Only, I think, when we have studied Pound's work in detail (taking account of Ezra Pound the man only when he interferes with Ezra Pound the poet and critic), and have weighed it against the tradition as a whole—not just the tail end of it—are we justified, if at all, in drawing a broad conclusion. The suggestion worked out in this book is that Pound's tragedy as a man of letters was in being born into a world which could offer him nothing to offset the extravagance of his mind: no system of thought worthy of the name, and no faith beyond a gentlemanly faith in the inevitable 'progress' of man. Pound accepted much of this world and at the same time revolted against it, but only in its own terms, so that his thought and work is, in a way, the plight of the modern Romantic incarnate. In a situation of increasing conformity, in which the old liberalism gradually merges with the absolute state and the law, Pound is two things at once, which are really stages in the same process. He is that very liberalism as it unconsciously becomes one of the things it thought it was opposing; and he is also that which gave birth to liberalism, namely 'private judgement'. He is the voice of 'private judgement', lost, and crying out in the twentieth century against a bewildering sea of matter and fact.

N. Stock

March 1963

CHAPTER I

Ezra Pound begins his Education

THE UNITY which binds the work of Ezra Pound is rooted in his early American years to a much greater extent than has hitherto been realized. My reason for treating this period of his life here is not that I am looking for an excuse to resurrect poetry and prose which Pound in his critical wisdom has cast away as not worth preserving, but in order to make clear certain things which have been obscured by those who have introduced, with great carelessness, irrelevant biography and psychology into the assessment of his work. The result has been a considerable piling-up over the years of only half-true assumptions about some of the essential history of modern poetry. Critics and historians have fed upon one another's assumptions, to produce in the end a number of thumping clichés, in which Pound—or what sometimes passes for his literary biography—plays a comparatively important part, to the neglect of his poetry, as poetry, and his contributions to other fields.

Literary biography, like history, has its dangers. It is almost irresistible at times, especially when it appears to illuminate some uncertain aspect of a poet's work; but this illumination is often deceptive, and biography is better left alone unless we are sure that it has direct reference to the main course of a poet's work. In this study I will try to confine myself to those aspects of Pound's life which are contained or referred to in his own writings, and throw light upon the unity of his work as a whole. And when I say 'unity of his work as a whole' I do not want to give the impression, which would be an entirely false one, that an examination of the poet's life—in this chapter, of his early American years and formal education—will explain the poetry which came later, for that work is, or is not, its own explanation, and no independent paraphrase or re-telling can enter into it. But what we may be able to do is to draw away some of the fixed ideas and the clouds of irrelevant opinion and half-truth which hamper the reader's approach to the poetry and sometimes darken his understanding of it. We are not going to dig into Pound's early years with the idea of synthesizing his 'state of mind', either then, or at a later and more controversial period of his life. What we are seeking are those things which helped to form the mind of Ezra Pound the poet; things, some of which, fifty years after he first read or heard about them at Philadelphia, Clinton or Crawfordsville, still seemed to him to be full of meaning or important milestones on the way.

Pound was born on 30 October 1885, the year in which Henry Adams began work on his *History of the United States of America during the Administrations of Jefferson and Madison.* It was a time when the old America was passing away and the new America, the one that is still with us, was finding her feet. The Civil War had brought many changes, not least those in the country's financial system; and about the time Pound was born the famous banker J. Pierpont Morgan began his reorganization of the American railroad system, which was the first step in the country's rise to leadership of the world of modern technology. Morgan's actual decision to change completely the whole structure of railway ownership and management was made during a trip to Europe in the early summer of 1885, when he came under pressure from dissatisfied investors in England. The close relation between Morgan's activities in the United States and the attitude of the English investor may be seen in the detailed examination of the American railroad problem in the London *Economist* of December 1885.

Pound was eight years old, living in Philadelphia, when Grover Cleveland was elected President in 1893. His father, Homer L. Pound, was an assayer at the Philadelphia mint. Forty years later Pound recalled this period of his life in a letter to Sir Montagu Webb, a British businessman in India who was interested in reforming India's monetary system: 'Silver I saw as no Aladdin, for when Cleveland was elected there was the recount of four million in the Mint vaults, the bags had rotted, and men half naked with open gas flares, shovelled it into the counting machines, with a gleam on tarnished discs.' Twenty years further on, in Canto 97, he could still see the coins 'lit by gas flares' in that Philadelphia vault. In the autobiographical prose work *Indiscretions*, which was first published in A. R. Orage's *New Age* in London in 1920, Pound sketches his early memories of New York, and these same scenes, of the white-wash and horse-cars, and the man throwing a knife at a fleeing figure past big baskets of peaches in the market, he records with great skill in the *Pisan Cantos*, first published in 1948. Another childhood memory was the family story of Captain Wadsworth, a distant relative who in the seventeenth century 'stole the Connecticut charter and hid it in Charter Oak, to the embarrassment', Pound says, 'of legitimist tyranny'. He touches on this story in some of the later Cantos, giving in Canto 109 a line from the vote recognizing Wadsworth's services which was later passed by the Connecticut Assembly.

When Pound first began to take an interest in literature we do not know, but his childhood attempts at composition, or those that remain, are said to be excruciatingly bad. What seems at least likely is that the intellectual level of the Pound household in Philadelphia was unexceptionable. 'I remember people talking about Bellamy when I was a kid,' he wrote to the English monetary reformer, Gladys Bing, in 1935 or '36, 'but hadn't ghost of idea what was in *Looking Backward*, it was just another book on shelf.' And in another letter about the same time, the one I have already quoted to Sir Montagu Webb, he said he remembered vaguely the 'Free Silver' campaign of 1896, when there was a nation-wide clamour against the bankers and the 'power of gold'. A poet who was popular during Pound's childhood and youth was James Whitcomb Riley who was born about 1853 and died in 1916. Pound mentions him as a respected figure in his essay 'The Renaissance' published in *Poetry* in 1915. There is also an affectionate reference many years later in Canto 80 where he asks whether Whitcomb Riley would still be found 'in a highbrow anthology'. Let us see if there is any concrete evidence suggesting Riley as an influence on Pound's poetry.

> Sapsucks gittin' down to biz,
> Weedin' out the lonesomeness;

> Mr. Bluejay, full o' sass,
>   In them base-ball clothes o' his,
> Sportin' round the orchard jes'
> Like he owned the premises!

That is Riley, from his poem 'Knee-Deep in June' published in the book *Afterwhiles* around the turn of the century. We find something similar in Pound's translation of the *Odes* of ancient China, first published in 1954:

> Yaller bird, let my corn alone,
> Yaller bird, let my crawps alone,
> These folks here won't let me eat,
> I wanna go back whaar I can meet
> the folks I used to know at home,
>   I got a home an' I wanna git goin'.

Another of the *Odes* reads:

> Ole Brer Rabbit watchin' his feet,
> Rabbit net 's got the pheasant beat;
>   When I was young and a-startin' life
>   I kept away from trouble an' strife
> But then, as life went on,
> Did I meet trouble?
>   Aye, my son;
> Wish I could sleep till life was done.

Of course what looks like influence here may simply be the result of Huckleberry Finn and a common American background. A great deal of what is referred to as influence is nothing more than some common air which both parties have breathed independently; and this may be so with Riley and Pound. But Riley's mastery within a certain narrow field makes it seem likely that Pound paid tribute to him in the *Pisan Cantos* because he was still able to taste the flavour of a new element which he had helped to add to English poetry. This new element must not be confused with the mere recording of dialect; there had been plenty of dialect before Riley and Twain. It was rather a new ease and naturalness brought into the language by writers who *made use* of dialect inside the texture of their poetry or prose, which is not the same thing as simply writing in dialect or trying to note it down. This distinction is important, for while those who just write in dialect are limited by the comparatively narrow range of their material—of necessity narrow, no matter how lively—the writers who make use of dialect to keep their diction in the living language are in effect extending the language to enable it to cover wider ground than before, or at least, new ground. These writers incorporate various aspects of dialect or common speech into the very essence of their work so that sometimes these elements are completely absorbed or invisible. They may appear as no more than a tone of voice, a cadence, or a raised eyebrow, or they may be clearly visible, as in the extracts from Riley and Pound just given. In the *Odes* Pound uses dialect and common speech in a number of different ways but this does not need pursuing here. All we need keep in mind is that writers like Riley were fairly popular reading in the America of Pound's schooldays.

In *Guide to Kulchur*, published in 1938, Pound mentions a man called Spencer, an instructor who recited a long passage of Homer to him in 1898 or thereabouts; declaiming it in such a way as to rouse the interest of the thirteen-year-old tennis player so that he remembered the incident in 1938, and later still in Canto 80:

> and it was old Spencer (,H.) who first declaimed me
> > the Odyssey
> with a head built like Bill Shepard's
> on the quais of what Siracusa?
> > or what tennis court
> near what pine trees?

Pound entered the University of Pennsylvania in 1901, about the time of his sixteenth birthday. In an article called 'How I Began', which he published in *T.P.'s Weekly* of 6 June 1913, Pound mentions that he already knew what he was doing with his life at the age of fifteen. As this article is little known I will quote from it here at some length:

I knew at fifteen pretty much what I wanted to do. I believed that the 'Impulse' is with the gods; that technique is a man's own responsibility. A man either is or is not a great poet, that is not within his control, it is the lightning from heaven, the 'fire of the gods', or whatever you choose to call it.

His recording instrument is in his own charge. It is his own fault if he does not become a good artist—even a flawless artist.

I resolved that at thirty I would know more about poetry than any man living, that I would know the dynamic content from the shell, that I would know what was accounted poetry everywhere, what part of poetry was 'indestructible', what part could *not be lost* by translation, and—scarcely less important—what effects were obtainable in *one* language only and were utterly incapable of being translated.

In this search I learned more or less of nine foreign languages, I read Oriental stuff in translations, I fought every University regulation and every professor who tried to make me learn anything except this, or who bothered me with 'requirements for degrees.'

Of course, no amount of scholarship will help a man write poetry, it may even be regarded as a great burden and hindrance, but it does help him to destroy a certain percentage of his failures. It keeps him discontented with mediocrity.

This article is helpful in two ways: it enables us to say with a fair degree of certainty that Pound was beginning to take an active interest in literature about the time he entered university to study 'Arts and Science'; and it also makes clear Pound's attitude towards scholarship, which has been a source of considerable misunderstanding. It shows that he did not, like so many of those who have found fault with his literary scholarship, set out to become a scholar, as such, but sought to learn as much as possible about the art of writing in order to become a 'flawless artist', which is another matter altogether. His attitude to universities was still much the same a quarter of a century later when in *Guide to Kulchur* he wrote:

The yoke of the universities has been heavy. . . .
Whether the nucleus of it is there in Prof. MacD's 'And besides, Mr Pound, we shd. have to do so much work ourselves to verify your results'?
Dated U. of Penn. 1906 when I suggested doing a thesis on some reading matter OUTSIDE the list of classic authors included in the curriculum, and despite the fact that Fellowships are given for research and that a thesis for Doctorate is supposed to contain original *research*.

One of the teachers at Pennsylvania whom he still remembered with affection in 1935 was Herman Ames, Professor of American Constitutional History. The volume, *Herman Vandenburg Ames,* published by the University of Pennsylvania Press in 1936 contains this tribute from Pound:

I don't remember how long he had been teaching in 1901, 1902, and there may be students with longer memories but this note and the one that missed him, at least prove over and above any mere opinion that his courses had a vitality outlasting the mere time of his lectures. After thirty years, I still have pleasant recollections of 'Reconstruction' and 'Foreign Relations' courses . . . The idea that a student might have a legitimate curiosity was in no way alien to his (Dr Ames') sensibilities.

After two years at Pennsylvania, Pound changed to Hamilton College, near Clinton, in the State of New York, where he came under the influence of William P. Shepard whose 'refined and sympathetic scholarship', wrote Pound in the preface to *The Spirit of Romance,* 'first led me to some knowledge of French, Italian, Spanish and Provençal'. Another teacher at Hamilton whose work he was thankful for in later years was Professor Ibbotson, who instructed him in Anglo-Saxon. Thinking back over his literary career in 1942, Pound wrote in his booklet, *A Visiting Card,* that he considered the 'hours spent with . . . copying a prose translation of Catullus by W. McDaniel; Ibbotson's instruction in Anglo-Saxon or W. P. Shepard's on Dante and the troubadours of Provence—more important than any contemporary influences'. Another thing he remembered from Hamilton was a remark by Dean Saunders which in later years seemed to be full of an old American wisdom—the sort of thing that John Adams might have said. This remark is recorded in *Polite Essays,* published in 1937, where Pound says that Dean Saunders once spoke to him of 'That fine old word "an independence", meaning sufficient income to live on, so that a man could do what he liked', and he mentioned it again years later in Cantos 87 and 104.

It was during his two years at Hamilton that Pound began to make some definite progress towards building the foundation

upon which his verse was to stand. His curiosity regarding history
had been mildly stirred by Professor Ames at Pennsylvania, but at
Hamilton, especially under the influence of Shepard, he entered
the Middle Ages. But not only did he begin work upon Dante,
the troubadours and Anglo-Saxon, he also discovered the English
verse of the late nineteenth century. According to his own
memory, as he recorded it in his 1915 essay on Lionel Johnson, he
was, between 1904 and 1906, drunk with 'Celticism', Dowson's
'Cynara' and some of the poems of Arthur Symons. Some of these
elements came, or were brought, together in 1905, to produce the
'Belangal Alba', a translation of a medieval Latin poem with
Provençal refrain, which was published in the *Hamilton Literary
Magazine* of May 1905. It is by no means outstanding and Pound
was certainly right to discard it, but there is something in it—no
more perhaps than some sign of his firm intention—which sug-
gests that he was already committed to a lifetime with poetry.
Here are the opening lines:

> Phoebus shineth e'er his glory flyeth,
>   Aurora drives faint light athwart the land,
> And the drowsy watcher cryeth,
>   'Arise!'

It may have been while he was at Hamilton that he read the
Canadian poet Bliss Carman. He made mention of the poets of
the 'Carman-Hovey period' in an essay written in 1909 and again
many years later in the *Pisan Cantos* where they are referred to in a
record of George Santayana's early days at Harvard. Carman,
who was born in Canada in 1861, studied Greek and Latin, and
entered Harvard in 1886 where he came under the influence of the
poet Richard Hovey and the philosopher Santayana. He published
more than thirty books of verse and prose before his death in
1929—eighteen of them between 1893 and 1904. He left Harvard
in 1888 and during the next nine years held editorial positions on
the New York *Independent*, the *Literary World*, *The Outlook*, the
Atlantic, *Cosmopolitan*, *Current Literature* and *The Chap-Book*. He
made his name as a poet with the publication of the *Songs of
Vagabondia* (in collaboration with Hovey) in 1894, after which he

was regarded as one of the most important figures in North American poetry.

Similarities between Carman's work up to 1904 and some of Pound's early poems may be due simply to common roots in Swinburne, Browning, William Morris and the English nineties. There is a resemblance between these lines in Pound's 'Famam Librosque Cano':

> the little rabbit folk
> That some call children
> Such as are up and wide,

and this from Carman's 'From an Old Ritual':

> arise,
> My little Brothers of the field,
> And put the sleep out of your eyes!

But Carman's best work is contained in *Sappho*, published in 1905 while Pound was in his final year at Hamilton; and when we turn to this book and examine it alongside some of Pound's early verse we find similarities which are probably due to the direct influence of Carman on the younger man. Compare these lines from *Sappho*:

> Will not men remember us
> In the days to come hereafter

with the following from Pound's *Ripostes* (1912):

> Let the gods speak softly of us
> In days hereafter.

It is only right to point out that in these two cases where I have isolated lines in order to draw attention to similarities, the poems from which those of Pound are taken are vastly finer and sharper than anything Carman ever wrote.

This is an appropriate place to recall that it was in 1904 that Henry Adams first published his *Mont-Saint-Michel and Chartres*. This was a private edition and it is most unlikely that Pound saw it at that time; but it is interesting to note that when Dr Shepard

was introducing Pound to the world of Dante and the troubadours, Adams was straining against his New England background
and attempting to find refuge in the art of the Middle Ages:

> Anyone can feel it who will only consent to feel like a child . . .
> your mind held in the grasp of the strong lines and shadows of the
> architecture; your eyes flooded with the autumn tones of the glass;
> your ears drowned with the purity of the voices; one sense reacting
> upon another until sensation reaches the limit of its range.

On what day, in what year, the young Pound first felt a correspondence with the Middle Ages, we do not know, but it is worth
noting that whereas Henry Adams, with his detailed knowledge
of the new industrial America coming into being, had despaired
of what is called progress and longed to lose himself in that distant
world, Pound soon wanted to devise a means of entering into the
Middle Ages so as to bring them to bear upon the present. Adams
belonged to the cultivated section of an upper class that had long
ruled but was gradually losing its grip on the power to set standards; Pound to a middle class that was exerting more and more
sway over the nation's tone. Both men wanted desperately to con-
quer history; both made the same mistake of fighting the battle
on history's own ground. Although defeated they wrested great
riches from their enemy, winning more in defeat perhaps than
some had been able to gain by maintaining a precarious peace
with that ever-present monster. This was true also of Henry's
younger brother, Brooks, who in later years would influence
Pound's thinking on monetary history.

After gaining his Ph.B at Hamilton in 1905 Pound returned to
Pennsylvania the following year to receive his M.A. There are a
few glimpses in his later writings of the teachers of this period.
One was Dr Hugo A. Rennert who introduced him to Lope de
Vega and made several remarks which Pound has preserved. One
of these occurs in an article by Pound in the *New Democracy* (New
York) of 15 October 1935:

> I remember Hugo Rennert remarking on some ballyhoo about 'the
> plant,' the U. of Penn. 'plant' was, according to the ballyhoo, not to

lie idle. Rennert observed on the part of himself and faculty: 'But damn it *we* are the plant.'

This remark is mentioned again in Canto 94. Rennert it was, whose *Life of Lope de Vega* was beside Pound when he wrote *The Spirit of Romance* (1910) and still among his books fifty years later, who sent him to Freiburg during his trip abroad in 1906 to see the Provençal scholar Emil Levy. Pound took with him on this visit two extracts from the work of Arnaut Daniel, words and music, which he had copied from a manuscript in the Ambrosiana library in Milan. This early concentration on Daniel, whom he was to translate and re-translate over a period of about seventeen years, was typical of Pound and helps to illustrate a difference between him and other American poets like Bliss Carman; helps us to appreciate that there was something in Pound which was not in the others, something the absence of which left Carman quite happy to potter around in New England and Canada, and the presence of which in Pound drove him on in search of perfection for half a century.

For whereas the Rev. Phillip H. Wicksteed and Mr H. Oelsner suggest in their notes to the Temple Classics edition of Dante— which was one of the books used by Pound at Hamilton and also in writing *The Spirit of Romance*—that Dante was wrong in his preference for Daniel over Guiraut de Bornelh, Pound followed Dante. Most readers would probably have been content with the solemn assurance by Wicksteed and Oelsner that 'the best modern criticism not only places Guiraut well above Arnaut (whose fame is at a very low ebb), but is almost unanimous in setting him at the head of the troubadours'. Pound however spent years taking Arnaut's verse to pieces and studying it in relation to music to see why Dante called him 'the better smith', the better craftsman. Many years later in *A Visiting Card* Pound described Dante's *De Vulgari Eloquio* as his 'baedeker in Provence'. He began to study it before he wrote *The Spirit of Romance* and was still looking into it in 1937 when he wrote the essay 'Immediate Need of Confucius':

Dante for a reason wrote *De Vulgari Eloquio*—on the Common Tongue—and in each age there is need to write De Vulgari Eloquio, that is, to insist on seeing words daily in use and to know the *why* of their usage.

The *De Vulgari Eloquio* was still on his bookshelf in 1959 when he took it up to check through some of the quotations used in the Confucius essay, a revised version of which is included in *Impact*, his most recent collection of essays.

Another influence which was important to Pound was that of Lionel Johnson whom he first heard of, he thought, 'in an odd sort of post-graduate course conducted by Dr. Weygandt' at Pennsylvania in 1906. Johnson's 'immortal things not made with hands' is echoed perhaps in Pound's 'house not made with hands', but the main influence consisted of a certain plainness and hardness which was taken over by Pound and made plainer and harder still. During his final year at Pennsylvania Pound was awarded a Fellowship in Romanics which enabled him to go abroad that year and study for several months in Spain and Italy and to visit France and Germany. Although his official duties at this time seem to have been centred round Lope de Vega, his interests were widening all the time and by the end of 1906 he was already engaged in what would be a life-long dialogue with French literature. He was also studying the latinists of Renaissance Italy who had an important influence on his attitude to the classics and religion. These two interests—French literature and the latinists—are reflected in the two items, 'Interesting French Publications' and 'Raphaelite Latin', which he contributed to the *Book News Monthly* of Philadelphia in September 1906. In the broadcasts he made on the B.B.C. Third Programme in July 1959, Pound recalled wandering about Paris in 1906 with the French poet Mathurin Dondo who was 'then doing most romantic stuff in the style of De Musset', and it was during this stay in the French capital that Pound discovered part of the library of another French poet, Catulle Mendès, for sale on the bookstalls on the *quais*. Introduced thus to a new world of recent French poetry he began there and then the process of trying to sort out the best of it.

Back in Philadelphia in January 1907, Pound wrote to Professor Felix Schelling about the progress of his work. This letter is interesting because in it Pound mentions his 'study of Martial' as something already completed. Many critics over the past forty years, in discussing the hardness and concision which Pound strove to get into his verse, have taken for granted that these qualities were due to T. E. Hulme or some other influence of the London years; but Pound himself was under the impression—in later years at any rate—that he first learnt to appreciate these qualities while studying Martial and Catullus in the United States. That same year, 1907, Pound was appointed a teacher at Wabash College, Crawfordsville, Indiana. He found the college library 'utterly useless', but if his memory twenty years afterwards can be relied on, he made at least one discovery there which was important for his later poetry. In his spacious and well-printed edition of Cavalcanti's works *Guido Cavalcanti: Rime*, published in Genoa in 1932, Pound points out that Dante's prosody in the *Divine Comedy* is 'composed of combinations of rhythm units of various shapes and sizes . . . put together in lines so as to make, roughly, eleven syllables in all. I say "roughly" because of the liberties allowed in elision.' He then goes on to say that he had discovered this fact for himself in Indiana twenty years before and 'made use of the knowledge continually'. A poem from the Indiana period which Pound has preserved in his later collections is 'In Durance' dated 1907. It shows that he was now beginning to acquire considerable skill in the art of writing:

> I am homesick after mine own kind,
> Oh I know that there are folk about me,
>   friendly faces,
> But I am homesick after mine own kind.

That is the opening; the final lines run as follows:

> And yet my soul sings 'Up!' and we are one.
> Yea thou, and Thou, and THOU, and all my kin
> To whom my breast and arms are ever warm,
> For that I love ye as the wind the trees
> That holds their blossoms and their leaves in cure
> And calls the utmost singing from the boughs
> That 'thout him, save the aspen, were as dumb
> Still shade, and bade no whisper speak the birds of how
> 'Beyond, beyond, beyond, there lies . . .'

Pound contributed a poem on the latinists to the *Book News Monthly* of January 1908 and an article on Keats and the latinist M. Antonius Flaminius to the issue of February the same year. In the article from *T.P.'s Weekly* already quoted, Pound had this to say about his career as a poet in America:

So far as the public is concerned my 'career' has been of the simplest; during the first five years of it I had exactly one brief poem accepted by one American magazine, although I had during that time submitted 'La Fraisne' and various other poems now held as a part of my best work. Net result of my activities in cash, five dollars which works out to about 4*s.* 3*d.* per year.

Early in 1908 Pound set sail for Venice and London. Although he would return home for about six months in the latter half of 1910, his life in America was over.

CHAPTER II

The Pagan Mystery Religions

WHAT I have to say can be reduced to this: in so far as Pound has concerned himself with religion his work has been a detour, an attempt to avoid the main claims of orthodox Christianity. This does not mean that Pound has not sometimes been sympathetic towards certain aspects of Christianity, or certain periods, tendencies or doctors of the Church, but the point to note is that his sympathy has always been that of a determined outsider who is not going to get involved except on his own terms.

Pound's thought and intuitions on religion have never been worked out into a system, with the result that a number of elements which inside a system might have been found to be incompatible, can take their place side by side in his work without embarrassment. For the most part his ideas and beliefs concerning religion have been built up from items selected—more by disposition or temperamental prejudice than reason—from the pagan mystery religions of Greece and Italy. His many remarks in favour of the Church must not lead us to suppose that Pound was ever a deep student of the Christian religion, as was that other sympathetic non-believer, George Santayana. He looked into certain things when the need arose, in connection with his *Cantos* or his other writings, but there is no evidence in his work that he ever considered carefully the dogmas of the Church or sought guidance as to their official meaning. He expresses his appreciation of the Church, when he discovers there some echo of paganism, or some current in Church history which seems to him to coincide with something in his own work, or thought, or feelings. But this regard for the Church, his anxiety over what he considers to be the corruption of the Church by certain diseases, or his eagerness to praise or embrace doctors whose attitude to usury appears to support his own work in that field, are touched with a peculiar zeal which is part of his American inheritance. One has only to

consider the following passage from *A Visiting Card* to see how
Pound approached the Church. It could only have been written
by an outsider who for all his solicitude is not really interested in
the truth or otherwise of the Christian religion. It is the work of a
man with a theory, and that theory, deriving after a fashion from
the mysteries of Eleusis, has no real connection with the 'Credo in
unum Deum':

> Latin is sacred, grain is sacred. Who destroyed the mystery of fecun-
> dity, bringing in the cult of sterility? Who set the Church against the
> Empire? Who destroyed the unity of the Catholic Church with this
> mud-wallow that serves Protestants in the place of contemplation?
> Who decided to destroy the mysteries within the Church so as to be
> able to destroy the Church itself by schism? Who has wiped the con-
> sciousness of the greatest mystery out of the mind of Europe, to arrive
> at the atheism proclaimed by Bolshevism?

It must be said that Pound's writings on religion, like his
writings on most other subjects, contain sentences which only he
could have written; which hold up to the light things we had
forgotten or overlooked, or which suddenly place in new perspective those we had been content to take for granted. All this is
undeniable, but it is undeniable also that Pound's religion, even
where it contains Christian elements, is not religion in the Christian sense. He has no interest in Grace, no idea of Sin or of that
feeling of religious community referred to in the phrase 'the com-
munion of saints'. The Pound who in Canto 94 wrote: 'pity, yes,
for the infected, but maintain antisepsis' could never have written
the words used by T. S. Eliot in recalling the collapse of Europe
in 1938:

> The feeling which was new and unexpected was a feeling of humilia-
> tion, which seemed to demand an act of personal contrition, of
> humility, repentance and amendment; what had happened was some-
> thing in which one was deeply implicated and responsible.

I do not mean to suggest that Pound is necessarily incapable of
such a feeling, but he could only experience it, if he allowed himself to do so, in isolation, or perhaps in relation to similar feelings

in others, but never as part of a vast system of thought and devotion to which the individual must submit himself.

Let us now examine some of Pound's main ideas and beliefs on religion with special attention to the Italian humanists. The reader would do well to keep in mind that the mysteries of Eleusis were first presented to the modern world by the Renaissance humanists, but the mysteries as they understood them had little to do with the original festival at Eleusis. This festival was a secret ritual in which the neophytes were purged of the fear of death and admitted into the company of the blessed. They were bound by a vow of silence. But later the Platonists adopted the language of the ritual for figurative use in philosophy, and this terminology was developed by the late Platonists to such a point that it ceased to be philosophy and became magic. One can imagine then the confusion which existed in the minds of the Renaissance scholars from whom Pound received his first instruction in the pagan mysteries. They saw the mysteries but obscurely through the contrivings and elaborations of Plotinus, Porphyry and the Cabbala. Professor Edgar Wind, to whom I am indebted for much of this information, says in his *Pagan Mysteries in the Renaissance* that the enjoyment a humanist like Pico della Mirandola derived from occult authors was vicarious and poetical:

> It never occurred to him, as it did to less speculative minds, that the turgid lore of the dialectical magi might be put to a more nefarious use than for amplifying the Platonic *mystères littéraires*. Black magic, in the sense that it appealed to Agrippa of Nettesheim, he rejected as a vile superstition.

It was some such mixture of the ritual, the figurative and magic which Pound took in when he began to read the humanists in or before 1906. Later, under the influence of Frazer and Frobenius, he concentrated more upon the original ritual aspect of the mysteries as restored by archaeology and anthropology, but our concern for the moment is with the pagan religions and associated matters as he first read about them while at university and during his early years abroad. We see from some of the poems, but especially the prose notes, in his first few books of verse that his interest in old religions was both wide and intuitive. As in his later years, so also in his early ones, we find him ranging far and wide looking for unity in diversity, grasping hold of nuggets of information that seemed indestructible. But neither then nor later did he work out or adopt a theological or philosophical system by which these nuggets might be tested, measured and arranged, for whatever may be said about Pound's version of Confucianism it does not constitute a system in the Western meaning of the word. If some item discovered by Pound in his reading or conversation seemed to fit, if it echoed some older text or appeared to, Pound would include it in his religion or hold it for future use. This is not to say that his method is entirely useless; there is evidence enough in his work to prove otherwise; but it has led to some silly blunders and unfortunate errors of emphasis which have distorted or ruined what might otherwise have been ordered passages of some importance. The prose notes in his first book *A Lume Spento* (1908) include a description of a mood in which he feels himself 'divided between myself corporal and self aetherial', a reference to the Egyptian *Book of the Dead*, a few lines on 'Bertold Lomax, English Dante scholar and mystic, died in Ferrara 1723', and the following note which I give in full:

> Referendum for contrast. 'Daemonalitas' of the Rev. Father Sinistrari of Ameno (1600 circ). 'A treatise wherein is shown that there are in existence in earth rational creatures beside man, endowed like him with a body and soul, that are born and die like him, redeemed by our Lord Jesus Christ and capable of receiving salvation or damnation.' Latin and English text, pub. Liseux, Paris, 1879.

Soon afterwards in *A Quinzaine for this Yule* there is a brief note about the origin of 'the ancient myths of the demigods' and 'the myths of metamorphosis'. But the most important of these notes, at least from the point of view of Pound's later work, occurs in *Personae* published in London in April 1909. It concerns the medieval theologian Richard of St Victor and his definitions of *cogitatio*, *meditatio*, and *contemplatio*, thinking, meditation and contemplation, which for a lifetime Pound has regarded as a high point in Western thought and something of a link between what he considers to be the better aspects of Christianity and the better aspects of Greece. Some thirty years after the note in *Personae* he wrote about this again in *Guide to Kulchur*:

There are three modes of thought, cogitation, meditation and contemplation. In the first the mind flits aimlessly about the object, in the second it circles about it in a methodical manner, in the third it is unified with the object.

That is something a man can check up on. It is a knowledge to be verified by experience. I mean ours with St. Victor's.

I will not concern myself here with the question of whether Pound's rendering of contemplation as a mode of thought in which the mind is 'unified with the object' is in fact an accurate presentation of Richard's thought, but with the assumption contained in his second brief paragraph, which suggests one of Pound's serious limitations when dealing with religion. Richard's definition, he says, is something we can check up on, a knowledge to be verified by experience. What Pound never seems to have realized in all the years he held these ideas is that *contemplatio*, contemplation, was for Richard a technical term in mystical theology. The word had an intricate context of asceticism and devotion, and included within it the idea of development, a hierarchy of ecstasies arrived at by the Grace of God, but under the strict supervision of a spiritual director, ending perhaps in the last heights of mystical ecstasy wherein all is from God and the mystic passive and in darkness. It is not for me to say whether Pound has ever experienced mystical ecstasy or known some state in which the mind is 'unified with the object', but it does seem that this is a case where he might have exercised his ability in the dissociation of ideas. It is not Pound's idea of a mind unified with an object that is in question here, but his action in reducing Richard of St Victor's system to a neat turn of phrase, and the definite invitation to regard *contemplatio* as a purely philosophical term rather than a term in mystical theology. This error is actually present in his original note on Richard in *Personae* where he says that 'Poetry in its acme is expression from contemplation'.

Now the fact that the young Pound collected ideas and fragments from the Talmud, Yeats, Richard of St Victor, Swedenborg
or Pico, or that he invoked the beryl stone (to which Nicolaus
Cusanus devoted his work *De beryllo*), means nothing by itself.
Even the fact that he successfully incorporated such elements into
early poems which have stood the test of half a century does not
give us licence to go digging into the history of these elements
themselves, for it is the poems which matter. But there is more to
it than that in Pound's case, and I will quote again from Professor
Wind who puts the substance of what I want to say in three clear
sentences:

> Had the cult of the incongruous produced nothing but monsters, it
> would have only a limited, anthropological interest. We could then
> be content to survey the *Hieroglyphica* of Piero Valeriano, and marvel at
> the ingenious piety of the author in evading the divine splendour he
> professes to worship. But in great Renaissance works of art, which
> often draw from the same sources as Valeriano, the splendour does
> shine forth through the disguise, and gives to the veil itself a peculiar
> beauty.

What Professor Wind says here about the artists of the Renaissance applies also to Pound. For it was due partly to his digging
around in these authors usually considered laborious that Pound
learnt to recognize the veiled splendour. Botticelli caught it and
held it in 'Primavera' and 'Mars and Venus' and Pound recognized
it in Botticelli. In the *Pisan Cantos* he writes of:

> all that Sandro knew, and Jacopo
> and that Velasquez never suspected
> lost in the brown meat of Rembrandt
> and the raw meat of Rubens and Jordaens

During his years in London, from 1908 until 1921, Pound read
and talked with a number of authors who were interested in
mysticism, the occult and old religions, among them W. B.
Yeats, G. R. S. Mead and Allen Upward. All three of these men
were well-read in their fields and Pound learned much from them.
Both Professor Wind and Jessie L. Weston have testified to Yeats's
knowledge of the Neoplatonists and associated matters, and Mead,

who was the author of books on Gnosticism, was also editor of *The Quest*, a quarterly dealing with the occult, religion and the mysteries. Upward, author of *The Divine Mystery* and other works on mystery in religion, was somewhat unorthodox even in that unorthodox field, but there is no doubt that he had considerable knowledge of the Gnostics and the Greek mysteries. It is as well then to keep these authors in mind when discussing Pound's attitude to religion, for they contributed to it and coloured his subsequent thinking. He was much interested in this subject before he arrived in London and the influence of people like Yeats, Mead and Upward kept his interest alive even when he was giving most of his attention to other matters.

I will have written to no purpose if I have given the impression that the mystery religions are important simply because they are to be found in early work most of which Pound has since discarded. It is that they are of more than passing interest because they play a considerable part in the *Cantos*. As most readers of Pound know, the *Cantos* got off to a false start in 1917 when he published three cantos which were later withdrawn. The first three cantos as they now stand in Pound's poem, when compared with the original three published in 1917, show that although his hesitation over the opening of the poem was largely technical, it was also related to his attempt to comprehend religion. In the original three cantos the poet presents the reader with a world of spirits, nymphs and Neoplatonists, and he is very self-conscious and uncomfortable about it. He keeps telling us that they are there ('the place is full of spirits') but we don't believe him for a moment, and the poet suspects that this is so. And all this is very embarrassing because he is trying to be serious and trying to believe in these various gods and spirits himself. I can best illustrate this unsatisfactory quality by quotations from the original Canto I:

> And the place is full of spirits, not *lemures*,
> Not dark and shadow-wet ghosts, but ancient living
>
> . . .
>
> Are they Etruscan gods?
>
> . . .

c

                                                    Metastasio
           Is right, we have that world about us.
                                             .   .   .
           Worlds we have, how many worlds we have.

Between the time he wrote these lines and the time he wrote the
first three cantos as they now appear, Pound not only reconsidered
the question of prosody, but of how to present gods and spirits in
a poem in which the main significance derives from the literal
surface meaning. What finally he did was simply to present his
gods, nymphs and other spirits, without comment or stage-
directions, as part of the world of the *Cantos*. There we see them,
there they exist, and there we accept them. The reader is no longer
troubled because he is no longer prodded into acknowledging them
as something real and apart from the poem. Whereas in the original three cantos the gods and spirits were *said* to exist, on testimony drawn from dealers in magic, Renaissance scholars and the
poet himself, in the later versions—and onwards for thirty or more
cantos—they are simply presented as part of the poem. And this
method works. Only towards the end of the poem does the original problem of literal belief intrude; but earlier we are quite
content to see the pale ankles of the goddess and to marvel at the
poetry.

   Two of the main figures running through the work are the
grain goddess, Demeter, and the goddess of love, Aphrodite. We
shall consider here Demeter, who was the central figure in the
'Greater Mysteries' of Eleusis. Pound's view of the mysteries is a
serious one: 'The mysteries are *not* revealed,' he wrote to Henry
Swabey in 1939, 'and no guide book to them has been or will be
written,' and one result of this attitude is that like Pico della
Mirandola he writes about them as an initiate in words that are
both 'published and not published', that are published to the
world and yet protect the mystery. Although he learnt much
from the Renaissance and the occultism of the early twentieth century, gradually, under the influence of anthropology and archaeology on the one hand, and his own readings among the Greeks,
troubadours and Tuscan poets on the other, Pound worked out a
view of the Eleusinian mysteries which is very much his own. He

expresses part of his view in two articles published in the early 1930's, both of which I will quote as they are not easy to find. The first, called 'Credo', was published in *Front* in December 1930 and is in the form of an answer to T. S. Eliot who several years before had asked what Pound believed:

Having a strong disbelief in abstract and general statement as a means of conveying one's thought to others I have for a number of years answered such questions by telling the enquirer to read Confucius and Ovid. This can do no harm to the intelligent and the unintelligent may be damned.

Given the material means I would replace the statue of Venus on the cliffs at Terracina. I would erect a temple to Artemis in Park Lane. I believe that a light from Eleusis persisted throughout the middle ages and set a beauty in the song of Provence and Italy.

The second article to which I refer was called 'Terra Italica'. It was published in the *New Review*, Winter 1931–2:

It is equally discernible upon study that some non-Christian and inextinguishable source of beauty persisted throughout the Middle Ages maintaining song in Provence, maintaining an enthusiasm, maintaining the grace of the Kalenda Maya.

And this force was the strongest counter force to the cult of Atys and asceticism. A great deal of obscurity has been made to encircle it. There are a few clear pages in Davidsohn's Firenze ai Tempi di Dante. The usual accusation against the Albigeois is that they were Manichaeans. This I believe after long search to be pure bunkumb. The slanderers feared the truth. I mean they feared not only the force of a doctrine but they feared giving it even the publicity which a true bill against it would have required.

The best scholars do not believe there were any Manichaeans left in Europe at the time of the Albigensian Crusade. If there were any in Provence they have at any rate left no trace in troubadour art.

On the other hand the cult of Eleusis will explain not only general phenomena but particular beauties in Arnaut Daniel or in Guido Cavalcanti.

The question as to what the mysteries of Eleusis actually were has been the subject of intermittent debate for two thousand years. There was a 'Sacred Marriage' involving the hierophant and the chief priestess of Demeter, but there are many views as to what this 'marriage' actually consisted of. Pound's view is unmistakeable: 'Sacrum, sacrum, inluminatio coitu,' he chants in Canto 36, sacred, sacred, the knowledge derived from coition, which is taken up again in the *Pisan Cantos*. This line, it should be noted, is in the same canto as his translation of Cavalcanti's 'Donna mi prega'; and in the same canto and in the same connection we find also the 9th-century philosopher Erigena whose presence much later, in Canto 90, is worth examining at this point, for it throws light upon Pound's idea of a sort of secret society transcending all societies and groups, whose members hand down 'the truth' to the initiates from age to age. In Canto 90 we find:

> And from the San Ku
>> to the room in Poitiers where one can stand
>> casting no shadow,
> That is Sagetrieb,
>>> that is tradition.
> Builders had kept the proportion,
>> did Jacques de Molay
>>> know these proportions?
> and was Erigena ours?

The general meaning of this passage is clear enough even if we have no idea of how Pound came to combine these various elements. But when we examine it in detail we find it is based upon the idea of an ageless 'secret society'. The San Ku was a sort of masonic council in ancient China in connection with which we find a grade of initiation called the 'Widow's Son' which is also to be found in some of the Romance literature of the Middle Ages and in the Masonic ritual of the present day. The town of Poitiers, which also crops up in the same Romance literature, is not only famous for its romanesque architecture but for its connection with the Order of Templars of which Jacques de Molay was grandmaster. And ceremonies remembering de Molay are also preserved today in some Masonic rituals. There are indications of some of these threads in Jessie L. Weston's book *From Ritual to Romance* which is concerned with Romance literature and the origin of the Grail. At one point she connects the Templars with pagan priests in Rome, known as the Salii, and later has this to say about the Templars and their possible connection with surviving pagan mysteries:

Had they, when in the East, come into touch with a survival of the Naassene, or some kindred sect? It seems exceedingly probable. If it were so we could understand at once the puzzling connection of the Order with the Knights of the Grail, and the doom which fell upon them. That they were held to be Heretics is very generally admitted, but in what their Heresy consisted no one really knows; little credence can be attached to the stories of idol worship often repeated. If their Heresy, however, were such as indicated above, A Creed which struck at the very roots and vitals of Christianity, we can understand at once the reason for punishment, and the necessity for secrecy.

Pound's approach is different of course from that of Jessie L. Weston, but the similarities are interesting. His question at the end of the passage from Canto 90, 'and was Erigena ours?' refers to his hunch that Scotus Erigena also was a member of the Eleusinian brotherhood. Actually the idea that the true religion, or parts of it, existed in an imperfect form before the coming of Christ is common to both St Paul and St Augustine; but whereas for them the earlier manifestations of it only made sense in the light of the Incarnation and all that that means, Pound takes a different view altogether. He places the core of the true religion in the Eleusinian mysteries and considers that the inner doctrines of Christians like Erigena only make sense when referred back to Eleusis.

Demeter's appearances all the way through the *Cantos* are so clear and her role as goddess of grain and fruitfulness so obvious that I will not dwell upon this aspect here. But I will refer to her connection with one of Pound's ideas about the origin of certain human dispositions or ways of thought. He believes that these dispositions and ways of thought derive from primitive ways of life. From agriculture we get the boundary stone and the beginning of ethics; from nomadic shepherds a disposition towards fattening for the kill; and from hunting tribes the first notions of religious rites. The shepherds, in contrast to those who take part in ritual combat with bulls, befriend and fatten helpless cows or sheep in preparation for slaughter, an idea which runs through the

Rock-Drill Cantos in particular: 'Butchers of lesser cattle,' he says,
'their villain the grain god.' His belief about the connection between agriculture and ethics seems to find support in the Old
Testament where the great prophets never cease to hammer on
the importance of boundary stones. As for the connection between Eleusis and agriculture, there is much evidence in favour of
this idea in Jane Harrison's *Prolegomena to the Study of the Greek
Religion* where she says that the cult of Eleusis was 'based on
agricultural conditions; the emergence of Eleusis was primarily
due to the fertile Rarian corn plain'. There is also much in the
Rock-Drill Cantos about the origin of religious rites in the hunting
rites of Diana, but we need not go into the details.

Another point to be noted is a certain similarity between
Pound's views on religion and those of the Emperor Julian the
Apostate who was initiated into the Eleusinian mysteries and
those of Diana. It is not surprising that Pound praises him in con-
nection with wheat storage and granaries. In his later work
Pound has been tracing his religious brotherhood back beyond
Eleusis of Attica to the Sumerians of Mesopotamia and the earliest
Egyptians. One example will suffice. In Cantos 94 and 97 there is
a drawing of a hawk or falcon, and there are a number of refer-
ences through the later cantos to the falcon-form and Frederick II
of Sicily. Pound's drawing is taken from an ancient seal found at
Abydos in Egypt and belonging to one of the earliest periods of
Egyptian history. He connects this with the falcon-form noted by
Frederick, and it is interesting to see that the falcon is mentioned
in Plutarch's *De Iside et Osiride* where he says it is a bird distinguished by the sharpness of its vision and the speed of its wings.
During the Renaissance the falcon was used as a symbol for insight and power, and is mentioned in Valeriano's *Hieroglyphica* in
connection with Horus and Osiris. Whether there is any meaningful connection between the seal from Abydos and Frederick II of
Sicily is a matter I am not competent to discuss. But what does
need saying about Pound's method, especially as he uses it in the
later cantos, and as it is often used by other writers on the occult,
is that there is no necessary connection between people who use
the same ritual or symbols. The use, for instance, of a certain

symbolism by Dante and its use again by some individual or group five hundred years later does not prove a connection between the two. It proves neither that there was a living tradition by which the symbolism was handed down, nor even basic similarities in belief. A tradition traced out by this method alone is based on nothing more solid than faulty reasoning. I will say no more for the moment on this or on Pound's apparent misuse of certain figures from mythology and ancient Mesopotamia, for these are questions which belong to a discussion on his method and its collapse in *Thrones* rather than to one on his belief in the pagan mysteries.

In summing up let me say that if we consider Pound's views on the subject as religious views, he may be classed—though in his own separate sub-category—with the Gnostics. Like them he seeks a basis in pagan mysteries, and like them, or some of them, considers that the Jewish religion because of its imperfections could never have had any connection with the God of the universe. But over and above this, Pound has consistently failed to see or admit that Christianity—the truth or otherwise of which has no bearing on what I am about to say—coincides with a great change in human sensibility. Something was already happening in Virgil's time which that sensitive soul perceived; with the establishment of Christianity some three centuries later that something was manifest. It was no less than the death of the old gods of the hearth and the city and the tribe—Eleusis it should be remembered was only a local religion—and their replacement by the conception of one God for all men. It is easy to show how men have sinned and still sin against this conception, but what I am concerned with is the fact that human sensibility changed to the point where societies, not just individual philosophers, were able to give up their old gods and face and acknowledge the existence of this new conception of the creator of the universe. The world had altered to such a point in the final years of paganism, that, as Cumont points out in the closing pages of his *Oriental Religions in Roman Paganism*, members of the Roman aristocracy who had remained faithful to their old gods did not have a mentality or morality very different from that of the Christians who sat with them in the senate.

But that above all else which casts serious doubts upon Pound's treatment of religion is his silence about Christ and the central Christian dogmas in a poem which purports to deal with human history over a great span of time. The closest he gets to the person of Christ is a tentative identification of Him, in Canto 98, with the Chinese barley god, Je tzu.

In Pound's case it is not the ingenuities or rituals of the mystery religions, the Gnostics, Cabbalists or Neoplatonists which matter, nor any of the other fragments he uses in order to bolster his religious 'system', but the fact that with these things he somehow creates a medium through which a great splendour shines. There is an amusing comment on the ingenuity of the Platonists in Gibbon's twenty-third chapter which I insert here for its relevance to what we have been discussing:

> The lascivious form of a naked Venus was tortured into the discovery of some moral precept, or some physical truth; and the castration of Atys explained the revolution of the sun between the tropics, or the separation of the human soul from vice and error.

And to this remark about Atys he attaches a footnote which might well be applied to the pagan mysteries and some of the poetry of Pound:

> But all the allegories which ever issued from the Platonic school are not worth the short poem of Catullus on the same extraordinary subject.

CHAPTER III

London, the Metropolis

IT IS true I suppose that poetry, possibly even great poetry, can be written almost anywhere, under almost any conditions; but this should not be allowed to conceal from us the fact that a certain kind of great poetry, which is a renewal and not in, or at the end of, an established line, can only be written at a particular time and place, under certain very definite conditions. And the poet who executes this renewal, who stirs a language into new life, is not only one who sees that certain things need doing, for there may be others who see this too, but thinks that it is worth doing and goes ahead and does it even while those about him are impotent, supercilious or uncomprehending. Now there is no doubt that it was Ezra Pound who stirred English poetry out of the condition of extreme stagnation it was in around the year 1910; and it is just as certain that he could never have done this, could never have written the poetry he did from *Ripostes* onward, or supported it and clarified his own mind and the minds of others with his prose, had he failed to make his pilgrimage to London, the metropolis.

When Pound arrived in London towards the end of 1908, he was the author of one book of verse, published in Venice a few months before, and of a few articles published in the United States. In bald terms his first year or so in London might be condensed as follows. His first publication in England was a booklet of poems, *A Quinzaine for This Yule*, issued by Pollock and Company in December 1908. Two things of interest in this booklet are the short poem 'Beddoesque' which shows that the basis for his remarks about Beddoes many years later in Canto 80 was already in his mind in 1908, and a prose note in which he says, speaking of beauty, that 'without curiosity and awe none find her'. This view of the importance of curiosity was to remain one of the central points in Pound's attitude towards the study of literature and

history. 'Their writings wither because they have no curiosity,' he
wrote in Canto 85, and a few years later in his B.B.C. broadcasts
he said it again: 'You cannot have literature without curiosity, and
when a writer's curiosity dies out he is finished—he can do all the
tricks you like, but without curiosity you get no literature with
any life in it.' Pound first made a name for himself as a poet with
the publication in April 1909 of *Personae* which caused a small but
definite stir in the world of poetry in London at the time. He met
and talked with writers like Laurence Binyon, Ford Madox Ford,[1]
Frederic Manning, T. E. Hulme and Maurice Hewlett; he reviewed Manning's *Brunhild* in the *Book News Monthly* of April
that year and published his poem 'Altaforte' in Ford's *English
Review* in June. One of the English poets of that period now almost forgotten whom Pound recalled for the B.B.C. was Margaret Sackville. He quoted for his English listeners a pair of lines
he remembered from one of her poems:

> The night forgets the day
> And there is no rumour left in any place of twilight.

Towards the end of 1909 he brought out another book of poems,
Exultations, met and impressed Yeats with his knowledge of the
troubadours, and went on learning all he could about the art of
writing.

That then is how we might summarize the first year from the
facts available, but it leaves out the awe which he felt when he
first arrived, and the lasting impression it made, for if Pound left
his mark on London, London just as surely left her mark on him.
'There is no town like London to make one feel the vanity of all
art except the highest,' he wrote to William Carlos Williams
in May 1909, and went on to suggest that Williams read Margaret Sackville, Rosamund Watson, Ernest Rhys and James Fairfax
if he wanted to know how good was the work of second rank
being done in the capital. About five years after his arrival he
wrote this account of London in the article 'How I Began':

I came to London with £3 knowing no one.
I had been hungry all my life for 'interesting people'. I wanted to

---

[1] He changed his name from Hueffer to Ford in June 1919.

meet certain men whose work I admired. I have done this. I have had good talk in plenty.

I have paid a certain price, I have endured a certain amount of inconvenience, enough to put an edge on my enjoyment. I believe I have had more solid pleasure in life than any fellow of my years whom I have ever met.

I have 'known many men's manners and seen many cities'.

Besides knowing living artists I have come in touch with the tradition of the dead. I have had in this the same sort of pleasure that a schoolboy has in hearing of the star plays of former athletes. . . . I have relished this or that about 'old Browning', or Shelley sliding down his front banisters 'with almost incredible rapidity'.

There is more, however, in this sort of Apostolic Succession than a ludicrous anecdote, for people whose minds have been enriched by contact with men of genius retain the effects of it.

I have enjoyed meeting Victorians and Pre-Raphaelites and men of the nineties through their friends. I have seen Keats' proof sheets, I have personal tradition of his time second-hand. This, perhaps, means little to a Londoner, but it's good fun if you have grown up regarding such things as about as distant as Ghengis Khan or the days of Lope de Vega.

The point about all this meeting and talking, watching and listening was that in Pound's case it was affecting an instrument of unusual genius; not one that would be content to tag on to the nineties indefinitely, producing beautiful poems, just a little more beautiful, a little sharper, a little more graceful perhaps than those of his contemporaries, but one who would quickly take the literary language away from those who held it in their keeping and refashion it according to the cadence of the living tongue. Already when he first reached England his thinking was in some ways ahead of his time, but it took him a year or two to get his bearings and to find out how much he knew, and after that another two years to put the required edge on his diction. There is an approximate and brief description in his *Gaudier-Brzeska: A Memoir* (1916) of the steps by which he advanced over some of the crucial years. Although written six years after the beginning of the process described, it seems to tally with as much as we are able to piece together independently. This is what he says:

In the 'search for oneself', in the search for 'sincere self-expression', one gropes, one finds some seeming verity. One says 'I am' this, that, or the other, and with the words scarcely uttered one ceases to be that thing.

I began this search for the real in a book called *Personae*, casting off as it were, complete masks of the self in each poem. I continued in a long series of translations, which were but more elaborate masks.

Secondly, I made poems like 'The Return' which is an objective reality and has a complicated sort of significance. . . . Thirdly, I have written 'Heather', which represents a state of consciousness, or 'implies' or 'implicates' it.

The first part of this process, the creation and 'casting off' of the masks of the 'self', is very clear in the early poems. What might go unnoticed is that as early as 1908 Pound already had in mind the beginnings of a method of articulation in poetry which would cause him to do away with intermediary explanation, as it is to be found in prose and so much poetry, and leave the poem free to concentrate its own proper virtues. In a letter to William Carlos Williams in October of that year he says that 'To me the short so-called dramatic lyric—at any rate the sort of thing I do—is the poetic part of a drama the rest of which (to me the prose part) is left to the reader's imagination or implied or set in a short note. I catch the character I happen to be interested in at the moment he interests me, usually a moment of song, self-analysis, or sudden understanding or revelation.' This of course was only the beginning of the method as developed by Pound and Eliot later. The idea as he held it in 1908 might have been developed along other directions or even left as it then was; all I wish to say at the moment is that the idea of setting aside the 'prose part' was already a rough working principle during his first year in London.

If we extract any one person from the 'general impression' which London had on Pound, the man who had greatest influence was Ford Madox Ford. Certain claims have been made over the years in favour of T. E. Hulme as the presiding genius who licked Pound into shape. These claims are unfortunate in at least two ways: (1) they give the innocent reader an entirely false impression of some of the essential history of modern poetry, leading him off in any direction except the right one; and (2) they have served to distract attention from Hulme's real importance, for some of his insights are of more than passing interest, and he was, incidentally, a man whose knowledge in fields other than literary technique, and in places where he is least popular, might have saved Pound from a number of errors in later years. All this is not to say that Hulme did not have an influence on Pound's verse, for I think it is almost certain that he did; and as far as Pound's interest in Hulme is concerned we have not only a number of statements to that effect by Pound himself but the fact that he edited Hulme's verse and preserved it in a book of his own. But if we examine Hulme's own writings as they apply to poetry and then turn to Pound's achievement in renewing English verse, the fuss over Hulme's part immediately falls into perspective. It is easy to see why Hulme appealed to Pound and how Pound might have learnt a number of things from him, when we read the remarks about poetry and images in Hulme's *Speculations*; but put these remarks alongside the achievement and it becomes clear that there was much more in the actual work than is contained in the philosopher's conceptions. It was not just a case of making images or writing 'hard, dry, classical verse', as Hulme puts it, but of forcibly cleaning each word and learning to register one's own time in terms of one's own time. And it was precisely with regard to these matters, the cleaning of the word and the learning of contemporary speech, that Ford showed Pound the way.

As Pound remembered in 1932 in his article on Harold Monro in the *Criterion*, it was Ford who 'knew the answer' and preached 'the simple gallic doctrine of living language and *le mot juste*'. About five years later in *Polite Essays* he again claimed that the really important man, so far as poetry was concerned, was Ford: 'The revolution of the word began so far as it affected the men who were of my age in London in 1908, with the LONE whimper of Ford Madox Hueffer.' And a year or two later he wrote for the *Townsman* an article called 'This Hulme Business' in which he tried to correct the balance in favour of Ford. But if these articles written twenty years after the events described, at a time when Hulme's reputation was enjoying what Pound regarded as an unwarranted inflation, are suspect, as the work of an interested party, let us leave this period and go back to a time when there was little or no argument about Hulme's position in the 'new poetry' and when he was still alive and well able to defend himself. It is June 1914, ten years before the publication of *Speculations*, and Pound is reviewing Ford's *Collected Poems* for *Poetry*. It was Ford, he writes, who 'insisted, in the face of a still Victorian press, upon the importance of good writing as opposed to the opalescent word, the rhetorical tradition'. And in the closing lines of the review, this: 'I find him significant and revolutionary because of his insistence upon clarity and precision, upon the prose tradition; in brief, upon efficient writing—even in verse.' In a review of D. H. Lawrence's *Love Poems and Others* published in *Poetry* for July 1913 he again referred to this question of good writing in both prose and verse, bringing in at the same time a reference to Ford and the *English Review* of 1909. It was almost as if Ford and the overall question of good writing were for Pound interchangeable terms:

Mr Lawrence was 'discovered' by Ford Madox Hueffer during the latter's editorship of the *English Review*, about four years ago. Some of his verses appeared then, and he has since made a notable reputation by his prose works, *The White Peacock* and *The Trespasser*.

His prose training stands him in good stead in these poems. . . .

Mr Lawrence has attempted realism and attained it. He has brought contemporary verse up to the level of contemporary prose, and that is no mean achievement.

But the clearest indication of Ford's usefulness as a teacher of important doctrine is to be found in the editorial 'Status Rerum' which Pound contributed to *Poetry* of January of 1913 at a time when he was writing some of the thoroughly 'modern' poems which later appeared in his book *Lustra*. I will give a large section of it here because it shows some of the things that were going on in Pound's mind at an important stage in the development of his poetry:

I would rather talk about poetry with Ford Madox Hueffer than with any man in London. Mr Hueffer's beliefs about the art may be best

explained by saying that they are in diametric opposition to those of
Mr Yeats.

Mr Yeats has been subjective; believes in the glamour and associa-
tions which hang near words. 'Works of art beget works of art.' He
has much in common with the French symbolists. Mr Hueffer believes
in an exact rendering of things. He would strip words of all 'association'
for the sake of getting a precise meaning. He professes to prefer prose to
verse. You would find his origins in Gautier or in Flaubert. He is
objective. This school tends to lapse into description. The other tends
to lapse into sentiment.

Mr Yeats's method is, to my way of thinking, very dangerous, for
although he is the greatest of living poets who use English, and though
he has sung some of the moods of life immortally his art has not
broadened much in scope during the past decade. . . .

Mr Hueffer has rarely 'come off'. His touch is so light and his attitude
so easy that there seems little likelihood of his ever being taken seriously
by anyone save a few specialists and a few of his intimates. His last
leaflet *High Germany* contains, however, three poems from which one
may learn his quality. They are not Victorian. I do not expect many
people to understand why I praise them. They are *The Starling, In the
Little Old Market-Place* and *To All the Dead.*

The youngest school here that has the nerve to call itself a school is
that of the *Imagistes.* To belong to a school does not in the least mean
that one writes poetry to a theory. One writes poetry when, where,
because, and as one feels like writing it. A school exists when two or
three young men agree, more or less, to call certain things good; when
they prefer such of their verses as have certain qualities to such of their
verses as do not have them.

Space forbids me to set forth the program of the *Imagistes* at length
but one of their watchwords is Precision, and they are in opposition to
the numerous and unassembled writers who busy themselves with dull
and interminable effusions, and who seem to think that a man can write
a good long poem before he learns to write a good short one, or even
before he learns to produce a good single line.

I must leave this topic for the present, although I have by no
means exhausted the evidence which secures for Ford a definite
place as a forerunner in the struggle to renew the literary language. It is quite clear from what I have just quoted that as far as
Pound was concerned there was a close connection between the

Imagist school of which he was leader ('one of their watchwords is Precision') and Ford who believed 'in an exact rendering of things' and in 'getting a precise meaning'. But more important for our purposes than this question of Ford and Hulme, if we are to understand what Pound was doing during these years, is his first prose book *The Spirit of Romance* which was published in June 1910. Let me say immediately that it is a book well worth reading for its own sake; it is still very much alive today, despite its faults, and it does not come under the heading of archaeology. It was undertaken late in 1909 or early in 1910 'at the instigation of Mr Ernest Rhys', and according to a note attached to it by Pound in 1929 it is 'a partial confession of where I was in the year 1910'. My reason for examining it here is to indicate how far ahead of his contemporaries he was in 1910 and why he was in such a good position to make use of what London had to offer. There is a sentence in his chapter on Camoens which we, in looking back, might now apply to Pound himself:

Every age, every lustrum, yields its crop of pleasant singers, who know the rules, and who write beautiful language and regular rhythms; poetry completely free from the cruder faults: but the art of writing poetry which is vitally interesting is a matter for masters.

It is my contention that in *Spirit of Romance* Pound was already saying things about the art of writing which none of his contemporaries in London could have written and which point as surely as signposts to the years ahead.

In the opening lines of his preface Pound immediately makes it clear that the book is not an attempt at literary scholarship in the accepted academic sense, but the work of a man 'interested in poetry' who is attempting to isolate 'certain forces, elements or qualities which were potent in the medieval literature of the Latin tongues, and are, I believe, still potent in our own'. It is a book about the poetry of the past by a poet who is very much concerned as a practitioner with the poetry of his own day and the immediate future. 'What we need', he writes, 'is a literary scholarship, which will weigh Theocritus and Yeats with one balance, and which will judge dull dead men as inexorably as dull writers of today, and will, with equity, give praise to beauty before referring to an almanack.' We see in this sentence the urge of the American to get things straight, to see some sort of unity in a diversity which others, knowing more than Pound ever did or could about individual compartments, had perhaps been too willing to accept as inevitable or ignore. His thrusting at Milton, his reverence for Dante, his insistence upon the importance of Arnaut Daniel or the greatness of Villon are all present in *Spirit of Romance* as part of a single-minded effort to discover and announce what literature is all about. He might not always be right, he might oversimplify or distort, but every so often some major point is made clear, which future criticism might seek to reject or qualify, but by means of a vision which has been altered by the thing it judges.

I have said above that there are things in the *Spirit* which point to the years ahead. I was not referring merely to pieces of information which turn up again in the prose or cantos of later years; there are many examples of these; but to ideas, already part of his general attitude to literature in 1910, which played a significant part in his conscious struggle with the language between 1911 and 1917. The best way for me to illustrate this is by isolating his line of thought on clarity of the word and the 'prose' element in verse which runs all the way through the early book, and, as we have already seen, was an essential part of his thinking later. In his first chapter he speaks of poetry as 'a sort of inspired mathematics' which gives us 'equations for the human emotions', and again of Ovid as urbane and sceptical, a Roman of the city who 'writes, not in a florid prose, but in a verse which has the clarity of French scientific prose'. In the chapter on Daniel he draws our attention to Daniel's refusal to use the 'journalese' of his day and subside, like some of the other troubadours, into a vocabulary stale and obvious. He also notes, in order to praise, that even in his most complex and difficult poems Daniel's words 'run often with an unperturbed order, almost that of prose'. But it is when we come to the chapters on Tuscan poetry and Dante that we have brought home to us the extent to which Pound was already thinking along lines which would lead to *Imagisme* and beyond. Referring to the precision of Guinicelli's descriptions he says that the use of a more

D

sophisticated epithet is an advance on the Italian's method only
when it suggests a vision not less clear, and remarks that in the
case of both Milton and Swinburne epithet 'is too often merely a
high-sounding word and not a swift symbol of vanished beauty'.
Speaking of the Tuscan period in general he says: 'The best poetry
of this time appeals by its truth, by its subtlety, and by its refined
exactness . . . it is not rhetorical, it aims to be what it is, and never
pretends to be something which it is not.' And finally, in the
chapter on Dante, he says that the *Vita Nuova* is 'strangely un-
adorned', and a few lines further on maintains that 'Dante's precision both in the *Vita Nuova* and the *Commedia* comes from the
attempt to reproduce exactly the thing which has been clearly
seen'.

This particular line of thought points towards the first of the
three principles of good writing formulated by Pound in the
Spring of 1912: 'Direct treatment of the "thing" whether subjective or objective', and towards the sharper poetry of the
volume *Ripostes* published in the Autumn of that year. There is no
need however to jump from 1910 to 1912, for some of the intermediate steps are available for inspection. These steps were: (1)
his translation of the *Sonnets and Ballate of Guido Cavalcanti*; and
(2) a meeting in Germany with Ford Madox Ford who protested
so strongly about Pound's use of artificial 'literary' language that,
as Pound remarked in his obituary on Ford many years later, it
sent him back to his 'own proper effort, namely, toward using the
living tongue'. It is the Cavalcanti that we will examine here,
leaving the story of his meeting with Ford to the next chapter.
Although not published until May 1912 the Cavalcanti was completed a year or more before the date of publication. The introduction, dated 15 November 1910, was probably written during
a visit to the United States. In it we read this:

Than Guido Cavalcanti no psychologist of the emotions is more
keen in his understanding, more precise in his expression; we have in
him no rhetoric, but always a true description. . . .

As for the verse itself: I believe in an ultimate and absolute rhythm
as I believe in an absolute symbol or metaphor. The perception of the
intellect is given in the word, that of the emotions in the cadence. It is

only, then, in perfect rhythm joined to the perfect word that the two-fold vision can be recorded.

It will be seen immediately that this is a development of Pound's earlier thinking as recorded in the *Spirit of Romance*. He is now thinking constantly in terms of precise expression and the 'perfect word' and of the problem of establishing some definite relationship between this expression and the rhythm. His concern with precision in the actual translations themselves is summed up by Anne Paolucci in an article called 'Ezra Pound and D. G. Rossetti as Translators of Guido Cavalcanti' which appeared in the *Romanic Review* for December 1960:

The fluency of Rossetti's translations is not sufficient reason to prefer his effort to that of Pound. If Pound is involved, he is also precise; if his imagery is sometimes strained, it is basically faithful to the Italian; his striving for the 'right' word makes us keenly aware of the special vocabulary of the 'dolce stil novo'—a vocabulary which is rooted deep in a rather elaborate philosophy of love.

That is enough to show that Pound at this stage was devoting considerable thought and effort to precision and rhythm. The book of verse *Canzoni*, published in July 1911, shows that he still had a long way to travel before he achieved in his own verse a language that was at once precise and natural. There is an attempt at 'naturalness' in 'Und Drang' but the effect is a long way short of what he was looking for:

> Only the restless will
> Surges amid the stars
> Seeking new moods of life,
> New permutations.
>
>   .   .   .
>
> Here in the flurry of Fifth Avenue,
> Here where they pass between their teas and teas.[1]

Between *Canzoni* in 1911 and *Ripostes* in 1912 Pound broke the

[1] It is worth noting that about the time *Canzoni* was published, a Harvard graduate student, T. S. Eliot, who did not meet Pound until 1914, was putting the finishing touches to his 'Love Song of J. Alfred Prufrock', which was not published until 1915.

back of the problem confronting him. But ransack the records as we may, read through his *New Age* articles of late 1911, dismantle poems like 'The Seafarer' (first published in November 1911), examine the work on music and the troubadours he did with Walter Morse Rummel in 1910—we are no nearer to an answer. All we know is that he did it, and that *Ripostes* is suddenly full of a new note, containing several poems perfectly worked in the 'modern cadence'.

It has been my aim in this chapter to show that London was responsible for a broadening and clarifying of Pound's attitude to literature and to suggest that it was a necessary part of his education. Pound had the ideas, but London was the necessary climate for their proper growth. Even in 1912, four years after his arrival there, he was still very much impressed by what it had to offer and eager to tell other Americans about it, as in this comment in *Poetry* for January 1913: 'There are men also, who are little known to the general public, but who contribute liberally to the "charm" or the "atmosphere", of London,' and he goes on to list Blunt, Rhys, Plarr and others whose work had 'given pleasure'.

Much of Pound's basic reading in English, the troubadours, Italian poetry, Renaissance and classical Latin, had already been completed when he arrived in England at the age of twenty-three. What London did, with its Museum reading-room, its literary world and conversation, was to provide him with the means of measuring where he had got to in poetry, and the opportunity to bring his partial, perhaps, but extraordinary grasp of past literatures to bear upon the problem of writing contemporary English verse. I have concentrated on his concern with language, speech, the word; but at the same time it is better if we realize that already he was exercising this concern within a cultural context which lasted through to his later work. This striking passage from *Spirit of Romance* will help to show what I mean:

> The Twelfth Century, or, more exactly that century whose centre is the year 1200, has left us two perfect gifts: the Church of San Zeno in Verona, and the canzoni of Arnaut Daniel; by which I would implicate all that is most excellent in the Italian-Romanesque architecture and in Provençal minstrelsy.

While the 'minds' of the age were legislating for orderly angles, and reconstructing the laws of God with an extreme precision, the architects were applying the laws of proportion to buildings 'meet for the new religion,' (or they were simply continuing the use of Byzantine stone forms, lacking the money to incrust the interior with mosaic) and the Troubadours were melting the common tongue and fashioning it into new harmonies depending not upon alternation of quantities but upon rhyme and accent.

Already stated here in clear language is a perception of cultural unity which is central to all Pound's later thinking on cultures and civilization. And while praising this quality of precision which he finds in the Middle Ages he also expresses in the same work another of his main ideas, namely that it was some current of the Renaissance which 'brought in rhetoric and all the attendant horrors', although in 1910 he used the word 'probably', which was dropped from his later statements.

CHAPTER IV

The Norm of Language

THE history of English poetry—one aspect of it—may be seen as a series of struggles by great poets to return to the norm of the language. The purpose of this chapter is to show how the operation performed early this century by Pound and Eliot was in this tradition. But first, having used the word norm, it is essential that I say something about it; if not to define it, at least to give some idea of what I am trying to express by means of it. It is clear, first of all, that not all important poets have waged this struggle; some have even concerned themselves with special developments of language away from the norm; but those to be discussed here are the poets who, in seeking to advance the art in order to keep it abreast of the natural changes of their time, have sought first a return to the natural grain of the language. For, consciously or unconsciously, they have known that this norm, in so far as it can be said to exist at all, is the best starting-point for any attempt to match the new feelings, new ways of looking at things, and the thousand small, almost imperceptible changes which accompany us from decade to decade, year to year, and sometimes even from hour to hour. Now the word norm, in this connection, whatever else one may say about it, certainly does not mean a style of writing which might have been popular or in fashion fifty or two hundred years ago; nor does it mean the language as it is being spoken by any person or group in England or elsewhere at the present moment. But it is possible to get close enough to what I do mean, by reference to a few of the poets in the past who have waged this struggle to freshen literature by contact with the spoken language of the day.

Let us begin with Chaucer. Despite the gap of six hundred years and the great changes that have taken place in language, sensibility and thinking since his time, we find Chaucer so implicated in some essentials of the language as to have produced cadences, tones of voice and emphases which are still with us, still naturally a part of our living language today. The following quotations speak for themselves in such a way, I believe, as to make any further comment on their link with our present language superfluous.

> As why this fissh, and naught that, comth to were

> That whoso stryveth with yow hath the werse

> For many a lovere hastow slayn and wilt

> My word, my werk is knyt so in youre bond
> That, as an harpe obeieth to the hond
> And maketh it soune after his fyngerynge

Shakespeare sometimes saves what would otherwise be disastrous situations by maintaining this relationship with the spoken language. Whereas Marlowe and some others sometimes display a tendency to match outrageous conceits or flights with equally outrageous language, Shakespeare manages somehow to anchor his contrivings to reality by remaining faithful to the language as spoken. Even the carefully contrived and elaborate passages of the later plays are rooted in the living tongue in a way that Milton's elaborations—stemming as they do from one of the directions pursued by the mature Shakespeare—are not. We see it clearly in this passage from *The Winter's Tale*:

> What you do,
> Still betters what is done. When you speake (Sweet)
> I'ld have you do it ever: When you sing,
> I'ld have you buy, and sell so: so give Almes,
> Pray so: and for the ord'ring your Affayres,
> To sing them too. When you do dance, I wish you
> A wave o' th' Sea, that you might ever do
> Nothing but that: move still, still so:
> And owne no other function.

If Milton went as far as it is possible to go in English with a certain kind of elaboration, Dryden fortunately returned to a more natural style and in doing so forged an instrument which proved its worth not only in his own hands—poems, plays and translations—but in the hands of Pope, Johnson, Goldsmith and Crabbe after him. It is no longer necessary to defend Dryden and his followers against the view that however well they wrote it was not poetry. What I do wish to draw attention to, as something easily missed in the search for other qualities, is the absence of strain in their writings, even when dealing with matters of high intensity, and their ability to contain and control these intensities with the greatest economy and to delineate large areas of meaning, justly, in a few words. It may not be the very highest poetry when Pope writes:

> Or stain her honour or her new brocade

or

> At every word a reputation dies

but it is poetry of a very important kind, and like the highest it brings together and relates several layers of meaning, and is similar to the highest in at least one other respect, in that it satisfies reason and common sense even while acting on us through other channels.

It is, however, when we come to Johnson and Goldsmith that we see more clearly the value of this norm, this closeness to the natural language. If great poets are men whom we are inclined to think of as helping to make their age, even while their age is making them, there are lesser figures like Johnson and Goldsmith who are sometimes regarded as distinctly products of their age—as men who made judicious use of what was on hand rather than as innovators who changed the course of literature. These two understood their own limitations, they did not try to do too much; and by carefully observing certain realities in the world around them, weighing those realities justly in the balance of their own learning, their own understanding of tradition and their own experience, and by working with, and modifying, the form left to them by Dryden and Pope, managed to create two small masterpieces, the *Vanity of Human Wishes* and *The Deserted Village*. Probably Crabbe is the last direct descendant of this particular line, though even Fitzgerald gains much by submitting his exotic learning to the discipline of Dryden, and by contriving phrases that move with the natural fall of the words.

Let us now take up this thread in our own century—about the year 1911 when the twenty-six-year-old Pound took his latest book of poems to Germany, there to present it to Ford Madox Ford whom the young American regarded as knowing more about the art of writing and the needs of the time than any other writer. Pound recalled this meeting in his obituary notice on Ford which was published in the August 1939 issue of the *Nineteenth Century and After*:

And he (Ford) felt the errors of contemporary style to the point of rolling (physically, and if you look at it as a mere superficial snob, ridiculously) on the floor of his temporary quarters in Giessen when my third volume displayed me trapped, fly-papered, gummed and strapped down in a jejune provincial effort to learn, *mehercule*, the stilted language that then passed for 'good english' in the arthritic milieu that held control of the respected British critical circles, Newbolt, the backwash of Lionel Johnson, Fred Manning, the Quarterlies and the rest of 'em.

And that roll saved me at least two years, perhaps more. It sent me back to my own proper effort, namely, toward using the living tongue. . . .

The influence of this incident and Ford's criticism generally is already visible in *Ripostes*, but it was not until *Lustra* in 1916 that his mastery over a new poetry became clear. Interesting light is shed on this change by Ford's own criticism; interesting because not only did he know much about the art of writing but was in the thick of London literary life for a number of years without being directly involved as a regular and active participant in the 'new poetry'. The little-known preface which Ford wrote for his own *Collected Poems* of 1914 contains many illuminating paragraphs on the problems of contemporary poetry. For a quarter of a century, he tells us, 'I have kept before me one unflinching aim—to register my own times in terms of my own time, and still more to urge those who are better poets and better prosewriters than myself to have this same aim.' Ford saw clearly that in practical terms this was 'a matter of diction', of diction that would not impede the contemporary flavour and that would enable the poet to register emotions born of contemporary happenings. The 'very strongest emotion' of this class he had ever had—I let him continue in his own words—

was when I first went to the Shepherd's Bush Exhibition and came out on a great square of white buildings all outlined with lights. . . . There were crowds and crowds of people—or no, there was, spread out beneath the lights, an infinite moving mass of black, with white faces turned up to the light, moving slowly, quickly, not moving at all, being obscured, reappearing. . . .

What we are in, that which is all around us, is the Crowd—the Crowd blindly looking for joy or for that most pathetic of all things, the good time. I think that that is why I felt so profound an emotion on that occasion. It must have been the feeling—not the thought— of all these good, kind, nice people, this immense Crowd suddenly let loose upon a sort of Tom Tiddler's ground to pick up the glittering splinters of glass that are Romance, hesitant but certain of vistas of adventure, if no more than the adventures of their own souls—like cattle in a herd suddenly let into a very rich field and hesitant before the enamel of daisies, the long herbage, the rushes fringing the stream at the end.

I think pathos and poetry are to be found beneath those lights and in those sounds—in the larking of the anaemic girls, in the shoulders of the women in evening dress, in the idealism of the pickpocket slanting through a shadow and imagining himself a hero whose end will be wealth and permanent apartments in the Savoy Hotel. For such dreamers of dreams there are.

That indeed appears to me—and I am writing as seriously as I can— the real stuff of the poetry of our day.

The poet playing for safety and the critic trying to find something safe to praise will be looking for love in country lanes, the song of birds, the comfrey under the hedge; looking, in short, for something to sentimentalize over, taking it for granted, says Ford, that sentimentalizing is the business of poetry:

But it is not really; for the business of poetry is not sentimentalism so much as the putting of certain realities in certain aspects. The comfrey under the hedge, judged by these standards, is just a plant—but the ashbucket at dawn is a symbol of poor humanity, of its aspirations, its romance, its ageing and its death. . . . The empty tin of infant's food stands for birth; the torn up scrap of a doctor's prescription for death. . . . And similarly, the anaemic shop-girl at the Exhibition, with her bad teeth and her cheap black frock, is safer than Isolde. She is more down to the ground and much more touching.

The past of course is important; we should soak ourselves in Sappho, Bertran de Born, Walther von der Vogelweide, the bardic chants of Patric: 'Let us do anything in the world that will widen our perceptions,' he says, in a passage that reminds us, in its way, of the essay 'Prolegomena' published by Pound in the *Poetry Review* of London in February 1912, several years before Ford's preface, and also of passages in *Spirit of Romance*. This impression of similarity is further strengthened when we read Ford's statement that although we are heirs of all the ages, the purpose of our studies with past writers 'is the right appreciation of such facets of our own day as God will let us perceive'.

Ford's preface is long, even long-winded, with his usual irrelevancies and whimsicalities; but he keeps coming back to the subject of modern poetry and when he does his grasp of the subject is obvious. For instance, poetry is 'the putting of the one thing in juxtaposition with the other . . . because such juxtapositions suggest emotions'. In another place he writes that 'It is, in fact, better to be vulgar than affected, at any rate if you practise poetry', and again that 'I prefer personally the language of my own day, a language clear enough for certain matters, employing slang where slang is felicitous and vulgarity where it seems to me that vulgarity is the only weapon against dullness'. Yet despite his knowledge and his own writing ability and the fact that he was 'breathless' at the new opportunities available to the poet in the modern world, he was, as he admits himself, unable to do anything about it: 'I am for ever on the look out for some poet who shall render modern life with all its values. I do not think that there was ever, as the saying is, such a chance for the poet; I am breathless, I am agitated at the thought of having it to begin upon. And yet I am aware that I can do nothing . . .' His reason for writing about it has been merely 'to voice what I imagine will be the views or the aspirations, the preferences or the prejudices, of the poet of my day and circumstances when he shall at last appear'.

Actually of course two such poets were already at work on the problem; but one of them, T. S. Eliot, whose 'Prufrock', 'Rhapsody on a Windy Night' and first three 'Preludes' had been completed several years before, spent a good part of 1914 as a Harvard graduate student studying philosophy on the Continent, and did not enter London literary life (and then only gradually) until he journeyed to England on the outbreak of war and met Ezra Pound in Kensington on 22 September 1914. 'Prufrock' was not published until the middle of 1915. The other poet, Pound himself, was probably too closely involved with Ford for the latter to be able to view his work with any sort of detachment—detachment not being his strong point in matters like this—or perhaps he would never have recognized it no matter who was the author, for he belonged essentially to the pre-war period, and, as Hugh Kenner has remarked, to an order 'incompatible with the very exertion by which it might save itself'. At a time when the complex of 'energies' which had made London the centre of power for such a long time was gradually slipping westward across the Atlantic, Ford, who saw a great deal of what needed to be done in order to create a 'new poetry', confessed his feeling of inadequacy, his inability to do anything about it. Nor is it strange perhaps that the job which he found beyond him should have been tackled successfully by two young men who belonged to the country which was taking over from England as the main centre of world power.

Leaving Ford on the threshold let us now examine some aspects of the 'revolution' performed by Pound and Eliot in the light of what has already been said about diction and the norm of language. Now there is no better introductory test of a piece of verse, I believe, than the impact of its rhythm. If the rhythm sounds right to the experienced ear on the first or second reading, we are justified in regarding that piece of verse as worthy of closer examination. And there is, further, a handy introductory test of rhythm, which is no certain proof that it is good but useful as a thumb-rule, in so far as all good verse seems to pass it, and the bad, never. It is this: a good line or passage you can recite in three or four different ways, placing your emphasis now here, now there, letting the words fall this way or that; and yet, no matter what variations one makes, the verse, if good, takes hold upon the reader, imposing itself, imposing a tone, imposing an inevitable rhythm. Bad or indifferent verse on the other hand admits of only one sure way of being read: one can force or distort it, but if the poet's intended rhythm is to be retained, then it has to be read one way and one way only. And turning to the poetry of Pound and Eliot we find that masterly use of rhythm is a distinguishing feature which sets it apart from most other poetry of the period 1911 to 1922, the period that concerns us here. They gave us a new tension and intensity, achieved by means of rhythms and images caught in the very gait of the language—a poetry intensified rather than lessened by the presence of 'prosaic' elements. There is lurking always, in or behind each phrase or line, the ghost or echo of something we may have heard somebody say, once, at some place we cannot recall, and preserved in our mind, just out of reach, as the wraith of a human voice.

Let us go back to an earlier period in our literature and compare a passage from *Gorboduc*—a landmark in the history of the drama —with a passage from Marlowe after he had 'revolutionized' blank verse:

> Your lasting age shall be their longer stay,
> For cares of Kings, that rule as you have ruled,
> For public wealth and not for private joy,
> Do waste man's life, and hasten crooked age
> (*Gorboduc*)

> Marriage is but a ceremonial toy;
> If thou lovest me, think no more of it.
> I'll cull thee out the fairest courtesans,
> And bring them every morning to thy bed:
> She whom thine eye shall like, thy heart shall have,
> Be she as chaste as was Penelope,
> As wise as Saba, or as beautiful
> As was bright Lucifer before his fall.
> (*Faustus*)

The difference is enormous; and yet we see that it is not simply a question of naturalness. Many would say that the first, although obviously inferior, is in a sense more natural than the second. Marlowe gets his variety by subjugating speech to the texture of his verse. *Gorboduc* is less 'artificial', less contrived perhaps, but the naturalness does not penetrate below the surface; in the Marlowe the natural speech rhythms are imprisoned in and made part of the very backbone of the verse. By keeping this comparison before us we shall be better able to appreciate the difference between the rhythms created by Pound and Eliot and those of a poet like Robert Graves, whose latest verse even is in many ways pre-Eliot in diction. Let us compare a fairly recent Graves poem with examples from Pound and Eliot about fifty years old.

> Were I to cut my hand
>   On the sharp knife you gave me
>   (That dangerous knife, your beauty),
> I should know what to do:
>   Bandage the wound myself
> And hide the blood from you.
>
>   (Graves, 'The Dangerous Gift')

> I am moved by fancies that are curled
> Around these images, and cling:
> The notion of some infinitely gentle
> Infinitely suffering thing.
>
> Wipe your hand across your mouth, and laugh;
> The worlds revolve like ancient women
> Gathering fuel in vacant lots.
>
>   (Eliot, 'Prelude IV')

> I would bathe myself in strangeness;
> These comforts heaped upon me, smother me!
> I burn, I scald so for the new,
> New friends, new faces,
> Places!
> Oh to be out of this,
> This that is all I wanted
>   —save the new.
>
>   (Pound, 'The Plunge')

We see immediately that the difference between the first of these passages and the other two is the same as that between the lines from *Gorboduc* and those from *Faustus*. The lines by Robert Graves are, like the *Gorboduc*, very natural in their way, but they lack the sense of muscle and sinew beneath the surface which we get from the lines by Pound and Eliot. All three make use of the spoken language, but the first in a manner quite different from that of the other two. Whereas Graves seems to imitate certain aspects of speech, so that his verse gives the appearance of being outwardly simple and natural, Pound and Eliot incorporate certain elements of the spoken language into the texture of verse which is contrived and 'artificial' and not at all simple.

In my previous references to the 'prosaic' elements in poetry, I was referring to those qualities which, as Eliot says in his 1930 essay on Dr Johnson, 'good verse shares with good prose'. As he points out in the same essay, a great deal of the inferior verse of the eighteenth century is inferior not because it is too prosaic, as the cliché has it, but because it is not prosaic enough. He puts the matter in a nutshell thus: 'To have the virtues of good prose is the first and minimum requirement of good poetry.' There is, however, another aspect of prose we need to discuss in examining the Pound-Eliot 'revolution'. For while they were responsible for a full-blooded reintroduction into English poetry of the prosaic virtues they were also responsible for delivering the poet from *exposition*; from the necessity of having to write verse after the manner of expository prose. They delivered poetry from reliance on explanatory passages linking together and commenting on the passages of greater intensity, and left it free to pursue its own proper business rather than compete with prose in the exposition of philosophy as such, or history or certain types of story-telling, for which prose is by far the best medium. This new step also made available to poetry a dangerous but sometimes effective method of articulation which had never been fully exploited in the past. By careful juxtaposition of passages no longer held apart by intermediary explanation the poet was enabled to produce an additional charge of meaning.

And as a result of these various changes, poetry, as a mirror of contemporary sensibility, was able to make up the ground it had lost to prose during the 19th century. There is, even in Eliot's 'Portrait of a Lady' written while he was still at Harvard, a strength, an ability to consume and transform reality, such as belongs to the best poetry, and which no amount of deftness in the novelist can ever quite match:

> returning as before
> Except for a slight sensation of being ill at ease
> I mount the stairs and turn the handle of the door
> And feel as if I had mounted on my hands and knees.

What Pound and Eliot brought back into our verse was that direct intensity which startles us in the best poetry of old. This intensity is impossible to define, but we know it as soon as we come across it, and we wonder at it, for it is usually simple with a blessed simplicity, quite different from that of *Gorboduc* or Graves, and which yields us nothing if we try to take it apart:

> The oddes is gone
> And there is nothing left remarkable
> Beneath the visiting moon.
> *(Anthony and Cleopatra)*

The reader may well seek at this stage the common thread to justify our ranging over the widely scattered elements that have been brought together in this chapter. The answer is *things:* an appetite for things, the ability of these poets to place a finger, at the right moment, upon some concrete thing, as a means of bringing to life some universal meaning which had previously remained dormant or unknown. Even Ford had this appetite; it shows in his novels, in some of his other prose, and there is also Pound's remark in the *Pisan Cantos* about Ford's conversation being better than Yeats's in that it consisted of *res* and not *verba*. There are certain types of poetry—those of Swinburne and Dylan Thomas for example—which produce brilliant effects by a process which may be described as the striking together of words. The intensity which I am trying to describe here, however, is of another kind, which—to pursue the figure just used—is produced by the striking together of things. Just as intellectual ideas cannot compete in effectiveness with the experience of concrete facts which stimulate the affections and the passions, so words unanchored in the concrete or 'reality' cannot compete with those fastened firmly to things. The strange power of things when handled by a master is evident when we compare the songs of Shakespeare with those of Campion. Campion is sometimes unsurpassed in his feeling for the movement of words—as in the opening lines of 'Kinde are her answeres':

> Kinde are her answeres,
> But her performance keeps no day;
> Breaks time, as dancers
> From their own Musick when they stray . . .

This is art of a high degree, but the fact is that Shakespeare's songs sting the mind in a way that Campion's do not, for the reason that they are composed of things which strike into the visual imagination and stay there:

> Between the acres of the rye

> And in sad cypresse let me be laide

> And winking Mary-buds begin to ope their golden eyes

> And merry larks are ploughman's clocks

> And Dick the shepherd blows his nail

In:

> Blow, blow thou winter wind,
> Thou art not so unkind
> As man's ingratitude

the poet evokes both the concrete and the universal, without giving us a list of examples: he summons echoes of concrete cases of ingratitude without any actual case intruding too far into the forefront of the imagination. There is a noteworthy description in Newman's *Grammar of Assent* of this realm of mind which

E

hovers between the apprehension of the concrete and abstract
thought, partaking of both as the mind acts upon the immediate
experience by drawing it into relation with past experience and
past abstractions. I can bring before me, he says, the music of
the *Adeste Fideles,* as if I were actually hearing it:

and the scent of the clematis as if I were in my garden; and the
flavour of a peach as if it were in season; and the thought I have of all
these is as of something individual and from without,—as much as the
things themselves, the tune, the scent, and the flavour, are from without,—though, compared with the things themselves, these images (as
they may be called) are faint and intermitting.

Nor need such an image be in any sense an abstraction; though I
may have eaten a hundred peaches in times past, the impression, which
remains on my memory of the flavour, may be of any of them, of the
ten, twenty, thirty units, as the case may be, not a general notion,
distinct from every one of them, and formed from all of them by a
fabrication of mind.

A little further on he describes how the mind handles direct
experiences:

Experience tells us only of individual things, and these things are
innumerable. . . . Instinctively, even though unconsciously, we are
ever instituting comparisons between the manifold phenomena of the
external world, as we meet with them, criticizing, referring to a standard, collecting, analysing them. Nay, as if by one and the same action,
as soon as we perceive them, we also perceive that they are like each
other, or unlike, or rather both like and unlike at once. We apprehend
spontaneously, even before we set about apprehending, that man is
like man, yet unlike; and unlike a horse, a tree, a mountain, or a monument, yet in some, though not the same respects, like each of them.
And in consequence, as I have said, we are ever grouping and dis-
criminating, measuring and sounding, framing cross classes and cross
divisions, and thereby rising from particulars to generals, that is from
images to notions.

His brief summary of the difference between real apprehension
and notional apprehension and their dependence upon one another
is also worth quoting for the light it throws on the power of
things to penetrate the mind when handled by a master poet:

To apprehend notionally is to have breadth of mind, but to be shallow; to apprehend really is to be deep, but to be narrow-minded. The latter is the conservative principle of knowledge, and the former the principle of its advancement. Without the apprehension of notions, we should forever pace round one small circle of knowledge; without a firm hold upon things, we shall waste ourselves in vague speculations. However, real apprehension has the precedence, as being the scope and end and test of the notional; and the fuller is the mind's hold upon things or what it considers such, the more fertile is it in its aspects of them, and the more practical its definitions.

It is largely by exploiting this middle ground, where our experience of the more or less immediate concrete meets not only with the abstract but with all that our mind has done with past experience and past thought and abstraction, that a small part of the poetry of one age lasts to become an acknowledged part of tradition. But sometimes the means used to exploit this ground in one age become the clichés of the next; and the only way that this can be overcome is by renewing the means to match the new situation. The Pound-Eliot 'revolution' was a return to the past in order to renew the links connecting past and present, but it also provided a new means of advance which was not available in such clear-cut form to any previous age. This consisted of the imaginative arrangement of poetic passages no longer held apart by intermediary explanation. Brought to its highest point so far in the *Four Quartets*, this method has not really been taken advantage of by the generations that have followed its introduction.

CHAPTER V

Good Writing and the Health of Society

WE MUST distinguish carefully among three different kinds of writing if we wish to make a just assessment of what Pound has had to say about the connection between art and society. These are: (1) writings on the social function of poetry, in which poetry is treated as itself and not something else; (2) writings which communicate or define some intuition or idea about the overall health of society, as it includes literature; and (3) those which deal more or less with politics or economics and must be labelled accordingly. In those of the first category Pound writes as a poet about poetry with the special qualifications and limitations of the poet in this field. His writings in the second category are harder to deal with, for here Pound still writes as a poet, as one with the language in his care, but the things he writes about are matters which sometimes come under the heading of politics, so that great skill is needed otherwise the poet finds himself involved in the third category, as a politician among politicians, no longer able to control the words he is using. Much of Pound's critical prose as collected in the *Literary Essays* falls naturally in the first category, while much of what he says in *Guide to Kulchur* wavers between the second and third and sometimes definitely crosses over into politics. Here I will deal with those writings in which he speaks as a poet about what he believes to be the social function of his art.

In so far as Pound has succeeded as a poet, he has done so, I believe, by virtue of his practical application of certain basic principles of good writing which he discovered while studying Dante, Catullus, Martial, Villon and perhaps Daniel very early in his career. These principles have remained with him as a sort of keel throughout his literary life. In an essay called 'The

Wisdom of Poetry' published in the *Forum* of April 1912, Pound
referred to poetry as strengthening the 'perceptive faculties' and
freeing them from such encumbrances as 'set moods, set ideas,
conventions; from the results of experience which is common but
unnecessary, experience induced by the stupidity of the experi-
encer and not by the inevitable laws of nature'. The language is
constantly wearing out under the grind of usage, and it is the
poet's job to renew it:

Thought is perhaps important to the race, and language, the medium
of thought's preservation, is constantly wearing out. It has been the
function of poets to new-mint the speech, to supply the vigorous terms
for prose. Thus Tacitus is full of Vergilian half lines; and poets may be
'kept on' as conservators of the public speech, or prose, perhaps, becoming more and more an art, may become, or may have become
already, self-sustaining.

. . . Now that mechanical science has realized his ancient dreams of
flight and sejunct communication, he is the advance guard of the
psychologist on the watch for new emotions, new vibrations sensible
to faculties as yet ill understood. As Dante writes of the sunlight coming
through clouds from a hidden source and illuminating part of a field,
long before the painters had depicted such effects of light and shade, so
are later watchers on the alert for color perceptions of a subtler sort,
neither affirming them to be 'astral' or 'spiritual' nor denying the
formulae of theosophy. The traditional methods are not antiquated,
nor are poets necessarily the atavisms which they seem. Thus poets may
be retained as friends of this religion of doubt, but the poet's true and
lasting relation to literature and life is that of the abstract mathemati-
cian to science and life . . .

A certain man named Plarr and another man whose name I have forgotten, some years since, developed the functions of a certain obscure
sort of equation, for no cause save their own pleasure in the work. The
applied science of their day had no use for the deductions, a few sheets
of paper covered with arbitrary symbols—without which we should
have no wireless telegraph.

What the analytical geometer does for space and form, the poet does
for the states of consciousness.

His speaking here of poetry in terms of science shows how he
was wrapped up in the idea of precision, even though it is wrong

to draw an analogy between scientific precision and the precision
of the poet, which are completely different and not to be treated
in this way.

Pound began the job of sorting what he wanted from modern
French literature during his visit to Paris in 1906, and as far as
earlier French poetry is concerned he was certain of Villon's
greatness by the time he wrote *Spirit of Romance*. It is hard to say
when exactly he saw how important modern French poetry was
in the struggle for precision in English; but towards the end of
1913 he felt confident enough to write in *Poetry* that 'practically
the whole development of the English verse-art has been achieved
by steals from the French, from Chaucer's time to our own, and
the French are always twenty to sixty years in advance'. The same
views about the social function of poetry which he expressed in
his *Forum* article he took up again in a series of short articles in
the *Little Review* a few years later. In an editorial in the issue of
May 1917 he wrote:

> If any human activity is sacred it is the formulation of thought in
> clear speech for the use of humanity; any falsification or evasion is
> evil . . . I see no reason for concealing my belief that the two novels, by
> Joyce and Lewis,[1] and Mr Eliot's poems are not only the most important
> contributions to English literature of the past three years, but that they
> are practically the only works of the time in which the creative element
> is present, which in any way show invention, or a progress beyond
> precedent work. The mass of our contemporaries, to say nothing of our
> debilitated elders, have gone on repeating themselves and each other. . . .
> I cannot believe that the mere height of the Rocky Mountains will pro-
> duce lofty poetry; we have had little from Chimborazo, the Alps or
> the Andes. I cannot believe that the mere geographical expanse of
> America will produce of itself excellent writing. The desert of Sahara
> is almost equally vast. . . . The Arts are not the mediocre habit of man-
> kind. There is no common denominator between the little that is good
> and the waste that is dull, mediocre.

For about five years the *Little Review* provided Pound not only
with pages in which he could publish Joyce, Lewis, Eliot and
himself, all together, without unnecessary delay, but also with

---

[1] *Portrait of the Artist* and *Tarr*.

an editorial soap-box from which he could lay down the law. Some of the summaries on writing which he produced at this time are no longer worth reprinting because Pound has said the same things better in other essays which are readily available, but one or two of them still deserve to be remembered, even if only in brief quotation. This distinction, for instance, between journalism and literature, which was published in the issue of October 1917:

The root of the difference is that in journalism the reader finds what he is looking for, what he, the reader, wants; whereas in literature he must find at least a part of what the author intended.

That is why 'the first impression of a work of genius' is 'nearly always disagreeable', at least to the 'average man'. The public loathe the violence done to their self-conceit whenever an author conveys to them an idea that is his, not their own.

The difference is lasting and profound. Even in the vaguest of poetry, or the vaguest music, where in a sense the receiver may, or must, make half the beauty he is to receive, there is always something of the author or composer which must be transmitted.

In journalism, or the 'bad art' which is but journalism thinly disguised, there is no such strain on the public.

He developed this idea in the issue of November of the following year:

The demand that the public shall agree with the author's utterance has become the curse of contemporary letters. . . .

The authentic presentation of his subject is job enough for any author; very few have attained it.

The intelligent man must fight the dominant imbecilities of his time, whether they are 'aristocratic' or 'democratic', mono-tyrannic or demo-tyrannic.

The man who states the fact as he sees it is of no more 'value to the state' than the man who receives a salary for uttering a set programme (religious, economic, political or literary, or 'educational'). His value is proportionate to the clarity and precision of his statement; to the closeness of correspondence between his statement and fact.

This of course is not a satisfactory definition of good literature, nor perhaps did Pound intend it as such, but it is something we

need to be reminded of, in one form or another, in every generation. It was about this time that Pound began to put his knowledge of modern French literature into some sort of order. He
published a translation of a poem by Laforgue in May 1917, and
a short but very important essay called 'Irony, Laforgue, and
Some Satire' about six months later. In February of the following
year he published another important article, 'The Hard and Soft
in French Poetry' and also his long 'Study of French Poets' which
was reprinted in *Instigations* (1920) and *Make it New* (1934), but
is now unfortunately out of print. Most of this concern with
modern French verse had to do with his search for literary precision. We see this particularly in the selections he made from the
works of the poets examined in his 'Study'. Take Rimbaud:
Pound's interest in this poet had very little in common with the
point of view of later critics. Pound was a maker of poems, and
so was Rimbaud. He visited Rimbaud's work as a visiting engineer,
interested no doubt in the final product, but with those special
interests which drive the craftsman to examine and tinker with
technical details and the means employed in arriving at a given
end. He wanted to know how Rimbaud achieved a certain type
of clarity. In the 'Study' he gave his quotations in French only,
not bothering to translate, but forty years later he re-read the
essay and translated five of these quotations into English verse.
The results are worth attention here for they show immediately
why Pound went to Rimbaud at a time when he was putting the
finishing touches on his own style and technique in preparation
for the *Cantos*. Rimbaud provided him with proof that some of
the effects he was looking for could best be obtained by the
presentation of objects unencumbered by comment.

This is how he translated 'Au Cabaret-Vert':

> Wearing out my shoes, 8th day
> On the bad roads, I got into Charleroi.
> Bread, butter, at the Green Cabaret
> And the ham half cold.
>
> Got my legs stretched out
> And was looking at the simple tapestries,

Very nice when the gal with the big bubs
And lively eyes,

Not one to be scared of a kiss and more,
Brought the butter and bread with a grin
And the luke-warm ham on a coloured plate,

Pink ham, white fat and a sprig
Of garlic, and a great chope of foamy beer
Gilt by the sun in that atmosphere.[1]

This poem shows the validity in at least one case of Pound's belief that 'the natural object is always the *adequate* symbol'. Simple objects arranged by the poet in a special context can take on an intensity of meaning which they do not possess in dull poetry or ordinary speech. Pound's choice of the word 'symbol' to describe this process is not a happy one, especially in view of the other uses to which it had already been put; but there is no doubt about the power of words denoting ordinary objects when selected and given a context by a great poet. I do not attempt to explain why this is so, I am content to draw attention to it. A method similar to that used by Rimbaud served Pound admirably at times in the early cantos:

> the sun-tanned, gracious and well-formed fingers
> Lift no latch of bent bronze, no Empire handle
> Twists for the knocker's fall
>
> (Canto 7)

> Air moving under the boughs,
> The cedars there in the sun,
> Hay new cut on hill slope,
> And the water there in the cut
> Between the two lower meadows; sound,
> The sound, as I have said, a nightingale
> Too far off to be heard.
>
> (Canto 20)

[1] First published in Ezra Pound, 'Five French Poems', *The Edge*, Melbourne, October 1956. With French text: Ezra Pound, *Rimbaud*, Milan, 1957.

This same method he used with great authority in the *Pisan Cantos*, investing it there with a new dignity or decorum:

> Judith's junk shop
> > with Theophile's arm chair
> > one cd/ live in such an apartment
> > seeing the roofs of Paris

In 1921 Pound said goodbye to London after twelve full years and moved to Paris; and it was during this period when Europe was in a state of collapse that he began the task of trying to knit his poetry to the whole world of human affairs and history. It is easy from our elevated position to pass judgement on Pound's decision to enter the world of history, politics and contemporary economics: it was a false step, he should have kept to matters within his own capacity: these are the things critics have said, and in a way they are right; but it should be remembered that in 1920 the pervading fatuity of the modern world was something new, it had not become as common as the air we breathe, as it is today. Pound, a Yankee with a strong Puritan streak in him, began naturally to think in terms of getting into the struggle and doing something about it. What he lacked was that ability to make a calm appreciation of human beings in their pursuit of power or prestige, which was granted to Ben Jonson, Dryden and Pope. Lack of this ability was probably the main reason why he was led up so many garden paths which might well have been the end of poetry in a lesser artist; but in Pound's case his dedication to the principles of good writing, such as I have been tracing, had such a hold on him, that when it came to the writing of 'political' cantos, fads and foibles had to pass through a stern recording instrument that was usually more accurate than the Pound of some of his prose outbursts. Some pieces may have got through into the *Cantos* which mar the work and detract from its coherence and beauty, but the achievement far outweighs the defects. In the 'Paris Letter' which he published in the *Dial* of September 1922 we notice that despite a certain shift of emphasis he is still the artist who in 1912 spoke of the importance of clear thought and language:

Civilization, as Flaubert had known it, appeared to be foundering; Gautier died, as Flaubert wrote, 'suffocated by modern stupidity' and Flaubert thinking of Gautier feels 'as if a tide of filth' were rising around him and submerging him. This tide of *immondices* must be considered as messy thought, general muddle. 'We pay for the long deceit in which we have lived, everything was false, false army, false politics, and false credit.' 'The present is abominable, and the future ferocious.' So run the phrases of his correspondence. . . .

With Dickens, with any provincial writer there is an 'answer', which the author and reader know; a touch of kindness, the payment of the instalment due on the mortgage, et cetera; but with Flaubert, with the writer of first magnitude there is no answer, humanity being what it is, and the given character moving inside its own limitations there is *no* easy way out; the given situation has arisen, and will continue to arise; the impasse is a biological impasse. Human capacity, perseverance, endurance continuing static, it will continue to be an impasse. Hence the idea of literature assuming the duties of a science—despite the sentimentalist's shudder and the lazy man's objection to the term 'science'. I take it that good poets have always believed this, but that the light has come to a few prose-authors.

When examining literature in which he was interested Pound was able to resist the whole trend of his own make-up towards finding 'answers'; anyone trying to understand Pound's work must face the fact that the man who wrote 'there is *no* easy way out' was the same who later claimed that the Second World War began 'in 1694 with the foundation of the Bank of England'. About seven years after this 'Paris letter' he published two articles, 'Mr Aldington's Views on Gourmont' and 'How to Read', both of which show that he still had an artist's interest in the social function of his art. Although he had moved to Italy in the intervening period and spent much of his time enquiring into such matters as the manufacture of armaments, Italian history and monetary economics, he still clung to the view that the artist's main job is with his art and not somewhere else. Only during the 1930's do we find him neglecting his art and spending a disproportionate amount of time and energy with politics and such fruitless side-issues as the internal dissensions of English and American monetary reform groups. What Pound lacked, as I have said, was the ability to look at human beings with a calm eye; but let me add immediately that this was not something which set him apart from his fellows, either inside or outside the arts, but something he shared with the greater part of mankind. But to return to his concern with his art, there is one passage in 'Mr Aldington's Views on Gourmont' published in the *Dial* of January 1929, which deserves to be read in full:

As to the inestimable value of Gourmont, inestimable in the sense of incalculable, and very great, we must consider him as a definite and actual force still operative. We cannot afford to lose sight of his value, of his significance as a type, a man standing for freedom and honesty of thought, a type rarer than the 'general reader' imagines, for the general reader does not know, and I doubt if even men of letters realize until they have been on their job a long time (say twenty years as a minimum) how many well known and so called 'critical' writers pass their whole lives in, and how many entire periodicals are given over to, the production of statements agreeable to editors, agreeable to the book trade (in the widest sense of the term, publishers, printers, bookshops) but having nothing whatever to do with thought, civilization, or honesty.

The article 'How to Read', which was first published in the books section of the *New York Herald Tribune* about the same time, contains what is probably the best summary Pound ever made of his beliefs about the part poetry plays inside the actual workings of society. It is an oversimplification, but within its limitations it remains one of the best attempts of its kind:

It [literature] has to do with the clarity and vigour of 'any and every' thought and opinion. It has to do with maintaining the very cleanliness of the tools, the health of the very matter of thought itself. Save in the rare and limited instances of invention in the plastic arts, or in mathematics, the individual cannot think and communicate this thought, the governor and legislator cannot act effectively or frame his laws, without words, and the solidity and validity of these words is in the care of the damned and despised *litterati*. When their work goes rotten—by that I do not mean when they express indecorous thoughts—but when their very medium, the very essence of their work, the application of word to thing goes rotten, i.e. becomes slushy and inexact, or excessive or bloated, the whole machinery of social and of individual thought and order goes to pot. This is a lesson of history, and a lesson not yet half learned.

During the late 1920's and early 1930's Pound devoted much of his time to preparing an Italian text of Guido Cavalcanti, with commentary, which was published in Genoa in 1932 under the title *Guido Cavalcanti: Rime*. This led him to publish the following note on precision in the *New Review* of August-September-October 1931:

Certain kinds of depth are obtainable only I suppose with a concision that produces an apparent obscurity. The test is probably: precision. If the phrase is exact the obscurity grows steadily less with increased attention from the reader. As with Guido's 'luce rade'. If however the expression is inexact, the longer and more intensely the reader considers it, the less he respects the author.

Several years later he made one of his periodic attempts to come to terms with teachers of English in the United States, by contributing an article on accuracy of statement, and the morality of ideas expressed in that statement, to the *English Journal* of May 1933. And a few months later he touched on a similar matter in *Poetry*: 'I do not believe that authors will attain interest merely by seeing the "LARGER" subject,' he wrote, and then went on to say that eighty per cent of 'the worst poetry in the world has been written about the largest possible subjects; infinity, God and eternity. The best poem on all these subjects is the *Paradiso*, which contains more precise and specific statements and more concrete exact presentations than all the rest put together.'

As one goes through Pound's prose during the 1930's it is impossible to escape the conclusion that as time went on and he became more and more interested in history and monetary economics, he tended to lose interest altogether in a great deal of important literature. This led to a falling off in the quality of his literary prose. The essay on Horace, which he contributed to the *Criterion* of January 1930, has some bright sentences—this one, for instance: 'Landor was almost unique in examining specific passages of verse to see whether they were well or ill written or if they could be improved'; but taken as a whole it is dull because he was not really interested in Horace nor in writing an expository essay. He shows up to better advantage in the correspondence pages of the issue of July 1931, where he was not under an obligation to explain himself at length:

> Heaven knows all English printed matter having to do with philosophy or aesthetics is sufficiently rotted by false dilemma, and by sloppy ideology unbased on any immediate and clear perception of the subject treated, but Spengler has reached a nadir where Bach and Wagner can be lumped into one category and said to express the same state of something or other.

Only once or twice, as in the essay 'Date Line', does he really concentrate and write a good literary essay, although even this is marred by an exercise of his incredible lack of judgement in non-literary matters. Even the death of René Crevel, a French writer whom he greatly admired, did not stir him to any great heights in the obituary essay he contributed to the *Criterion* of January 1939; it is a dull affair, although it does show that his belief about the social function of writers had not changed since 1912: 'The social function of writers is to keep the nation's language living and capable of precise registration.' Where once he had enjoyed writing about literature, he had now lost interest in literature as such and was trying to treat all subjects as part of one large subject, the process of history.

At this point I shall break off temporarily from Pound's own writings to review his part in discovering, recognizing and promoting other writers now generally acknowledged to be among the most important of the twentieth century. Such a review has a place in our attempt to sort out and label the various elements in Pound's literary career, for several reasons. In the first place his talent as an entrepreneur has often been confused with his literary talent—a confusion which needs resolving at the outset. There is a connection between the two, in Pound's case, but the one does not follow automatically from the other. Once this is understood it is then possible to examine the work of Pound the entrepreneur, carefully, to see whether or not it can help us to appreciate his achievement as a writer. And we do in fact discover that his activity as a promoter of good writing was part of the 'atmosphere' in which he carried out some of his own most important work as a poet and critic. It does not explain this work, but it does help us to see it better in its natural habitat.

It should be borne in mind that the sum of the parts we are attempting to disentangle and name in this book, does not add up to an Ezra Pound. Discover all the elements and put them together again, but you still will not have the creator of great poetry. The analysis is necessary, because Pound's work, the actual texts from which criticism draws its meaning, has long been obscured by a preference for biography over the real business of the critic, which is the sensitive weighing of a poem against relevant texts drawn from, and related to, the body of tradition. What may at first appear as merely another attempt to introduce biography by the back door, is really something quite different. It is a clearing away of some of the accumulated rubbish of half a century so that the reader who wishes to appreciate Pound's work may have at his disposal the text plus an accurate sketch of its immediate context. I am not attempting to *explain* Pound's work, or even to rule out biography entirely: at most I hope to leave the reader in possession of such facts as may encourage him to read Pound through his own eyes without too much distraction from outside. Nobody can read with completely innocent eyes, and it is probably true that a certain amount of 'accepted opinion' causes tension and heightens one's enjoyment of any good book, so long as one makes, at the same time, an effort to pull in the opposite direction and to see the text for the first time. The trouble in the case of Pound is that 'accepted opinion' is all-powerful; the reader is smothered in assumptions of a compelling nature even before he starts, and unless he has special gifts, reads Pound through the eyes of others without having any idea of the extent to which this is so. We are providing the reader here with the means to struggle free. The reader who assumes that the only really important literature of the present century is that promoted, or approved of, by Pound, is just as much mistaken as the one who believes that anything touched by Pound is probably hollow or pretentious. As we shall now see, his ability to pick important new work, out of a mass of writing that was simply 'new' and nothing else, was not unrelated to his striving after clarity and precision in his own work, and his critical activity on behalf of these same qualities. If generally his judgements were limited by his preoccupation with these qualities, almost to the exclusion of others, yet this was not so in all cases. Occasionally he was capable of seeing the importance of work lying almost completely outside his own critical categories, or at any rate outside the application he gave them.

CHAPTER VI

Central Judgements
on Contemporary Literature

'I WANT a place where I and T. S. Eliot can appear once a month (or once an issue) and where Joyce can appear when he likes, and where Wyndham Lewis can appear if he comes back from the war.'

These words occur in a letter written by Pound to Margaret Anderson of the *Little Review* early in 1917. I have begun with this quotation because it sets out clearly what is, I suppose, the most important of all Pound's judgements on contemporary work, and is a fitting reminder of the certainty with which he put it forward at a time when the world of English letters was not even mildly concerned at the existence, let alone the merits, of Lewis, Joyce or Eliot. In the title of this chapter I speak of 'central' judgements. In other words Pound's judgements were not all of the same kind or quality. It is enough for our present purposes if we distinguish between his 'central' judgements, meaning those where he meant absolutely what he said, at the very uppermost, so to speak, of his technical and professional faculties, and secondly those judgements which are not really judgements at all, in the strict sense, but pronouncements uttered as literary propaganda, with some practical end in view. Obviously this twofold division is not completely satisfactory, for some of the judgements which fall into the first category were sometimes put forward by Pound later for reasons of propaganda; but the judgement preceded the use to which it was later put, whereas those in the other category are not really distinguishable from Pound's general aim of putting new life into the arts, and sometimes may have been distorted by it.

In considering Pound as one who sought out and found the best work available during his London years, and then forced it into print, we must take into account, at least in passing, the state of English literature when Pound first began his struggle to enliven the literary language by bringing it into contact with both the spoken language of his own day and with certain high points in past literature which had been increasingly neglected. The path of the man who wishes to conserve in this sense, is not easy: it is like walking a tight-rope. He must preserve as much of the relevant past as he is able to master, without falling into the error which overtakes most so-called conservatives, the mere worship of dead modes and ideas; but he can do this, can preserve the relevant past and give it a meaning, only by recreating it here and now in the flesh and blood of contemporary speech. The danger on this side of the problem is of falling into novelty or destruction for its own sake, as has happened so often in the arts during the past fifty years.

There is an instructive attack upon conservatism in David Hume's two essays on the 'Rise and Progress of the Arts and Sciences' and 'National Characters'. According to Hume, societies adopt certain modes of conduct and thought under the pressure of association and education, and these modes are maintained by the force of authority, superstition and public opinion. 'I have sometimes been inclined to think,' he wrote, 'that interruptions in the periods of learning, were they not attended by such a destruction of ancient books, and the records of history, would be rather favourable to the arts and sciences, by breaking the progress of authority, and dethroning the tyrannical usurpers over human reason. In this particular, they have the same influence as interruptions in political governments and societies.' It is not in order to discuss or challenge this view that I bring it forward, but because it illustrates so well the dangerous path which the conservative must negotiate. Both errors he must avoid: stagnation on the one hand, and Hume's narrow distrust of what he calls 'the weight of authority, superstition, and public opinion' on the other. His task is one of constant renewal and reassessment of tradition, in a world which is forever in transition. In many ways Pound himself was liberal in thought and feeling, with a disposition towards destruction and interruption, but he knew so much about certain areas of past literature, and loved them so well and deeply, that he understood their relevance to the stagnant condition of English literature in 1910, and was a fitting instrument for what was in effect a conservative reassessment of the tradition.

The period of this struggle was one in which even some of those who were theoretically well disposed towards the 'new' in literature and the arts found the work of men like Eliot and Joyce rather hard to take at the start. It was a period in which editors who were 'progressive' struggled against 'Prufrock' and some of the poems in Pound's *Lustra*; in which friendly publishers turned away from some of the best work of the time, having no taste for what Pound described as treating 'actual things in a simple and direct manner'. Editors who objected to so-called *vers libre* when it was written by skilled artists who understood both the living language and the English tradition, were the same who later, when *vers libre* had become established, allowed the incompetent almost free rein. If we look at Pound's published correspondence for the year 1918 we find him having to defend *Ulysses* against the doubts of John Quinn, a generous patron who made great efforts to keep abreast of the arts, and was later to stand by that work when it got into legal difficulties in the United States. The best way perhaps to describe the tone of the decade 1913–23 is to say that not only did it object to its first dose of Robert Frost, but was a time in which the established publishing houses left the job of putting out such works as Joyce's *Portrait of the Artist*, Eliot's *Prufrock and Other Observations*, Lewis's *Tarr* and Pound's *Quia Pauper Amavi* to Harriet Shaw Weaver and the Egoist Ltd. The fact that Pound eventually gave up and went into a sort of exile on the Continent is well known. The fact that T. S. Eliot almost did the same thing, a year or so later, is not so well known, but it is a useful pointer to the state of the publishing world at that time.[1] Pound's opposition to the age, where it was not based upon minor and inexplicable irritation, misapprehension arising out of impatience, or on national or personal factors—all of which were

[1] See for instance letters from Vivian Eliot and T. S. Eliot to Richard Aldington, items 6j. and 6k. in *An Exhibition of Manuscripts and First Editions of T. S. Eliot*, Humanities Research Center, University of Texas, 1961.

present—was due to an important difference of opinion with literary London about technical matters. It is, as Eliot has observed, a perpetual heresy of English culture to believe that only the Genius, the Great Man, really matters; and it follows from this that the Genius is one who pops up at any odd time and creates masterworks out of the air or his own imagination or personality. For Pound, on the other hand, the masterwork is the drawing together by a very great artist of threads manufactured for him by the great artists of the past, and by lesser men and specialists as well. He expressed this idea in *Spirit of Romance*, where he drew attention to the debt which the Elizabethans owed to earlier Italian poetry, and the way in which the troubadours and early Italian writers prepared the means by which Dante created his *Commedia*. This same idea he put forward again in the *Poetry Review* of February 1912. 'I am constantly contending,' he said, 'that it took two centuries of Provence and one of Tuscany to develop the media of Dante's masterwork, that it took the latinists of the Renaissance, and the Pléiade, and his own age of painted speech to prepare Shakespeare his tools.' Seen from this point of view the Great Man is no longer a sort of inane spark from a divine fire but one who makes a fitting summary of the tradition, or part of it, in terms of his own time and all that that implies. Lesser works by men of genius and minds of the second order, are, in one sense, a creation, renewal or repairing of the means or the tools which some future genius will take up and turn to the cause of another great summary or masterwork.

One of Pound's earliest successes in 'picking the rising talent' was with the work of Robert Frost, the first mention of whom in Pound's published correspondence is in a letter to Alice Corbin Henderson of *Poetry* in March 1913. In this he says that he has just reviewed an advance copy of Frost's first book, *A Boy's Will*. Shortly afterwards he directed the attention of *Poetry*'s editor, Harriet Monroe, to Frost's merits and set about procuring him an audience. Reading over the reviews he wrote in 1913 and 1914 of *A Boy's Will* and *North of Boston*, we see that today's critical opinion and general impression of Frost's work is really only an elaboration (and exaggeration) of what Pound set down nearly fifty years ago, although Pound, it should be pointed out, saw limitations in Frost's poetry which too many later commentators have tended to overlook.

Probably the best glimpse we get of Pound's determination, in those days, to select the best work available regardless of his own personal prejudices, is in his treatment of D. H. Lawrence. There was something about Lawrence and his work which Pound disliked; it was a sort of irrational dislike which he never, so far as I know, defined, but it was very strong and almost always came to the front when he discussed Lawrence's work. 'Detestable person but needs watching', he wrote to Harriet Monroe in March 1913, which is an almost perfect summary of Pound's attitude over a period of twenty years or more. In reviewing a book of Lawrence's poems in 1913, Pound praised him as a writer of both verse and prose, remarking that 'when Mr Lawrence ceases to discuss his own disagreeable sensations, when he writes low-life narrative, as he does in *Whether or Not* and in *Violets*, there is no English poet under forty who can get within shot of him'. Three months later he explained his general attitude in a letter to Harriet Monroe about the publication of some of Lawrence's work in *Poetry*: 'Lawrence, as you know, gives me no particular pleasure. Nevertheless we are lucky to get him. Hueffer, as you know, thinks highly of him. I *recognize* certain qualities of his work. If I were an editor I should probably accept his work without reading it. As a prose writer I grant him first place among the younger men.' This, it should be noted, was before Pound had had an opportunity to judge Joyce's prose. Early the following year, after he had seen *Dubliners*, he wrote to Amy Lowell that he thought Lawrence and Joyce were the 'two strongest prose writers among les jeunes'.

Before going on to outline Pound's association with Joyce and Eliot, it will be instructive, I think, to glance over some of Pound's other activities on behalf of the arts and literature during 1913 and 1914, and also to examine the growth of his outlook under the influence of the American scholar Ernest Fenollosa, so that we get something like a balanced view of this part of his career. He described Epstein at this period as 'a great sculptor', the young

Gaudier-Brzeska as '*the* coming sculptor', and promoted the work of Tagore. Verhaeren he described as 'not so much Whitman as a sort of lesser Wordsworth, with a sense of Flamand country and of people of labour'. Blunt was the 'last of the great Victorians' and Rupert Brooke the 'best of all that Georgian group'. He isolated a fine quatrain by Padraic Colum, described the troubadours 'their sorts and conditions' for the *Quarterly Review*, praised two poems by Bridges, the cadence of one of them as 'exquisite', and pointed to pleasing qualities in the work of Sturge Moore. These and other activities of a like nature he engaged in at a time when he was gradually impressing Yeats with the virtues of clarity and simplicity, and conducting a precise technical campaign which is partly summarized by his famous three principles, agreed to, he later wrote, by H. D., Richard Aldington and himself in the spring or early summer of 1912:

1. Direct treatment of the 'thing' whether subjective or objective.
2. To use absolutely no word that does not contribute to the presentation.
3. As regarding rhythm: to compose in the sequence of the musical phrase, not in sequence of a metronome.

A great deal has been written about *Imagisme* and also the meaning of Fenollosa's work as it affected Pound, and through Pound, modern poetry. Neither Fenollosa nor Pound knew very much about either medieval philosophy or the so-called 'method' of modern science, so that there is no coherent philosophical validity in their application of these matters to poetry. Unfortunately, however, some commentators have wrestled with them on some such ground, with the result that part at least of the meaning which Fenollosa held for Pound during a formative period in his poetic career, has been lost in a flood of discussion which is irrelevant if what we are looking for is Fenollosa's impact on Pound at a particular time, rather than the meaning of what Pound said about Fenollosa in later years. My aim here then is merely to indicate the true nature of Fenollosa's original impact on Pound's poetry and technical thinking. The theorizing which Pound did later on the basis of Fenollosa's essay on the 'Chinese

Written Character', and the use to which he sometimes put his theories in his translation of Confucius, the Chinese *Odes* and the *Sacred Edict* (Canto 99), has nothing to do with his own poetic practice in 1914, and is a question which awaits a sympathetic enquirer who has a thorough knowledge of both modern English and ancient Chinese.

In the 1949 edition of the *Unwobbling Pivot* and *Great Digest* of Confucius, published in India, and also in his B.B.C. broadcasts in 1959, Pound said that Fenollosa's widow gave him the Fenollosa papers after meeting him at the home of the poetess Sarojini Naidu in London. This appears to have taken place in 1913. In a letter to William Carlos Williams in December 1913, Pound speaks of having 'all old Fenollosa's treasures in mss.' and a little over a month later sent a translation of the Japanese Noh play 'Nishikigi', which he had worked out from Fenollosa's notes, to Harriet Monroe for publication in *Poetry*. In April 1914 he wrote to Amy Lowell: 'I am on my head with Fenollosa's notes', and a year later published his book of Chinese translations, *Cathay*, which he described in a note as being 'from the notes of the late Ernest Fenollosa, and the decipherings of the Professors Mori and Ariga'. These latter were Japanese scholars from whom Fenollosa derived his idea that the literature and feeling of ancient China were better preserved in Japan than in China itself. According to an article by Professor Norman Holmes Pearson in *Shenandoah* for Autumn 1955, Fenollosa was from Salem, a young man still fresh from Harvard when he went to Japan before the turn of the century as instructor in rhetoric to the Imperial University. He took an increasing interest in oriental art and languages and finally rose to be Imperial Commissioner of Art in Tokyo. He died in 1908, and his book *Epochs of Chinese and Japanese Art* was published by his widow in 1911. The papers which Mrs Fenollosa gave to Pound included an unfinished manuscript of the essay on 'The Chinese Written Character as a Medium for Poetry', literal or rough translations of a number of Noh plays into English, together with notes about the Noh, which Pound first published in book form in 1916 (now available in *The Translations of Ezra Pound*), and a series of notebooks containing notes which Fenollosa made while studying ancient Chinese literature under Professor Mori. These notes are similar in form to those published by Pound at the back of his 1936 edition of *The Chinese Written Character*.

A month or so before the appearance of *Cathay* Pound had some interesting things to say about Fenollosa in *T.P.'s Weekly* of 20 February 1915. I insert a long passage from this article because it makes clear Pound's main attitude to Fenollosa at a time when he was actively absorbing this oriental material into his own work. It shows that at this stage he regarded Fenollosa as complementary to *Imagisme* and in a sense its justification. The article is called 'Imagisme and England':

'There are two sorts of poetry which are to me the most interesting, the most *poetic*. The one is that sort of poetry where music, sheer melody, seems as if it were *just coming over into speech*; the other, where painting or sculpture seems as if it were just forcing itself to words.' The first has long been called lyric. You are able to discern a *lyric* passage in a drama or in a long poem not lyric in its entirety. The second sort of poetry is as old and as distinct, but until recently no one had named it. We now call it *Imagist*, it is not a new invention, it is a critical discrimination.

Apart from this new and more articulate designation of 'The Image' certain writers have dared to say openly that poetry ought to be written 'at least as well as prose', and if possible with greater concentration and pertinence. . . .

The English language is composed, roughly speaking, of Anglo-Saxon, Latin and French. Imagisme exists in all three of these languages; in the Anglo-Saxon 'Seafarer', in Catullus' 'Collis o Heliconii', and in 'Charles D'Orléans'. It is ridiculous to say that a form of poetry, a form of beauty, which is possible in each of these three main components, is *impossible* in the language which results from picking the best and the strongest elements from each of the others.

As for Chinese, it is quite true that we have sought the force of Chinese ideographs *without knowing it*. As for the unsuitability of English for that purpose, I have now by me the papers of the late Ernest Fenollosa, sometime Imperial Commissioner of Art in Tokyo. He certainly knew more about this matter than anyone else whose opinion we are likely to get at.

In his essay on the Chinese written character he expressly contends that English, being the strongest and least inflected of the European languages, is precisely the one language best suited to render the force and the concision of the uninflected Chinese.

Fenollosa was, in fact, a sort of chemical agent who helped to bring together, relate and solidify a number of elements individually present in Pound's work or thought. A part of Pound's own donation and some of the things he took over from his earlier teachers are clearly visible in two letters he wrote to Harriet Monroe in January 1915. In one he speaks of the editing of the anthology *Des Imagistes* as a 'delicate operation . . . managed by the most rigorous suppression of what I considered faults', and in the other he writes of 'objectivity and again objectivity', and insists that 'Poetry must be as well written as prose. Its language must be a fine language, departing in no way from speech save by a heightened intensity (i.e. simplicity). There must be no book words, no periphrases, no inversions. It must be as simple as De Maupassant's best prose and as hard as Stendhal's.' Actually Pound had been concerned with the problem of objectivity and images as early as *Spirit of Romance*, as we see from the following paragraph taken from the chapter on Daniel:

The second stanza is of the major importance, and those who are trying to trace the sources of Dante's style would do well to consider how much he owes to Daniel's terse vigour of suggestion. Three times in this stanza the Provençal makes his picture, neither by simile nor by metaphor, but in the language beyond metaphor, by the use of the picturesque verb with an exact meaning. Firstly, 'pools himself'—the natural picture. Secondly, after the comparison of gold and lead, the metal worker's shop gives tribute, and is present to the vision in the technical word 'refine'. Thirdly, the feudal ceremony and the suggestion of its pageantry are in the verb 'invest'.

What Fenollosa brought from Japan and China—whether he brought over something that really existed there, or simply rhapsodized upon his own impressions and perhaps imperfect knowledge of oriental languages, does not matter here—was a new elucidation of the question of images and objectivity in verse.

In June 1915 Pound told Professor Schelling that Fenollosa's essay on the Chinese written character provided 'a whole new basis of aesthetic', and in his essay 'The Renaissance', published in *Poetry* the same year, he wrote: 'It is possible that this century may find a new Greece in China', and again that 'Liu Ch'e, Chu Yuan, Chia I, and the great *vers libre* writers before the Petrarchan age of Li Po, are a treasury to which the next century may look for as great a stimulus as the renaissance had from the Greeks'. In his book '*Noh*', *or Accomplishment*, published in 1916 from the Fenollosa papers, Pound touched on the connection he saw between the Noh plays and his own ideas about *Imagisme*:

When a text seems to 'go off into nothing' at the end, the reader must remember 'that the vagueness or paleness of words is made good by the emotion of the final dance', for the Noh has its unity in emotion. It has also what we may call Unity of Image. At least, the better plays are all built into the intensification of a single image: the red maple leaves and snow flurry in Nishikigi, the pines in Takasago, the blue-grey waves and wave pattern in Suma Genji, the mantle of feathers in the play of that name, Hagoromo.

And in a footnote he makes this comment:

This intensification of the Image, this manner of construction, is very interesting to me personally, as an Imagiste, for we Imagistes knew nothing of these plays when we set out in our own manner. These plays are also an answer to a question that has several times been put to me: 'Could one do a long Imagiste poem, or even a long poem in vers libre?'

What I have said about Fenollosa being a 'justification' of ideas which Pound was pursuing before he ever set eyes on the Fenollosa papers—ideas connected with his own poetic practice and immediate thinking about the art of writing, rather than independent theorizing about aesthetics—is confirmed, I believe, in his brief introduction to the essay on the Chinese written character. It is obvious that by 1918 when this note was written, Pound was already beginning to think of Fenollosa as a philosopher in his own right, who had made 'a study of the fundamentals of all aesthetics', and would be even more important in the future than in the past; but it is also obvious that he saw the orientalist as one who, a year or two before, had provided independent confirmation of the validity of the 'new' poetry and art with which Pound had been associated since about 1911. Fenollosa was, according to the introduction, 'a forerunner without knowing it and without being known as such', and the 'later movements in art' had 'corroborated his theories'. Pound regarded Fenollosa as the highest possible authority, and this authority had confirmed his own views; he was therefore supremely confident of his position when he came to pronounce on the work of Joyce and Eliot. There was no hesitation, this was something new, but exciting and genuine as well. Let us take the case of Joyce first.

Pound got in touch with Joyce, through Yeats, in 1913 when he was preparing the anthology *Des Imagistes*. He wrote an article about him in the *Egoist* of January 1914, and soon afterwards arranged for the same paper to begin publishing *Portrait of the Artist* in serial form. In July of the same year he reviewed *Dubliners*; here is an extract, which shows the economy of his judgement:

Freedom from sloppiness is so rare in contemporary English prose that one might well say simply, 'Mr Joyce's book of short stories is prose free from sloppiness', and leave the intelligent reader ready to run from his study, immediately to spend three and sixpence on the volume.

Unfortunately one's credit as a critic is insufficient to produce this result. . . .

Mr Joyce writes clear and hard prose. He deals with subjective things, but he presents them with such clarity of outline that he might be dealing with locomotives or with builders' specifications . . .

. . . He accepts an international standard of prose writing and lives up to it.

Already in his essay 'The Serious Artist' published in the *Egoist* during October and November of 1913 Pound had insisted upon how important it is for the poet to understand good prose formulation, and spoke of the labour necessary for a verbal artist to be able to say 'Send me the kind of Rembrandt I like' in terms of

'Send me four pounds of ten-penny nails'. Both *Dubliners* and the *Portrait* must have seemed like an answer to his own highest hopes. I will not go on to describe Pound's activity on behalf of Joyce's material needs, for this is now well known, but I will give a brief sketch of his opinions about Joyce's work between 1915 and the appearance of *Ulysses* in book form in 1922. 'The prose writer I am really interested in', he wrote to H. L. Mencken in February 1915, 'is James Joyce', and about a year later he suggested to the critic Kate Buss that she 'keep an eye out for Joyce'. He reviewed the *Portrait* for the *Egoist* early in 1917 and again in the *Future* for May 1918. In this latter article he says:

On almost every page of Joyce you will find such swift alternation of subjective beauty and external shabbiness, squalor, and sordidness. It is the bass and treble of his method. And he has his scope beyond that of the novelists his contemporaries, in just so far as whole stretches of his keyboard are utterly out of their compass.

As London editor of the *Little Review* Pound arranged for the serial publication of *Ulysses*, beginning in 1918, and in his correspondence with Joyce about the same time, made some suggestions about the possibility of chapter headings and other matters, most of which Joyce did not accept. On 25 January 1918, soon after the first two chapters had arrived from Joyce, Pound wrote to Mencken that 'Joyce's new novel has a corking 1st Chap. (which will get us suppressed), not such a good second one'. In a published note in mid-1918, while *Ulysses* was still incomplete, he referred to it as Joyce's 'profoundest work' and said: 'He has done what Flaubert set out to do in *Bouvard and Pécuchet*, done it better, more succinct. An epitome.' Looking back twenty years later, he described in *Guide to Kulchur* what he remembered of his feeling of excitement as the work began to arrive from the author:

The katharsis of 'Ulysses', the joyous satisfaction as the first chapters rolled into Holland Place, was to feel that here was the J O B D O N E and finished, the diagnosis and cure was here. The sticky, molasses-covered filth of current print, all the fuggs, all the foetors, the whole boil of the European mind, had been lanced.

After receiving a new chapter from Joyce in October 1919, he wrote to John Quinn that 'Our James is a grrreat man', and later, in June 1922, published articles in praise of the whole work in both the *Dial* and the *Mercure de France*. If, in looking back, Pound's criticism of Joyce now appears rather thin and narrow, as if he saw only one aspect of the work, yet it was unhesitating and amazingly precise within its own limitations. Today's broader views owe much to Pound's original insights; without them, the broader views might not exist at all.

The fact that Pound had a decisive 'influence' on the literary career of T. S. Eliot is well known, and does not bear repeating merely for its own sake; nor am I concerned here with correcting the distortion to which this event, or series of events, has been subjected, which would require a long and detailed analysis outside the scope of this book. All I will do here is make a brief reconstruction of their association between the time of their first meeting in 1914 and the publication of the *Waste Land* in 1922, in order to show that from the very first Pound understood that Eliot's poetry was something out of the ordinary, and did not hesitate to place it in a category apart from that of the other poets of the time.

He wrote to Harriet Monroe on 22 September 1914 saying that an American by the name of Eliot had called on him that day and seemed to have 'some sense'. This letter was followed about a week later by Pound's well known outburst on first seeing 'Prufrock': 'I was jolly well right about Eliot. He has sent in the best poem I have yet had or seen from an American', and a few days later he sent 'Portrait of a Lady' to Mencken saying, 'I enclose a poem by the last intelligent man I've found—a young American, T. S. Eliot ... I think him worth watching. ...' Miss Monroe received a copy of 'Prufrock' towards the end of October, and objected to it. She and Pound exchanged letters on the subject for six months—*Poetry* was a monthly—before she finally tucked it away towards the back of the issue for June 1915; and it was through Pound's continuing efforts that Eliot's first book, *Prufrock and Other Observations*, was published by the Egoist Ltd. in 1917. His review of this book in *Poetry* of August 1917 leaves no shadow of doubt that Pound, while he may not have penetrated fully into Eliot's poems, recognized them as finished products, not to be confused with the other 'new' poetry of the time:

> After much contemporary work that is merely factitious, much that is good in intention but impotently unfinished and incomplete; much whose flaws are due to sheer ignorance which a year's study or thought might have remedied, it is a comfort to come upon complete art, naïve despite its intellectual subtlety, lacking all pretence.
>
> It is quite safe to compare Mr Eliot's work with anything written in French, English or American since the death of Jules Laforgue. The reader will find nothing better, and he will be extremely fortunate if he finds much half as good. . . .
>
> . . . And, above all, there is no rhetoric, although there is Elizabethan reading in the background. . . .
>
> For what the statement is worth, Mr Eliot's work interests me more than that of any other poet now writing in English. . . .
>
> . . . Eliot's work rests apart from that of the many new writers who have used the present freedoms to no advantage, who have gained no new precisions of language, and no variety in their cadence. His men in shirt-sleeves, and his society ladies, are not a local manifestation; they are the stuff of our modern world, and true of more countries than one. I would praise the work for its fine tone, its humanity, and its realism; for all good art is realism of one sort or another. . . .
>
> . . . And, 'confound it, the fellow can write.'

I will not go over the well-known ground about Pound's editing of the *Waste Land*, but if we turn to the letter he wrote to Eliot on that subject on 24 December 1921 we see clearly that he was able to appreciate the fact that it was something more than just another good poem: 'Complimenti, you bitch. I am wracked by the seven jealousies, and cogitating an excuse for always exuding my deformative secretions in my own stuff, and never getting an outline.' In July 1922 he wrote to Felix Schelling, 'Eliot's *Waste Land* is I think the justification of the "movement", of our modern experiment, since 1900.'

The *Waste Land* was a poem outside Pound's own range which he himself could never even have thought of composing; but the great accumulation of professional skill which underwrote his central judgements bade him praise and admire it quite irrespective of his own theories and his own personal likes and dislikes. It is easy enough to find fault with some of Pound's critical ideas, if that is one's aim, or to neglect the solid sense that so often underlies the cranky exterior, but no amount of critical talk can hide the fact that as a judge of new talent his performance between the years 1913 and 1922 was unique in its own time and remains so to this day.

CHAPTER VII

Words and Music

I

WHAT IS perhaps Pound's best general statement on the connection he believed existed between poetry and music occurs in a short essay called 'Vers Libre and Arnold Dolmetsch' which he published in the *Egoist* during 1917 and reprinted in his book *Pavannes and Divisions* in 1918. In this he states clearly his belief that a poet's interest in melody must extend beyond the 'music' of verse, to music itself:

> Poetry is a composition of words set to music. Most other definitions of it are indefensible, or metaphysical. The proportion or quality of the music may, and does, vary; but poetry withers and 'dries out' when it leaves music, or at least an imagined music, too far behind it. . . .
> Poets who are not interested in music are, or become, bad poets. I would almost say that poets should never be too long out of touch with musicians. Poets who will not study music are defective. I do not mean that they need become virtuosi, or that they need necessarily undergo the musical curriculum of their time. . . .
> It is too late to prevent vers libre. But, conceivably, one might improve it, and one might stop at least a little of the idiotic and narrow discussion based on an ignorance of music. Bigoted attack born of this ignorance of the tradition of music, was what we had to live through.

He expressed the same idea later in the opening pages of his *ABC of Reading* (1934), where he extended it and put it into a broader perspective by remarking that 'music begins to atrophy when it departs too far from the dance', and poetry 'when it gets too far from music'. Bach and Mozart were 'never too far from physical movement'. The roots of this concern with the connection between poetry and music are to be found, more than anywhere else in Pound's work, in his early investigations into the art of the troubadours.

According to Pound's own account written some five years

afterwards, it was under Dr William P. Shepard of Hamilton College, between the years 1903 and 1905, that he first gained some knowledge of the troubadours. During his trip abroad in 1906 as a Fellow in Romanics from the University of Pennsylvania he visited Provence and also examined some of the troubadour material in the Ambrosiana library in Milan. A few years later in Paris he worked on the subject of troubadour words and music with the pianist and composer Walter Morse Rummel. In the preface to his *Neuf Chansons de Troubadours*, published in 1913, Rummel thanked Pound for providing him with two Daniel melodies from Milan. Beginning about 1903, Pound studied Provençal on and off for about twelve years, during which time he made translations and adaptations, wrestled with Provençal forms in his own verse, and wrote about the troubadours at some length in his prose. In the poems 'Provincia Deserta' and 'Near Perigord', first published in 1915, we see that not only was he fond of the poetry of the troubadours but had explored Provence on foot, measuring the distances between castles and putting the landscape against what he found in the verse. He took the matter up again with a burst about 1918 when he produced more translations and adaptations, wrote the essay on Arnaut Daniel, with bilingual texts, which appeared in his book *Instigations* in 1920, and also did some more work on the problem presented by what is left of the early musical settings of Provençal verse. We will now see what influence the troubadours had on the 'music' of his own verse, looking first at the article 'How I Began' in which he discussed his sestina 'Altaforte', an adaptation from the Provençal of Bertran de Born. This poem was written some time between Pound's arrival in London in the Autumn of 1908 and its publication in the *English Review* of June 1909. Here is what he said about its composition some four years afterwards:

My other 'vigorous' poem, the 'Altaforte' was also written in the British Museum reading-room. I had had De Born on my mind. I had found him untranslatable. Then it occurred to me that I might present him in this manner. I wanted the curious involution and recurrence of the Sestina. I knew more or less of the arrangement. I wrote the first strophe and then went to the Museum to make sure of the right order

G

of the permutations, for I was then living in Langham Street, next to the 'pub', and had hardly any books with me. I did the rest of the poem at a sitting. Technically it is one of my best, though a poem on such a theme could never be very important.

It will be seen that while this poem was for Pound a means of 'presenting' De Born to a modern audience, it had also a technical aspect—'the curious involution and recurrence of the Sestina'. Pound did not attempt a close or literal translation of the Provençal into English. He sought first to get the feel of Bertran de Born and his poetry in general and then to bring this over into English by adapting a particular poem. But since Provençal was another language, very different from English, and de Born a long way from the British Museum reading-room of 1909, the work of adaptation, like the bringing over of de Born's 'personality', required of the poet that he get the feel of the original form rather than simply transfer it literally into English. Pound's success in hitting on terminal sounds which leave a fairly strong residue in the ear in wait for the succeeding stanza, can be seen very clearly in this poem, which needs to be read in full.[1] It is of course an early and fairly crude example of Pound's use of the 'music' of Provençal verse in English; and there is often a gap of some years between the moment he appreciates some finer point in Provençal sonority and his creation of a satisfactory equivalent for it in his own verse. And such equivalents, when they did come, were not usually to be found in his translations, but in poems having no outward connection with Provençal as such. 'Altaforte' is not really an equivalent, but one in a series of intermediary experiments.

In *Spirit of Romance*, which he described as 'an attempt to define somewhat the charm of the pre-Renaissance literature of Latin Europe', he devoted one chapter to the troubadours in general and another to Arnaut Daniel in particular. Some of the insights in this book were ahead of Pound's own poetic practice at the time, as we shall see in a moment. Following Dante, Pound prized Daniel above all the other singers of Provence. Not only did his canzoni 'satisfy the modern ear, gluttonous of rhyme, but also the

[1] 'Altaforte', *Personae: Collected Poems of Ezra Pound*, New York, 1926; London, 1952.

ear trained to Roman and Hellenic music, to which rhyme seemed and seems a vulgarity'. Daniel 'was the first to realize fully that the music of rhymes depends upon their arrangement, not on their multiplicity', and out of this perception he 'elaborated a form of canzone where stanza answers to stanza not boisterously, but with a subtle persistent echo'. One of Daniel's canzoni reminds him 'of a chord struck repeatedly in crescendo'. Here are two stanzas from Pound's 'Canzon: The Yearly Slain', which is an attempt to reproduce Daniel's 'persistent echo'. This poem was first published in the *English Review* of January 1910 about the time he was writing *Spirit of Romance*:

> Ah! red-leafed time hath driven out the rose
> And crimson dew is fallen on the leaf
> Ere yet the cold white wheat be sown
> That hideth all earth's green and sere and red;
> The Moon-flower's fallen and the branch is bare,
> Holding no honey for the starry bees;
> The Maiden turns to her dark lord's demesne.
>
> Fairer than Enna's field when Ceres sows
> The stars of hyacinth and puts off grief,
> Fairer than petals on May morning blown
> Through apple orchards where the sun hath shed
> His brighter petals down to make them fair;
> Fairer than these the Poppy-crowned One flees,
> And Joy goes weeping in her scarlet train.

This poem does indeed catch some of Daniel's 'music', but in a verse which was divorced from both the spoken language and the sharp perfection of sound which we find in the best English songs. Pound's problem in those days was that the literary language he had inherited was a dry shell, no longer a living thing in touch with the world around it. As Pound remembered it in 1934, the 'common verse of Britain from 1890 to 1910 was a horrible agglomerate compost, not minted, most of it not even baked, all legato, a doughy mess of third-hand Keats, Wordsworth, heaven knows what, fourth-hand Elizabethan sonority blunted, half-melted, lumpy'. Before being able to transfer Provençal elements

successfully into the contemporary world, he would have to make
a new literary language in touch with his own time; and this is
what he did do in a series of poems beginning with his adaptation
of the Anglo-Saxon 'Seafarer' in 1911 and reaching fulfilment
with *Mauberley* in 1919. Few of these poems have any outward
connection with the more obvious aspects of Provençal. I lay
stress upon this point because two different processes have to be
kept in mind if we are to understand Pound's assimilation of
Provençal verse: (1) a wrestling with Provençal forms, rhythms
and blending of sounds, carried out by means of translations
and adaptations; and (2) the creation of a new literary language
compact of his own time. The former was important in his
poetic development, for the light it threw on the subject of
rhythm and sound, but it was not until he had fully accomplished
the latter in *Homage to Sextus Propertius* and *Hugh Selwyn Mauberley* that he was able to give new life to the Provençal 'aesthetic of
sound', in the texture of modern English verse. But of course
there were times, even before the final success, when these two
processes came together and were indistinguishable one from the
other. In the introduction to his *Sonnets and Ballate of Guido
Cavalcanti*, written, it will be recalled, in November 1910, Pound
put forward an idea, arising out of his study of the troubadours
and Cavalcanti, about the possibility of a verse rhythm which
would be part of the poem's total meaning. 'I believe', he said, 'in
an ultimate and absolute rhythm as I believe in an absolute symbol
or metaphor.' And this belief was at the same time one of a number of converging ideas which set him in opposition to the clichés
arising out of the misuse of English 'iambic pentameter'; and
again, it was this same mounting dissatisfaction which caused him
to re-examine the whole question of contemporary speech in
verse and to look for a means of avoiding rhythms which forced
the poet to adhere to conventional and accepted 'thought'.

In December 1911 at a time when he was writing some of the
poems which appear in *Ripostes*, his first 'modern' book, Pound
was also working on an essay called 'Prolegomena' which was
published in *Poetry Review* of February 1912. I give an extract
here to indicate the stage he had reached in his criticism:

Rhythm.—I believe in an 'absolute rhythm,' a rhythm, that is, in poetry which corresponds exactly to the emotion or shade of emotion to be expressed. A man's rhythm must be interpretative, it will be, therefore, in the end, his own, uncounterfeiting, uncounterfeitable.

Symbols.—I believe that the proper and perfect symbol is the natural object, that if a man use 'symbols' he must so use them that their symbolic function does not obtrude; so that *a* sense, and the poetic quality of the passage, is not lost to those who do not understand the symbol as such, to whom, for instance, a hawk is a hawk.

Technique.—I believe in technique as the test of a man's sincerity; in law when it is ascertainable; in the trampling down of every convention that impedes or obscures the determination of the law, or the precise rendering of the impulse.

Form.—I think there is a 'fluid' as well as a 'solid' content, that some poems may have form as a tree has form, some as water poured into a vase. That most symmetrical forms have uses. That a vast number of subjects cannot be precisely, and therefore not properly rendered in symmetrical forms.

. . . I think the artist should master all known forms and systems of metric, and I have with some persistence set about doing this, searching particularly into those periods wherein the systems came to birth or attained their maturity.

In the same issue of the magazine in which this essay was published there appeared several poems which Pound later included in *Ripostes*. A development in control and the use of language, as well as of rhythm, shows out in 'Doria':

> Be in me as the eternal moods
>   of the bleak wind, and not
> As transient things are—
>   gaiety of flowers.
> Have me in the strong loneliness
>   of sunless cliffs
> And of grey waters.
>   Let the gods speak softly of us
> In days hereafter,
>   The shadowy flowers of Orcus
> Remember thee.

Four months later Pound's poem 'The Return' was published

in the *English Review*. It is one of his best poems and shows, in its perfect movement, the poet's feeling for the weight and duration of words and the good effect of time spent with music and the blending of sounds.

> See, they return; ah, see the tentative
> Movements, and the slow feet,
> The trouble in the pace and the uncertain
> Wavering!
>
> See, they return, one, and by one,
> With fear, as half-awakened;
> As if the snow should hesitate
> And murmur in the wind,
>   and half turn back;
> These were the 'Wing'd-with-Awe',
>   Inviolable.
>
> Gods of the wingèd shoe!
> With them the silver hounds,
>   sniffing the trace of air!
>
> Haie! Haie!
>   These were the swift to harry;
> These the keen-scented;
> These were the souls of blood.
>
> Slow on the leash,
>   pallid the leash-men!

The beauty of this poem echoed for many years in T. S. Eliot's head before coming to light in a completely new and different context, in the third and fifth sections of *Little Gidding*. In Paris shortly after the First World War, 'The Return' was tested by the French phonetics expert, the Abbé Jean Pierre Rousselot, who according to Pound 'had made a machine for measuring the duration of verbal components. A quill or tube in the nostril, a less shaved quill or other tube in the mouth, and your consonants signed as you spoke them.' When 'The Return' was read into the machine each letter of the words 'they return, one, and by one,

With fear, as half-awakened' made 'a double registration of quavering'. But 'The Return' was only the beginning of his search for a language both natural and at the same time musical, ordered, and capable of comprehending extreme poetic precision and intensity. In April 1913, within a month of telling the readers of *Poetry* to 'dissect the lyrics of Goethe coldly into their component sound values', he was able to prove by his own verse that he had left the overripe and blurry sound of Swinburne and the nineties behind him and was restoring to the language a clearer, older richness, properly controlled. The dozen short poems published in that issue and later included in *Lustra*, contain such lines as:

> There is none like thee among the dancers;
> None with swift feet.

> You were praised, my books,
>   because I had just come from the country;
> I was twenty years behind the times
>   so you found an audience ready.

> Dawn enters with little feet
>   like a gilded Pavlova.

His advice to apprentice poets at this time was that they should learn 'assonance and alliteration, rhyme immediate and delayed, simple and polyphonic, as a musician would expect to know harmony and counterpoint and all the minutiae of his craft'. The poet who has a feeling for 'music' will not chop his lines into 'separate *iambs*', he will not stop dead at the end of each line and then begin the next line with 'a heave'. Rather, he will begin a line by catching 'the rise of the rhythm wave', unless, that is, the music seems to call for a 'definite longish pause'. Although taken up with that part of poetry which has parallels in music, Pound was too good a poet not to see that there is more to the sound of human speech than a variety of syllables: speech is made up of words, and words tend to impress themselves on their neighbours or exert an attraction; so the apprentice was warned to watch out that his rhythms did not destroy the shape of his words, or their natural sound or meaning. In the poems Pound wrote between

the beginning of 1913 and the end of 1915 and published in
Cathay and *Lustra*, the musical elements and the things he learnt
from Provençal and other verse to be sung are not always in the
foreground, but they are present nevertheless to give it a freshness, intelligence and clarity of sound which had too long been
absent from English verse. There is sometimes a pleasant hardness
about the work of Crabbe and Lionel Johnson, but the quality
Pound recovered includes also—my terminology is not satisfactory, but it is the only one to hand—a certain glint or brightness
as well. This quality is present in a wide variety of poems—just as
much in a poem like 'Epitaph':

> Leucis, who intended a Grand Passion,
> Ends with a willingness-to-oblige.

as in one like 'The Spring':

> Cydonian Spring with her attendant train,
> Maelids and water-girls,
> Stepping beneath a boisterous wind from Thrace,
> Throughout this sylvan place
> Spreads the bright tips,
> And every vine-stock is
> Clad in new brilliancies.
>   And wild desire
> Falls like black lightning.
> O bewildered heart,
> Though every branch have back what last year lost
> She, who moved here amid the cyclamen,
> Moves only now a clinging tenuous ghost.

This is already the language of one who knows what he wants to
say and is not held up for want of knowing how to say it. The
word is given its due, but as part of a cadence, part of a line, and
part of a sentence. There is no less of 'music' in 'Society' than in
'The Exile's Letter'; it is just that they have a different movement,
towards a different end, in each case perfectly controlled. 'Society'
is ironically reticent in both 'thought' and 'music':

> The family position was waning,
> And on this account the little Aurelia,

> Who had laughed on eighteen summers,
> Now bears the palsied contact of Phidippus.

In 'The Exile's Letter' the poet is just as meticulous, but this time in finding a just notation for the unburdening of a pent-up emotion associated with retrospect. The writer of the letter is recalling something that can never come again:

> With boats floating, and the sound of mouth-organs
>   and drums,
> With ripples like dragon-scales, going grass green
>   on the waters . . .
> And then the crowd broke up, you went north to
>   San Palace,
> And if you ask how I regret that parting:
> It is like the flowers falling at Spring's end
>   Confused, whirled in a tangle.
> What is the use of talking, and there is no end of
>   talking,
> There is no end of things in the heart.

But even lines at first glance similar yield differences of 'music' under examination. The field is one thing in this:

> The wind moves above the wheat—
> With silver crashing,
> A thin war of metal.

and something else again in this:

> Over fair meadows,
> Over the cool face of that field,
> Unstill, ever moving
> Hosts of an ancient people,
> The silent cortège.

The advance we see in the poetry of this period over the adaptations from Provençal quoted earlier, was more than an advance in the use of language. Certainly Pound had rediscovered the living language during this period of transition, but he had done so, partly at least, *because* of his interest in music and Daniel's 'aesthetic of sound', and not in spite of them. If the language of his early poetry was false, a purely literary language, its 'music' also was comparatively monotonous. And these two problems were connected, for in solving the first he had to take account of the second and make use of his knowledge of music; and again it was partly because of his knowledge of music and song that he became dissatisfied with his own early performances. The two problems, first that of finding a natural language, and second of learning how to compose verse with a flexible 'music', may be considered separately, but taken in the context of his advance between the beginning of 1911 and the end of 1915 they are inseparable.

The years 1911 to 1920 were for Pound the most important in his literary career. During this time he wrote most of his best literary prose, renewed the language of poetry, and himself crossed over from being an interesting minor poet into the realm of major poetry. If we follow through the vast amount of prose he wrote for English and American periodicals during these years we find that he often returned to the subject of music and its importance to poetry. Thus, writing about 'The Tradition' he says that in Greece and Provence poetry attained its highest rhythmic and metrical brilliance at times when the arts of verse and music were most closely knit together; and as to quantity, 'it is foolish to suppose that we are incapable of distinguishing a long vowel from a short one, or that we are mentally debarred from ascertaining how many consonants intervene between one vowel and the next'. The reader is informed that Jannaris in his study of the Melic poets came to the conclusion that they composed according to the cadence and were not influenced by the discussions of the grammarians in Alexandria some centuries after their deaths. 'No one is so foolish', Pound says, 'as to suppose that a musician using "four-four" time is compelled to use always four quarter notes in each bar, or in "seven-eighths" time to use seven eighth notes uniformly in each bar.' For anyone to say that such and such combinations of sound and tempo are not proper 'is as foolish as to say that a painter should not use red in the upper left hand corners of his pictures'. It all depends, he says, on the nature of the syllables and articulate sound and the 'laws of music'. In order to learn these things a poet must undertake a first-hand examination of all kinds of verse and 'profound study of the art and history of music'.

In a review of Ford's *Collected Poems* in 1914 he devoted several paragraphs to words and music and the different kinds of 'music' in verse, and four years later in a review of a new edition of Joyce's *Chamber Music* remarked of one of the poems that 'If Henry Lawes were alive again he might make the suitable music, for the cadence is here worthy of his cunning'. We find him reviewing Dolmetsch's *The Interpretation of the Music of the XVIIth and XVIIIth Centuries*, translating a libretto for Beecham, and writing a note on the singer Raymonde Collignon; and towards the end of 1917 when he once again took up his study of Arnaut Daniel and the problem of translating Provençal, he began a period of three years as music critic for the *New Age*, under the pseudonym of William Atheling.

But returning for a moment to the poems in *Cathay* and *Lustra*, we see that from the point of view of prosody Pound had achieved the articulation of some definite 'music' within the line, passage, or poem, but with little or no 'modulation' or significant change inside the musical unit. Many of these poems are perfect in themselves, but were only steps on the way towards something else. What Pound wanted was to write poetry which required the whole of his art, not in separate poems, a piece at a time, but the whole of it woven together in the articulation of a single work, with each aspect of technique and ability coming into play as the rise or fall of the composition called for it. But when I say 'the whole of his art' I do not mean the piling-up of every form, every technique into a single work regardless of what is being conveyed, for that would be to ignore the essential point about technical skill, namely that it has no real meaning outside the end to which it is employed. Skill in the sense I mean it, is critical as well as creative. It means knowing what to leave out as well as what to put in, how to arrange and group the parts of a poem towards a definite end.

Pound's first major work of this kind, which required the whole of his art, was *Homage to Sextus Propertius*, which the author has dated 1917 although it was not published in either periodical or book until 1919. Although I have been speaking in terms of the 'music' of verse, I do not wish to give the impression that *Propertius* was the result of an underlying musical impulse only, for it was not. In so far as we are able to say anything at all about the 'origins' of art, it was the result of a convergence of at least three things: a musical impulse, a necessary subject matter, and a mature technique—all of which were essential to its creation. *Propertius* is London and the British Empire of 1917 as seen by Pound through the eyes of Propertius, using and adapting the Roman poet's words about Imperial Rome to a similar situation in the twentieth century. For Pound, London was the metropolis, the great centre, and for this reason its faults, its sluggishness, spurred him on to thought much more than the faults of San Francisco, say, or Melbourne. 'I don't see why you shouldn't live half the year in London', he wrote to Amy Lowell in March 1914. 'After all it's the only sane place for any one to live if they've any pretence to letters.' Two years later he wrote to Iris Barry that the value of Latin poets like Catullus and Propertius was that they were 'the only ones we know of who had approximately the same problems as we have. The metropolis, the imperial posts to all corners of the known world.' In a letter to the *English Journal* of January 1931, he summarized *Propertius* by saying that 'it presents certain emotions as vital to me in 1917, faced with the infinite and ineffable imbecility of the British Empire, as they were to Propertius some centuries earlier, when faced with the infinite and ineffable imbecility of the Roman Empire. These emotions are defined largely, but not entirely, in Propertius's own terms.'

In *Propertius* Pound's music and his subject are very nearly one. His technical resources were such by this time that they were able to place, without embarrassment, any subject they happened to encounter, no matter what turns, twists, changes of pace, or modulations were necessary for its proper apprehension in verse. The poem may be said to have brought a new 'music' into English, not a louder or bigger 'music' exactly, but, if we turn to symphonic music for a rough parallel, some definite change as we find in the later symphonies of Mozart:

                                    Now for a large-mouthed
        product.
Thus:
'The Euphrates denies its protection to the
                Parthian and apologizes for Crassus,'
And 'It is, I think, India which now gives necks to
        your triumph,'
And so forth, Augustus. 'Virgin Arabia shakes in
        her inmost dwelling.'
If any land shrink into a distant seacoast,
        it is a mere postponement of your domination.
And I shall follow the camp, I shall be duly
                celebrated for singing the affairs of your
                cavalry.
May the fates watch over my day.

                            .   .   .

If she goes in a gleam of Cos, in a slither of dyed
        stuff,
There is a volume in the matter; if her eyelids sink
        into sleep,
There are new jobs for the author;
And if she plays with me with her shirt off,
        We shall construct many Iliads.

Pound was still at this time improving some of his earlier translations from the Provençal and making new adaptations, and when
he published *Propertius* in *Quia Pauper Amavi* in October 1919 he
also included a group of Provençal poems, the idea being to show
up the contrast between the feeling of the troubadours, which he
regarded as archaic, and the feeling of Imperial Rome, which he
saw as something very similar to that of the modern world. These
later poems from the Provençal show a much firmer grasp of song
writing than do his earlier attempts; yet strangely, for all his interest in words and music Pound never managed to write a song
of the highest quality. He has written words to be spoken and
words to be chanted which are as melodic and perfect as almost
anything in the language; and yet his songs, despite the time he
gave to this question, have never been of the highest quality, for
the reason, I believe, that against his own advice he gave too much

attention to the blending of sounds and not enough to the joining
of words in phrases. This failure is all the more remarkable in that
the making of phrases is one of the things he did so well in his other
poetry. That there was a weakness in his theorizing about poems
to be sung is suggested by this distinction in *Guido Cavalcanti:
Rime*:

> There is opposition, not only between what M. de Schloezer dis-
> tinguishes as musical and poetic lyricism, but in the writing itself there
> is a distinction between poetic lyricism, the emotional force of the ver-
> bal movement, and melopoeic lyricism, the letting the words flow on
> a melodic current, realized or not, realizable or not, if the line is sup-
> posed to be sung on a sequence of notes of different pitch.[1]

Instead of going back to examine the best songs in English he
made the mistake of separating 'verbal movement' from another
thing he called 'letting the words flow on a melodic current',
thus introducing a new and perhaps non-existent problem—I
mean non-existent as far as the poet is concerned. In his Provençal
adaptations of 1918, which he made as songs to be sung, the stanzas
are fashioned to avoid monotony and they are very pleasant; but
the sounds, although blended, are blended as syllables rather than
as words in the phrase, so that they lack what he usually managed
to get into his other verse, a 'music' strung together in phrases,
each phrase made of words which fall in what, for brevity, I will
call the natural cadence. Syllables which go together when
blended as syllables do not always hold together when read or
sung as words, so the poet who would make a perfect song must
first of all make a perfect poem. Here is the opening of one of
these later adaptations from the Provençal, which shows that a care
for vowel 'music' without a proper gauging of the weight and
duration of words in the phrase seriously limits words to be sung:

> O Plasmatour and true celestial light,
> Lord powerful, engirdlèd all with might,
> Give my good-fellow aid in fools' despite
> Who stirs not forth this night,
>   And day comes on.

[1] Pound's translation of Boris de Schloezer's *Stravinsky* was published in the
Dial during 1928 and '29.

'Sst! my good fellow, art awake or sleeping?
Sleep thou no more. I see the star upleaping
That hath the dawn in keeping,
    And day comes on!

'Hi! Harry, hear me, for I sing aright
Sleep not thou now, I hear the bird in flight
That plaineth of the going of the night,
    And day comes on . . .'

Turning to Dryden's 'Lady's Song' we see that the vowel 'music'
is not an isolated thing but moves in phrases and depends on them
for its very life:

A Quire of bright Beauties in Spring did appear,
To chuse a *May*-lady to govern the Year;
All the nymphs were in White, and the Shepherds in
 Green,
The Garland was giv'n, and *Phillis* was Queen;
But *Phillis* refused it, and sighing did say,
I'll not wear a Garland while *Pan* is away.

While *Pan* and fair *Syrinx*, are fled from our Shore,
The Graces are banish'd, and Love is no more:
The soft God of Pleasure that warm'd our Desires
Has broken his Bow, and extinguished his Fires,
And vows that himself, and his Mother, will mourn,
Till *Pan* and fair *Syrinx* in Triumph return.

Forbear your Addresses, and Court us no more,
For we will perform what the Deity swore:
But, if you dare think of deserving our Charms,
Away with your Sheephooks, and take to your Arms;
Then Lawrels and Myrtles your Brows shall adorn,
When *Pan* and his Son, and fair *Syrinx* return.

But of course the 'Lady's Song' was written towards the end of
his life by one who had lived in the time of Henry Lawes and on
through the age of Purcell. Pound on the other hand had had no
such encouragement. He wrote at a time when poets gave little or

no thought to the essentials of this matter, and what is more, at a time when there were practically no English composers or singers interested in the kind of setting and singing which this art requires. In such circumstances it is hardly fair to criticize Pound because he fell short of his goal, for this art seems to require a society saturated in music and song before its practitioners can reach perfection. But given such a society even a poet like Waller may turn out a masterpiece 'Go lovely rose' or an anonymous writer produce the remarkable pastoral 'Bewailing the Death of the Earl of Rochester', which Pound printed in *ABC of Reading*. It perhaps needs saying at this point that it is largely because of Pound's work that we are able to discuss the art of song in these terms at all.

I have allowed myself this digression on song in order to emphasize the fact that the knowledge and aural education which Pound gained from listening to music and the study of song, went much more successfully into the making of poems to be spoken or chanted than into his Provençal translations and attempts at song. His fifteen-year effort towards a more intelligent and orderly, a more musical arrangement and zoning of sound in verse, was finally realized in *Hugh Selwyn Mauberley* and the *Cantos*. *Mauberley*, which was first published in June 1920, was the focusing of many years of technical training upon the indentations and impressions which London literary life of the post-war years had effected on the faculties of a sensitive observer. It is not a mere record of this or that shoddy piece of writing or politics, but the selection, orderly arrangement and crystallization of these things, and the emotions and thoughts they engendered, by means of a technique raised and groomed in objectivity. In these few pages meet the long hours spent with Daniel, Cavalcanti and Leopardi; the wrestling with Heine, Sappho and Propertius and the notes of Ernest Fenollosa, and also his more recent preoccupation with the French of Gautier and the Greek of Bion. But the result of course was something quite unlike any of the individual elements:

> The age demanded an image
> Of its accelerated grimace,
> Something for the modern stage,
> Not, at any rate, an Attic grace;

Not, not certainly, the obscure reveries
Of the inward gaze;
Better mendacities
Than the classics in paraphrase!

The 'age demanded' chiefly a mould in plaster,
Made with no loss of time,
A prose kinema, not, not assuredly, alabaster
Or the 'sculpture' of rhyme.

If we examine again some of Pound's early poetry it is possible here and there to see some of the elements which became transfigured in *Mauberley*. If we take the various effects which Pound achieved in 'Altaforte', the line-endings which remain in the ear; add to these the lines from his translation of de Born's 'Si tuit li dol':

The world o'ershadowed, soiled and overcast,
Void of all joy and full of ire and sadness

and this quatrain from Heine:

O ye lips that are ungrateful,
Hath it never once distressed you,
That you can say such *awful* things
Of *any* one who ever kissed you.

it is fairly clear how, under the pressure of increasing consciousness of sound elements and rhythm, and a growing desire for their more orderly arrangement, things learnt consciously and unconsciously in the making of the early poems were incorporated and made new in *Mauberley*:

Beneath the sagging roof
The stylist has taken shelter,
Unpaid, uncelebrated,
At last from the world's welter

Nature receives him;
With a placid and uneducated mistress
He exercises his talents
And the soil meets his distress.

Something of this new mastery is also to be found in such lines as 'Saffron sandal so petals the narrow foot' in Canto 4, which was written about 1919, and in the 'Hell' cantos, probably drafted, according to Pound's memory of it in 1960, in that same year 1919. Somewhere about the beginning of 1921 Pound left London for good and went to live in Paris. It is not always wise to mark out a literary career according to a writer's geography and the accoutrements of his mundane life, but in Pound's case the publication of *Mauberley*, his leaving London after twelve or more years, and his going to Paris, marked the end of the first half of his literary career, and the beginning of the second.

II

In a letter from Paris in April 1921, Pound discussed his opera *Villon* with Agnes Bedford, the English musician with whom he had collaborated the previous year in producing a book of words and music called *Five Troubadour Songs*:

> Sat through *Pelléas* the other evening and am encouraged—encouraged to tear up the whole bloomin' era of harmony and do the thing if necessary on two tins and wash-board. Anything rather than that mush of hysteria, Scandinavia strained through Belgium plus French Schwärmerei. Probably just as well I have to make this first swash without any instruments at hand. Very much encouraged by the *Pelléas*, ignorance having no further terrors if that damn thing is the result of what is called musical knowledge. . . .
>
> I haven't been able to exclude violins altogether; and I suppose there will eventually be a few chords in the damn thing. Fortunately Satie's *Socrate* is damn dull (and people endure it) and Auric, whatever he knows, is certainly out for even less system than I am. (I really having a damn definite system, which may bring up against Les Six.) They will hang me possibly as an academic but scarcely as a dynamitist.

For a person of Pound's disposition the composition of opera and music was the natural outcome of his earlier interest in music generally and the problem of words and music. Composers since the time of Lawes, he believed, had lost the art of setting words properly to music, and since Rossini the art of combining songs with an orchestra. Given this belief it was only a matter of time before he rolled up his sleeves and started to do the job himself. The suggestion that a single hearing of *Pelléas* had set him to tearing up 'the whole bloomin' era of harmony' should not of course be taken at its face value; Pound's correspondence is not always a good guide to his final decisions in matters of art; but it should not on the other hand be waved away as necessarily meaningless, for some of the flaws in Pound's major work, the *Cantos*, are due to a tendency, under certain conditions, to assume the world on the strength of some single item the accuracy or context of which he has made no effort to check or understand. In the case of music and the setting of words, his primary object was clarity of line and clarity of words. Harmony and counterpoint seemed to him to obstruct both at times, or at any rate were matters of secondary importance. In another letter soon afterwards he gave a further outline of his position:

Continuing in desperation and despite the outrageous postal rates—

What in your exalted opinion is the least amount of tarabiscotage the thing will stand? Answer to be as technical as possible. After the *Pelléas*, as aforesaid, I feel ready to make a *Partition pour deux Casseroles et une plance de buis*. Remembering that the accords, or rather identical note is built up of several instruments forcement giving VERY different overtones, how much bloody chord-harmony is necessary? . . .

Premier principe—RIEN that interferes with the words, or with the utmost possible clarity of impact of words on audience. . . .

Even an *instrumental* counterpoint developed ANYwhere near enough to satisfy mere contrapuntalist would presumably bitch the words?

Given the play for the eye, and the song, how much of the actual orchestration DOES the audience hear?

It was in 1922 or '23 while Pound was composing *Villon* that he met the young American concert pianist and composer George Antheil. Pound liked Antheil's compositions so well that he prepared, partly from Antheil's own notes apparently, a small book called *Antheil and the Treatise on Harmony*, which was published during the first half of 1924 in Ford's *Transatlantic Review*, and then in book form by the Three Mountains Press of Paris in

November of the same year. It would be outside the scope of this
book and my own competence to discuss it here. I mention it
merely as an indication of his interest in music with a particularly
vigorous rhythmic outline. The first performance of Antheil's
Ballet Mécanique—a work for pianos, player piano, xylophones,
electric bells, etc.—in Paris in June 1926 was attended by a riot and
a certain amount of relevant or irrelevant publicity, depending on
how you look at it. Pound continued to write about Antheil's
work in literary and other journals for a number of years and in
Guide to Kulchur defended the composer as follows:

> Musical moralists have damned in my presence that very tough baby
> George Antheil. He has gone to hell and to Hollywood a 'sub-Medean
> talent', he has made himself a motley and then some. He was imper-
> fectly schooled, in music, in letters, in all things, but he nevertheless did
> once demand bits of SOLIDITY, he demanded short hard bits of rhythm
> hammered down, worn down so that they were indestructible and
> unbendable. . . .
> This is in accord, though not contained in Jean's *Rappel à l'Ordre*.
> Cocteau there demanded a music to be like tables and chairs.
> That goes with Mantegna's frescoes. Something to be there and
> STAY there on the wall.

Parts of *Villon*—words by François Villon, music by Pound—
were performed in Paris in 1924. The work was given more fully
two years later at the Salle Pleyel, with the tenor Yves Tinayre,
the bass Robert Maitland, and a small group of instruments which
included a violin and a large French *corne* with only two notes.
It was performed by the B.B.C. in 1931 and again in 1962. In
a comment on it in the *Townsman* of April 1938 Pound re-stated
his belief that the problem of words and music, *motz el son*,
having occupied the best auditors in South Europe, namely the
troubadours and Dante, for at least a couple of centuries, it was to
that particular epoch that one had to go for the ABC of the subject. Other composers, he said, even if they wanted to go on from
where he had got to in *Villon* could not do so for want of satisfactory verbal texts. When Antheil and the Hungarian composer
Tibor Serly wanted operatic texts in English there were simply
none available; none, that is, composed of words written to be

sung. Pound himself in the absence of such texts wrote a second
opera using the Italian of Cavalcanti and the Provençal of Sordello. In the same *Townsman* article he wrote:

I am not merely being captious and heaping mud on the lousy
writers of British bilge, the frumpy Victorians and arid preceders of
the hoop skirt. When the island was still mentionable in a society of
technicians, Henry Lawes found the same paucity. Having exhausted
the frail and limited gamut of British metric invention in the cantabile
sector, Lawes went on to set Greek and Latin.

Turning to Debussy he claimed that French concert-hall songs
of the 1890's were mostly all on one tune:

The unending series of mist and mashed potatoes in the French
metric didn't give the composer a chance. Having squshed up his lips,
stuck them two inches forward, squeezed his voice through a sort of
sponge in his nozzle, the singer and/or composer had exhausted the
possible varieties of intoning THAT kind of verse. The café chançon
was alive. Yvette was heiress of the ages, and Debussy went back to
Villon and Charles D'Orleans for his song masterwork.[1]

What may strike the reader as curious, in view of Pound's fuss
over the lack of suitable operatic plays, is why he did not concentrate his attention on the writing of such texts, instead of composing operatic music. After all, the former was a job for which
he had full professional equipment in working order, whereas
composition of music was a field in which he could never be more
than an untrained, if gifted, amateur. I cannot pretend to answer
this question with any certainty, but I would point to his irrational
urge to get things done, which sometimes led to a scattering and
impoverishment of his work instead of to concentration and en-
richment. But whatever we may think of this exercise or over-
reaching of his talents, we must not lose sight of the fact that his
venture into opera was founded on his belief in the close connection between words and music, which he summarized in a letter

---

[1] It is interesting to note that Pound contributed English translations to a
book called *Selection from Collection Yvette Guilbert*, arranged by Gustave
Ferrari and published in London in 1912.

to Agnes Bedford in 1933 by saying that the whole point about his setting of Sordello's Provençal was that the 'music fits the words and not some other words'. It was after a re-examination of some of the troubadours about this time that he came to prefer Sordello above all the others, including Daniel. The reason for this change, he wrote in *Guide to Kulchur*, had to do with his 'long domesticity' with music: 'Above other troubadours, as I feel it *now*, Sordello's hand (or word) "deceives the eye" honestly. The complete fluidity, the ease that comes only with mastery in strophes so simple in meaning that they leave nothing for the translator.' But much more important than this, what he gained from all this study was a finer and finer sense of timing in his own poetry. In the Cantos written during the late 1920's and 1930's this refined sense is almost everywhere present. We notice it in the catching of a certain type of voice in a certain situation:

> Pokes his head in the doorway: 'Iz there any,'
> He says, 'Gar'
> Damn
> Man here
> Thet kan speak ENGLISH?'

and in the incantation of the following:

> Time is the evil. Evil.
>   A day, and a day
> Walked the young Pedro baffled,
>   a day and a day
> After young Ignez was murdered.
> Came lords in Lisboa
>   a day, and a day
> In homage. Seated there
>   dead eyes,
> Dead hair under the crown,
> The King still young there beside her.

Pick up a volume containing the first seventy Cantos and even one who knows them well may be surprised anew at the many varieties of 'music' perfectly executed on page after page. Only a very sure hand can turn from a verbal movement like this:

　　　better there with good acorns
Than with a crab for an eye, and 30 fathom of fishes
Green swish in the socket . . .

to the totally different 'music' of:

　　　the sound always of drums and trumpets
crying VIVA FERDINANDO and in all parts of the piazza
were flames in great number and grenades burning
to sound of bombs and of mortaretti and the
　　　　　shooting of
guns and of pistols and in chapel of the Piazza
a great number of candles for the publication of
　　　　　this so
provident law and at sundown were dances . . .

Merely thumbing through the pages it is possible to find three
other kinds of 'music' all totally unlike each other. In the first
there is no sign of the poet; it is as if the words had been brought
back from beyond recorded history:

　　　Evening is like a curtain of cloud,
　　　a blurr above ripples; and through it
　　　sharp long spikes of the cinnamon,
　　　a cold tune amid reeds.

The second is the voice of the Chinese sage:

　　　　　No house is
　　durable if perched on yr neighbour's ruin
　　An honest peasant is a prognostic . . .

And the third a very definite pronouncement by the author of the
poem:

　　　But for the clearest head in the congress
　　　　　　　1774 and thereafter
　　　　　pater patriae
　　the man who at certain points
　　　　　made us
　　at certain points
　　　　　saved us
　　by fairness, honesty and straight moving
　　　　　　　ARRIBA ADAMS

It was at the Italian seaside town of Rapallo where he had gone to live in 1925 that Pound organized a series of musical concerts which demand some notice here for the light they throw on his serious approach to music. From the playing of twelve Mozart sonatas for violin and piano at the opening concerts in 1933 to the final concerts of Purcell and Mozart in 1938 and '39, these programmes were arranged with one thing specially in mind: rigorous musical education. Here first is a general survey by Desmond Chute which appeared in the *Pound Newsletter* of October 1955:

Fanned by his disinterested and unflagging enthusiasm, rare and unforgettable little concerts sprang up according to the frequency and incidence of performers. One remembers blocks of music. *Block* in this context was a great word with Ezra; not only did he insist at rehearsals on 'blocks' of light and shade in the performance of old music, he also demanded integrated and consecutive programmes. The Rapallo musical seasons started as weeks, begun under the sign of Mozart, all of whose violin sonatas were played at least once by Olga Rudge and Gerhart Munch. One wonders when the whole series had last, if ever, been heard in its entirety. There followed all Bach's and all Pergolesi's. In a similar spirit, though more informally in a private house, Munch gave a reading on three consecutive afternoons of the complete *Wohltemperierte Clavier*. Meanwhile the weeks went on with Purcell's *Twelve Sonatas in Three Parts* (with basso continuo, 1683) and William Young's for strings and bass ('the first printed English Sonatas, 1653'). For the latter, absolute priority of execution may be claimed for Rapallo, actually in advance of the 'first' performance under the editor, W. Gillies Whittaker, at Oxford. In the 1930's Pound developed an intense interest in the vast unpublished output of Antonio Vivaldi, much of which, largely thanks to Olga Rudge's research and to microfilm technique, has since been made available to the public. Some Vivaldi *inedita* were given at Rapallo. Particular interest attaches to Gerhart Munch's transcriptions of MSS. embodying researches by the late Oscar Chilesotti into old music (e.g. Dowland, Janequin, Francesco da Milano).

The Bartok played here by the Hungarian Quartet, though published, was as yet seldom played and little known. As far as possible Ezra decided on local talent. Yet he was far from excluding good or excellent professionals on condition the programme was not made up to show off the performers, but rather based on intrinsic musical worth . . .

Besides the artists already mentioned, we heard Tibor Serly in Mozart's *Sinfonia Concertante* and Sonata for *Violin and Viola*, and some compositions of his own; Renata Borgatti in Bach, Haydn, Mozart and Debussy; Chiara Fino Savio singing *Arie Antiche*, and Lonny Mayers, Hindemith. Lugini Franchetti and Giorgio Levi were due to come when war cut short so many things more important (but how few rarer!) than concerts memorable for music and innocent of banality and display.

Let us now look at some of the programmes in more detail to see what Pound was aiming at. Two of the concerts for 1933 he listed in *ABC of Reading*:

October 10th.
From the Chilesotti MSS. Munch transcription: Francesco da Milano: 'Canzone degli Uccelli', recast from Janequin.
Giovanni Terzi: Suite di Ballo.
Corelli: Sonata in La maj., two violins and piano.
J. S. Bach: Sonata in Do maj., two violins and piano.
Debussy: Sonata per piano e violino.

December 5th.
Collezione Chilesotti: Severi: due Arie. Roncalli: Preludio, Gigua, Passacaglia.
Bach: Toccata (piano solo, ed. Busoni).
Bach: Concerto Re maj. for two violins and piano.
Ravel: Sonata per violino e pianoforte.

In his comment on these two concerts he says there was nothing fortuitous about the selection of the works to be played:

The point of this experiment is that everyone present at the two concerts now knows a great deal more about the relations, the relative weight, etc., of Debussy and Ravel than they possibly could have found out by reading ALL the criticisms that have ever been written of both.

Other programmes included a Scriabin recital, the music of Albert and Telemann, Ferroud, Boccherini, Honegger and Berg. Writing to Gerald Hayes in November 1937, Pound remarked that he was hoping to present 'rather more of Whittaker's 12 new Purcells than W. seems to think advisable in one lump', and went on to enquire whether there was 'anything of Jenkins (or enough for a whole evening) that could be played as it stands?' He also sought information about the works of Dowland and Lawes. It was about this time in two different books that Pound made several statements about music which help us to understand his point of view. The first occurs in a three-page article called 'Civilization' which he included in *Polite Essays* (1937). In this he is concerned with the relation of music to civilization, and after the general statement, 'Civilization begins when people start preferring a little done right to a great deal done wrong', he turns to opera. Falstaff, he says, is vindication of all Verdi's objections to Wagner:

> It is vindication of all Verdi's drive towards making a unity out of that heteroclite chaos of stage, orchestra, and caterwauling. Everything in it fits and belongs. It needs Toscanini, BUT it is second rate music. . . .
> Turning to Dr Whittaker's edition of William Young and his prefaces, we revive. Botticelli's 'Zephyrus' placates our parched audition. Young wrote for performers who were not virtuosi, but musicians capable of reading (that is of understanding) the musical line set before them. . . .
> At the risk of thumping the pulpit, I reassert this distinction between art made for USE—that is painting to have painted into the plaster and stay while one lives there—and painting to stick in an exhibition to catch the eye of the passing possible buyer or vendor; music for who can play it as distinct from music made for the least common, and most vulgar, denominator of the herd in the largest possible hall.

About a year later in *Guide to Kulchur* he distinguished between what he called 'music of representative outline' and 'music of structure':

> In music there is representation of the sole matter wherein music can be 'literally' representative, namely sound. Thus the violinist reading Janequin's music transposed said: a lot of birds, not one bird alone.
> Down on through Vivaldi and Couperin there is this kind of music, music of representative outline.
> And in distinction to it music of structure, as J. S. Bach in fugue or keyboard toccata, or Hindemith today in his Schwannendreher.

Not contradictory, not hostile one to the other, but two blessed categories, each for a particular excellence.

I will give one more example of Pound's writing on music during this same period. It is from a letter he sent to the *Musical Times* in December 1938:

I would say to composers, that the really great composers have been interested in line, that is in melody and in theme, and they have been diligent in expressing their ideas so that one, two or very small groups of players can represent them. . . .

As corollary to or emphasis . . . I would say that a composer who is really good can make a musical statement in a violin and piano sonata that will distinguish him from duds, duffers, second rate composers and the general soggy mess of nineteenth century music, as it slogged along after Chopin and Rossini. . . .

Good composers write down what they want played, but duds (meaning most of the composers since Rossini) simply have not had any clear intentions as to the duration of their notes. Stravinsky has. The rest of them being too utterly and damnably incapable of hearing the finer divisions of time have, confound it, left a sort of general stage direction and the performer must 'interpret', I.E. do one of the most vital parts of the composer's job for him. Almost any ass, or even a middle-aged literary gent can hunt around on a clavichord until he finds the pitch of the note he wants in a melody, but the job of writing music is something more than mere imagining of a melodic line or an harmonic progression, it requires the capacity for registering the duration of notes and pauses. All of which most musicians will grant and not one in ten thousand realize. . . .

What would you think of a painter who left a portrait vague and expected the photographer or engraver to put in the real likeness to the sitter when making reproductions. The analogy is inexact, but may start some readers toward what I am driving at.

What Pound gained by his study of music was a finer sense of timing; but this was not all. He gained also in his conscious or analytic knowledge of prosody. In the 'Treatise on Metre' attached to *ABC of Reading*, he says things which it is hard to imagine anyone being able to set down with such clarity without a considerable musical background. 'Rhythm', he says, 'is a form cut into time', and after suggesting that the section on Greek metric in the *Laurencie et Lavignac Encyclopédie de la Musique et Dictionnaire du Conservatoire* is better than one is likely to find in the Greek language department of a university, remarks that in making a line of verse (and thence building the lines into passages) the poet has certain primal elements, consisting of the 'articulate sounds' of the language, and the various groups of letters in syllables. These syllables have differing weights and durations; first of all their original weights and durations, and secondly the weights and durations 'that seem naturally imposed on them by the other syllable groups around them'. It is by arranging these elements that the poet cuts his design in time, not forgetting however that the poet is not a musician, as such, and must also take into account 'the varying qualities of sound inseparable from the words of his speech'. These 'varying qualities' might seem at first to be included under his earlier definition of weights and durations that seem naturally imposed on syllables by the other syllable groups around them, and in a sense they are; but unless the poet keeps the peculiarities of speech always in mind, peculiarities which may or may not exist in the realm of sound, but which certainly resound in the ear and mind of the auditor, he is likely, even as Pound has done in some of his attempts at song writing, and sometimes in his translation of the Chinese *Odes*, to exalt sound above speech, to the detriment—strange as it may seem at first—of the cantabile quality of his verse.

It has been my view throughout that the development of the 'music' of Pound's poetry, in so far as the 'music' is separable from the poetry and admits of separate examination, was partly at least the result of his interest in music for its own sake. This interest, which was strong at the beginning of his career, continued to grow stronger, and, if I may use such a term, more concrete over the years, providing him with the means of achieving greater and greater precision or effectiveness in the timing of his own verse. But if this is indeed so, it should then be possible to isolate examples in his later work which show this gain in precision of timing. If we turn to the *Pisan Cantos* written at the end of the Second World War and published in 1948, his mastery is evident in the control of pace, and the pauses:

> Lordly men are to earth o'ergiven
>   these the companions:
> Fordie who wrote of giants
>   and William who dreamed of nobility
>   and Jim the comedian singing:
>   'Blarrney castle me darlin'
>   you're nothing now but a StOWne'
> and Plarr talking of mathematics
>   or Jepson lover of jade
> Maurie who wrote historical novels
>   and Newbolt who looked twice bathed
>   are to earth o'ergiven

It was only through such mastery, the knowing how far he could go, that he managed to compose sometimes out of 'material' that by its nature was in danger of crumbling; that he managed, for example, to give a medallion-like quality to the following, without either changing it substantially into something too monumental, or letting it slide away to become trivial:

> But Tosch the great ex-greyhound
>   used to get wildly excited
>   at being given large beefsteaks
> in Tolosa
>   and leapt one day finally
> right into the centre of the large dining table
> and lay there as a centre piece
>   near the cupboard piled half full
> with novels of 'Willy' etc
>   in the old one franc editions
> and you cd/ hear papa Dulac's voice
>   clear in the choir that wd/ ring ping on the high altar
> in the Bach chorals
>   true as a pistol shot . . .

Pound's translation of the *Odes* of ancient China, first published in 1954 under the title of *The Classic Anthology Defined by Confucius*, is a mixed bag, but with enough of beauty and skill among the lapses to confirm our view of him as the possessor of a rare ear for the 'music' of verse. The *Classic Anthology* is a collection of

305 poems some of which were already ancient in the time of Confucius, that is the fifth century B.C. Whether Confucius selected the poems or merely touched up the old music here and there is still, apparently, a matter for discussion among specialists, but at least one thing seems certain—that the poems were meant to be sung. Now while Pound managed to translate some of them into beautiful English this is not so with all. In fact we probably need to divide the book somewhat after the following manner: poems which are beautiful in their own right, though not always good songs; those which are not particularly good as poems but seem to suggest certain beauties in the original; poems in which Pound lapses into bad English verse; and finally, poems which no amount of skill on the part of the translator could possibly bring to life, the original material being intractable—I mean consisting of material which is of absolutely no interest except to a specialist in philology or archaeology. If this division is regarded as unsatisfactory, others are free to make their own, but some such division is necessary, I think, if we are to get Pound's accomplishment into perspective.

It might seem strange that a poet of Pound's ability should have got himself bogged in such a collection; that he chose to translate all of them instead of selecting those he knew he could handle. The reason for this, I believe, has nothing to do with Pound's poetry at all, so it is not, in one sense at least, a blot upon his critical faculties. As far as I understand it, from what I have read and from my own conversation with him, he accepted the whole collection because Confucius recommended it. That is to say, as a follower of Confucius he was not interested in using his own critical faculties as a poet, not interested in weeding out the unsuitable poems and making a compact selection of his own; but preferred to believe, since Confucius had said so or seemed to imply it, that every poem was essential to the collection as a whole. In its own day, in the context of Confucian philosophy, this may have been so; and if, following Pound, we continue to regard the collection in this light as a philosophic, almost as a religious document, then it may still be true that every poem in it is essential. If, on the other hand, we judge the collection as poetry then quite a few poems in it cannot pass the test. The material I have referred to as intractable has been treated by Pound with complete seriousness. Both my use of the word intractable and Pound's attitude to this material, call for brief comment before we pass on to consider some of the better poems in the collection.

It is a fact that no material is intractable, given a poet who is master of it, and no man has done more to prove this than Pound himself. But in translating the *Odes*, Ezra Pound the poet was at the mercy of Ezra Pound the Confucian, so that whereas the former might well have taken this material in hand and satirized or punctured it in some way, he was forced by the other Pound to swallow it all with complete solemnity. Some of the sentiments in the *Odes* are such as Emily Post might have expressed, etiquette for people who do not wish to disturb the social surface, let alone the mind; but having accepted Confucius in a particular way, Pound was no longer free to exercise all his critical faculties upon the work he was making.

Now to the poems. Many of them Pound has translated into a loose ballad form. The words do not impose themselves, not strongly at any rate, upon the voice and there is plenty of room for the ballad singer to move around, without pulling the words too far out of shape. The first poem in the book is a good example of this type of translation; it is noteworthy for the clear strong sound of the final line:

> 'Hid! Hid!' the fish-hawk saith,
> by isle in Ho the fish-hawk saith:
> > 'Dark and clear,
> > Dark and clear,
> So shall be the prince's fere.'
>
> Clear as the stream her modesty;
> As neath dark boughs her secrecy,
> > reed against reed
> > tall on slight
> as the stream moves left and right,
> > dark and clear,
> > dark and clear.

> To seek and not find
> as a dream in his mind,
>> think how her robe should be,
>> distantly, to toss and turn,
>> to toss and turn.
>
> High reed caught in *ts'ai* grass
>> so deep her secrecy;
> lute sound in lute sound is caught,
>> touching, passing, left and right.
> Bang the gong of her delight.

Some of the poems impose themselves on the singer or speaker for a time, but the poet is unable to maintain his authority. In the following extract, the rhythm peters away after 'haunted pool' and by the time we get to 'sounding to perfect rule and rote' the movement is as clogged and stodgy as the bad English verse of any age:

> The king stood in his 'Park Divine,'
> deer and doe lay there so fine,
> so fine so sleek; birds of the air
> flashed a white wing while fishes splashed
> on wing-like fin in the haunted pool.
>
> Great drums and gongs
> hung on spiked frames
> sounding to perfect rule and rote
> about the king's calm crescent moat,
>
> Tone unto tone, of drum and gong.

The reason I think why this collection misled so many people, myself among them, when it first came out, was the sheer brilliance of so much of its 'music' compared with the general run of English verse in the postwar years. It was such a pleasure and a change to read a poet who relished and at the same time respected the language, who neither threw words around him like fireworks, nor indulged in the meanness of those who were too busy avoiding the wrong ever to do right. In my own case a number of years went by before I returned to the *Odes* to make a careful study of them, and discovered that the brilliance, which was there right enough, in single lines or quatrains, and in the use of many different styles, was seldom maintained throughout a whole poem. Even so, out of the collection of some three hundred poems, there are dozens which testify to Pound's genius for direct statement conveyed in supple rhythms. In poems of lament he ranges from:

> Cold wind, and the rain,
> cock crow, he is come again,
>   my ease.

> Shrill wind and the rain
> and the cock crows and crows,
> I have seen him, shall it suffice
>   as the wind blows?

> Wind, wind and the dark
> as it were the dark of the moon,
> What of the wind, and the cock's never-ending cry;
> Together
> again
> he and I.

to this:

> The erudite moon is up, less fair than she
> who hath tied silk cords about
>   a heart in agony,
> She at such ease
>   so all my work is vain.

> My heart is tinder, and steel plucks at my pain
> so all my work is vain,
>   she at such ease
>   as is the enquiring moon.

Or again, from:

> I walk the waste, these weeds my food;
> I came invited, as I construed,
> Let me go as I had come,
> You do not feed me,
>   let me go home.

I

to this, with its artfully simple conclusion:

> Let the Great Cart alone,
> 'ware dust.
> Think not on sorrows
> lest thy heart rust.
>
> Push no great cart
> lest dust enflame thine eye,
> brood not on sorrows
> lest joy pass by.
>
> Push not the great wheel-spoke in moil and sweat
> lest thou make thy troubles
>   heavier yet.

In some cases he takes over a traditional English song style adding some twist of his own to the sonority:

> What hour is this? the court-yard flare burns bright,
> we hear a chink of bit-bells thru the night.
>
> We hear it faint: 'chin-chink' across the night,
> he comes not yet, the court-yard flare flicks bright.

The 'chink' effect is at least as old as Ben Jonson's 'To chime in a man's pocket and cry chink', but it is unlikely that Pound remembered it from Jonson, or ever saw it there, and in any case there is an interesting difference in the method used to hold the 'chink' sound in the reader's ear: Jonson by fortifying it with the word 'chime' in the same line and the words 'quire' and 'chirp' close by; Pound by incorporating the word 'chink' itself into a direct imitation of the jingling bit-bells. Yet for all his skill there is nothing in Pound's book approaching the delicacy of Jonson's 'Still to be neat, still to be dressed' or the sound of Campion's 'Thrice toss these oaken ashes in the air'; nor is there any poem in it which imposes not just a rhythm but a complete and ordered pattern on the voice, like Campion's 'Love me or not':

> Love me or not, love her I must, or die;
> Leave me or not, follow her needs must I.

But the songs of Jonson and Campion, as I said earlier about those
of Dryden, rose out of an age which was saturated in music and
song, whereas Pound had to struggle in a society afflicted by a
coarsening of the ear and insensitive to many delicacies of sound.
How wonderful it was then that he managed, despite this handi-
cap, to add to both our knowledge of timing in verse and the
range of English sonority. As late as Canto 97, written about 1955,
he continued to give evidence that his sense of time was undimin-
ished:

> 'As THAT!' said Ungaro,
> > 'It is just as hard as that'
> (jabbing a steel cube with his pencil butt
> > and speaking of mind as resistant).

We have here an almost perfect example of poetry that is lucid
and at the same time verging on the movement of music.

> 'As THAT!' said Ungaro,
> > 'It is just as hard as that'

The rhythmic emphasis in the first line is both underwritten and
balanced by the melodic flow of the second; and the lines which
follow:

> (jabbing a steel cube with his pencil butt
> > and speaking of mind as resistant).

bring the whole to a conclusion that is right and just, from the
points of view of both 'music' and meaning. And strange as it may
seem, when we think of Pound's abuse of Milton, he achieved this
particular rhythmic effect, and a number of others like it, by using
a construction which imitates, in English, the delayed endings of
Latin and German. The ultimate strength of these lines resides in
the fact that they do not come to rest until the final words 'mind
as resistant'. Although Pound's insistence upon 'natural' language
without inversions was right for English poetry at the time he put
it forward, his own practice in later years suggests that under certain circumstances at least, Milton's way may be the right way. In
the end, the musical donation we owe to Milton, which Pound

forcibly excluded from the 'tradition' outlined in his criticism, crept in again by way of his poetry, without his knowing it. This is perhaps only one more example going to prove that there is more to tradition than one man is able to discover and hold on to with his conscious mind.

CHAPTER VIII

Some Dangers of Literary Biography

WE HAVE seen something in the preceding pages of the immense amount of purely prosodic training and general preparation that went into the production of Pound's verse. His maturity as a poet occurred, it will be noted, about 1920, when he was thirty-five years old; and up to this time his work holds together as an unmistakable unity, despite possible flaws or shortcomings. Of the poetry and prose up to 1920 it is possible to say that it makes sense both on and below the surface, and there is no need for us to go hunting for out-of-the-way explanations to substantiate this claim. When, however, we turn to the second half of Pound's career—from the time he left London in 1921 until the *Thrones* Cantos in 1959—we are faced with something different. There is still much that is great in his poetry after 1920—and the *Cantos* is a major work, no matter how harshly we may have to treat certain aspects of it—but the prose begins to disintegrate and there are ominous signs on the surface of the poetry which suggest that all is not well below. The young man who at the age of twenty-five measured out the roads of Provence and wrote so compellingly of the poetry of the Romance languages, has been replaced, by the time he is forty, by another who at the drop of a hat will lecture the world on almost any subject from monetary systems to the real meaning of Confucius; and there is a corresponding turn in his poetry. He begins to insert, here and there, lines which cannot bear the weight of meaning he intends, and while individual passages, and whole cantos, taken by themselves, may be perfectly lucid, the meaning of the whole work becomes no clearer as he passes Canto 50, and then Canto 70, and actually begins to recede after he passes into the *Rock-Drill* section (Cantos 85–95). It is not that the poetry weakens—in some ways it is stronger, and firmer, and better, than the poetry up to and including *Mauberley*—but that the job of giving a major form to such a vast undertaking is beyond him, and when cracks begin to show he tries to fill them with hasty and inferior material. Something obviously has happened, the real meaning of which may be impossible to discover. But one thing at least is clear: in moving through the second half of Pound's career we must tread very carefully. Before going on to deal directly and in detail with some of the more troublesome aspects of the later Pound, I will look at some of the problems to be encountered, and the danger of literary biography generally, so that the reader may understand why I have chosen to treat Pound's biography in such a highly selective way in the chapters that follow.

There is nothing which prejudices Pound more in the eyes of those who have a fairly detailed knowledge of his work than his tinkering with subjects he was not equipped to handle. In his books, his pamphlets, isolated articles or letters it is possible to find, in addition to expressions of undoubted good sense, others which look like evidence that Pound has once again been jumping to conclusions which he could not support for a moment if he were challenged. The reader who would untangle completely Pound's errors and bad guesses from his good sense and good guesses must make the examination for himself, even if it is only to discover that the quest was not quite what he had expected, and that some at least of Pound's errors of fact and judgement, especially in his literary essays, are merely annoying rather than fundamental. It is, in fact, a mark of the second-rate writer that he burdens his subject with his own ignorance. The important writer, like Pound, even if he does not always achieve complete lucidity, tends towards it and towards the establishment of unity; the errors in Pound's earlier prose are marginal, and even some of those in the later prose, errors which inhere not only in what he is saying but in the style as well, are still marginal in the sense that they do not interfere with his main drift—about clarity of expression, for instance, or the importance of literature to society. The reader who will profit most is the one who keeps an eye on the main direction of Pound's thought, rather than on the errors, the exuberant illustrations, the careless or wrong-headed asides or apparent switches of subject matter, which by causing irrelevant annoyance or delight may deflect the reader's mind from an underlying and important truth.

Like most artists born since that great change in European sensibility which included the Romantic 'revolution', Pound has not always been clear about how to interpret his own intuitions or sudden and unaccountable realizations. He has sometimes read into them more than was perhaps there, or confused mental constructions based on these intuitions, or desires produced or stimulated by them, with the intuitions themselves. But where we find them free from, or not too encumbered by, these later additions of thought or emotion, they sometimes prove to be of greater use than pronouncements on the same subject by those who are scholastically impeccable, for the reason that whereas the scholar's remarks, no matter how just in themselves, inevitably relate to a vast and impersonal subject without any real definition, and over which he has no control, those of the artist relate to a world over which he has, in proportion to his greatness perhaps, strict personal supervision. I am not suggesting that they are necessarily contradictory, for the world of the artist, although it obeys the logic of imagination, is not unconnected with the world of the scholar; but the difference is important. One of the troubles with literary biography is that it does not take this difference into account: it cannot, because it is dealing with parts which can never equal the whole. By literary biography I mean, of course, books which 'explain' a work of art by constant reference to what passes for the biography of its creator.

The situation was relatively simple in 1923 when T. S. Eliot pointed out that 'the multiplication of critical books and essays may create . . . a vicious taste for reading about works of art instead of reading the works themselves, it may supply opinion instead of educating taste'. This is still true, but we have to face now a more formidable network of interests pandering to this taste, and a literary public still more barbarous than that of the 1920's, given to belief in superstitions harder to pierce than before and supported by 'scientific' assertions increasingly null by people who are farther and farther removed from an awareness of their nullity. Among these superstitions is the one that biography is woven in such a way into a man's creative work that it need only be disentangled by an expert in order to provide the lay reader with all necessary clues and keys to a full and satisfying enjoyment of its artistic merit. Or in other words the best way to make sense out of the work is by first of all making sense out of the life. There appears at first sight to be a considerable difference between the entertaining biographer with a journalist's flair and the serious scholar who will track his facts down even if it takes him years to do it. And yet, I believe that the difference between them is usually not one of kind, but simply that the scholar digs much deeper; he is not necessarily getting any closer to the meaning of the artist's work than the other, any more than a scientist is closer to the meaning of the universe than his predecessor simply by obtaining a bigger and better microscope. It is possible for a critic who already knows a poet's creative work to return to that work refreshed and with some new ideas by virtue of a spell with his biography and peripheral work: he may use a little biography to reinforce his point that the poetry is in the poems and not the life, no matter how much of the life may have got into the poems. But to approach creative work by way of biography and the periphery, to see the creative achievement through these latter, is a perversion and ought to be treated as such.

Now while Pound's biography may be regarded as an extreme case, it may be possible, because it is extreme, to illustrate more clearly from it some of the dangers inherent in the biographic approach to literature. In Pound's case the difficulties stand out, whereas in an outwardly less eventful life, they may be more dangerous because less obvious. Literary biographers often rely a great deal on letters in order to explain the man or the work, ignorant of, forgetting, or misunderstanding the fact that all men are liars in their correspondence: it is a social convention, a necessary evil. As Pound says in his essay 'The Economic Nature of the United States', 'A signed letter proves what the writer wanted the recipient to believe on such and such a day'. In recent years I have examined Pound's own files containing his correspondence and papers, both published and unpublished, including many uncollected and inferior articles and letters published in fly-by-night periodicals; and I feel compelled to say that it would be next to impossible to do justice to such material simply by printing large quantities of it and 'explaining' it on the way by means of editorial comment and footnotes. In the case of many letters written with private purposes in view it is impossible for the scholar, no matter how painstaking, to restore them from the dead. To publish even a selection of his correspondence without carefully relating the method of selection to the meaning of his work would be to present a distorted picture. It is known, in a rough sort of way, that quite apart from his activities with and on behalf of Joyce, Lewis, Eliot, Yeats, Gaudier-Brzeska and a number of other artists, Pound in his role as catalyst and stimulant encouraged a host of lesser known creative, critical and other activities of a serious nature. But in order to draw any real meaning out of a great mass of letters written to others during the past half century, urging them to do this, that, or the other, one would have to know certain outside facts which are not mentioned in the letters at all; one would have to know that Pound's assistance is acknowledged, for instance, in such widely different books as R. McNair Wilson's *Mind of Napoleon* and Raymond Preston's *Chaucer*, that he turns up in Marianne Moore's introductory note to her translation of La Fontaine or in H. A. Mason's *Humanism and Poetry in the Early Tudor Period*; and one would have to know something about these books and the nature of the poet's influence, and about a great number of other books as well; and from there one might be able to attach some real meaning to a selection of letters. I happen to know, quite by chance, of two books on the diplomatic history of the present century, written and published because of two men, one an acknowledged academic historian in the United States, the other a European writer, brought together by Pound's correspondence during his detention in St Elizabeth's Hospital, Washington, D.C., after the Second World War. But it would be very difficult to link him with these books unless one happened to know about the matter independently. I certainly do not understand his poetry any better for knowing about this, although the knowledge may help me in a negative way and prevent me from jumping to a wrong conclusion.

It was during my examination of Pound's unpublished correspondence that I was brought face to face with the enormous dangers involved in publishing letters, and the unreliability of letters as a guide to an artist's work. There are a few men—not many artists among them—whose lives would encourage us to rely upon their letters as a safe guide to history; but they are exceptions. People generally, including artists, write to other people for many different reasons and the reasons sometimes die the day the letter is posted, leaving for the future scholar, a letter, yes, nicely phrased perhaps, carrying with it some special quality such as an air of urgency, and yet, the real reason for its origin having been lost, it becomes a false document even where no falsity was intended. This is even true, up to a point, of some published work; but generally speaking the man who sits down to write a book, even a book for his own entertainment, is quite different from the man who sits down to write a letter.

The danger with letters so often lies in the fact that so many of them have a plain surface meaning which is not necessarily the one they originally carried, or were intended to carry, to the person they were written to. Nor is it sufficient to reply that it is precisely the job of the future scholar to rescue the hidden and real meaning; this may be the ideal, but it is unlikely ever to be carried out in fact. Even the principals themselves forget and sometimes begin to believe the surface meaning of their own notes and letters. Also, biographers and critics rely too heavily on the letters and published comments of a poet's friends and contemporaries. A number of people who knew Pound personally in 1914 have been critical of some of the poems on contemporary life in *Lustra*, unable to match Pound's own unsure or sometimes eccentric behaviour at that time with the calm voice at the centre of the poems. These critics have read into the poems something that was not there and which does not, so far as I know, occur to later readers who did not know the poet when he wrote *Lustra*.

And there is the danger also of relying too much on a man's secondary work, a great deal of which in Pound's case is in the nature of range-finding. We find him firing off one day a statement that is excessive. Later he publishes a similar statement, this time undershooting the mark; and then another and another until he gets somewhere near the meaning he is seeking. The final statement, the one that really matters, supple and natural, with an unexpected twist, or a qualification or new context, turns up two or twenty years later in the *Cantos*. All the earlier attempts may be said to have played a part in the final statement, but to accept them, as critics have done, uncritically, at their face value, as throwing light upon Pound's thought or poetry is obviously dangerous and sometimes defeats the commentator's purpose.

In the same way Pound's many and sometimes bewildering interests must be seen not as final products with a life of their own, although some of them may have this independent life, but as part of the same process of range-finding and exploration. What distinguishes Pound is not that he took an interest in Vortographs, Fr Coughlin, the Just Price, Communism, Swedenborg, the Noh drama, *New Democracy*, endocrine glands, Confucius, Schwundgeld, Vivaldi, Fascism (and the variety of opinions and ideas inside the Italian party), the ironwork above certain London doorways, A. G. Street on Piccadilly or Sir Montagu Webb on Indian currency, but that he was able in some cases to make use of these interests—to draw together threads which had not previously been appreciated, and by range-finding and refining of his notation to set down a record of certain areas of meaning or coherence not previously visible or for which others had not been able to find the right words. What distinguishes Eliot and Pound from lesser poets who remain for the most part in the limbo of understatement, or overstatement, or even non-statement, is that they have so often hit the target dead centre.

When one comes to consider the relationship between Pound and Fascism, the field is strictly limited by the temper of our time. My own view is that there is little that can usefully be said on this subject at the moment, nothing certainly which deals with Fascism directly, for this is a topic upon which one is expected to utter a simple 'yes' or 'no' whether one knows anything about it or not, which puts it outside the bounds of rational and civilized discussion. Rather, I invite the reader to consider several points which seem to have been neglected in the welter of discussion on

Pound and Fascism. The following paragraphs are in no sense offered as an 'answer' to this question, but may be thought to clear a little of the dead wood.

There is no doubt in my mind that Pound as publicist, because he was trying to publicize certain economic ideas from the realm of ideas towards action, slipped into the realm of practical politics; but what should not be overlooked is that his usefulness to us has been in the direction of clarification of terminology, the clearing away of clichés and in pointing out relationships previously ignored. A little chronology may help towards a more accurate assessment than has so far been offered in respect of his interest in politics. He gave thought to the problem of war, peace and disarmament just after the First World War when the world might conceivably have come to some arrangement and been saved some of its later excesses, without the complete loss of national sovereignty in World Government. He was also interested in the part played in world affairs by the manufacturers of armaments, before that matter was turned into a political and ideological instrument with which to hook the unwary. Again, during the 1920's and 1930's he contributed to all manner of publications: to Communist and Fascist papers, to monetary reform journals, to musical journals, to the *Biosophical Review* and many others. Nor, when we consider what he was trying to do, was there necessarily any inconsistency in the fact that he was interested in the American negro, for which interest he was thanked by the negro poet Langston Hughes, while at the same time he was conscious of a need to preserve certain elements of white civilization that might still have existed in the southern states of the U.S. If Pound was interested in Mussolini, he was also interested, though to a lesser extent, in Stalin and Congressman George Holden Tinkham of Massachusetts. In Italian Fascism he saw two things which engaged him at the core of his mental life: (1) The idea that in modern industrial societies it is better for a man to be represented in Parliament by one of his own trade or profession rather than by geographic area; and (2) The idea that it is good for a nation to stay out of debt. At times he thought he saw also a healthy tendency towards genuine local control in matters purely local.

It is true that towards the beginning of the Second World War, when he saw the America and the Europe which he loved heading towards what he thought was certain destruction, he lost control of his own situation and became involved in something which he was powerless to control or even modify to the slightest degree, and that he was swept along by the current. It is true also that his Rome Radio broadcasts look rather foolish to us when we read them at ease, ten or twenty years after, despite the fact that they contain some enjoyable literary criticism and shrewd comment on other matters, among the nonsense; but of course the broadcasts and the rest of the Pound paraphernalia of the late 1930's and early 40's have been welcomed as an opportunity to keep the spotlight on Pound the ranting, puritanical, 'do-gooding' American, born of Rousseau and I don't know what else—an opportunity to keep the spotlight upon the eccentric showman rather than on the poet and his achievement.

As a result what is truly remarkable and of abiding interest has been lost: the fact that the same man could, and did, at the same time, preserve at the centre of his faculties a firm critical spirit which rescued, and continued to rescue throughout these troubled years, unity and order and beauty from the chaos both around him and in him.

CHAPTER IX

Prose Style and Method of Thought

ONE DAY in London about the year 1917, Ezra Pound was sitting in the office of Charles Granville, editor of the magazine *Future*. G. K. Chesterton was in an adjoining room. Granville came in to Pound, told him who was there, and asked whether he would like to meet him. Pound in his pursuit of perfection regarded himself as opposed to everything that Chesterton stood for, and declined the invitation. Ringing in his head were Chesterton's words: 'If a thing is worth doing, it is worth doing badly', which he found himself unable to forgive. Shortly after this near-encounter Pound wrote to John Quinn, 'I should probably like G.K.C. personally if I ever met him.' And sure enough, when he did finally meet him on 10 May 1935, at Rapallo, he was considerably impressed.

Pound as a young man in London, in his historic fight for hardness and clarity and perfection in verse, had driven as straight and as hard as he could to his goal, and as is only natural in a young man intent upon such a problem, had failed to see the breadth and the calm of Chesterton's wisdom, which was not narrower than his own, but in a way comprehended it. By the time he wrote his long essay on the Jefferson–Adams correspondence (about 1936) he had come to see Chesterton as a symbol for breadth of culture, as opposed to the 'impoverishment' of the Encyclopædists and the Enlightenment, and finally in the *Pisan Cantos*, he thought of an older England as: 'Chesterton's England of has-been and why-not.'

This was characteristic of Pound, to be thrown into fierce opposition by an aphorism, and twenty years later to be won over by a single meeting. This is not the whole story of course: monetary reform had brought the two men closer in the intervening years and Chesterton had published Pound in *G. K.'s Weekly* during 1934; and apart from that, Pound as he grew older had come to appreciate the fact that the world was a bigger and more various place than he had imagined in 1917. Nevertheless his treatment of Chesterton was typical of his way of going about things and leads us directly to the rift in his prose; good prose, sometimes brilliant prose, lifting the reader into the realm of clarity, but liable the next moment to drop him into a swamp.

The best and bulk of Pound's literary prose was written before 1920. Whatever shortcomings it may have, it was written by one who was interested not only in what he was writing about, but the literary world in which he was working as well. The later prose, even the best of it, even essays like 'How to read', 'Date Line' and those on Monro and Housman, lack the freshness of the earlier pieces, despite the chatty and occasionally effective style; but more than that, they are the work of a man who for critical purposes has lost touch with the literature he is discussing and the literary world for which he is writing, and is engaged in the arbitrary arrangement of categories and often disembodied guesses. Despite the tone of succinct wisdom with which these categories and guesses are laid out and related—related, that is to say, in the sense that Pound puts them together—there are no filaments of thought binding them into a whole. Relationships, all sorts of strange relationships, are thrust upon them by Pound's short sharp prose, which has a habit of outrunning both Pound and reality and creating a sealed-off world of its own.

Poetry is one thing, prose another: in prose you must explain part at least of what you mean or else say nothing at all. But Pound dispensed with explanation to the point that he was left with a form of writing that was not really prose at all, not in the sense of being the articulation of explanations and arguments, but a series of thrusts without any body of knowledge or core to which the reader might refer them. At its worst this prose is a form of hypnotism which takes hold of both writer and reader. One remembers Pound writing in this fashion on one occasion, to explain that whereas the medieval theologian and scientist Hugh of St Victor was a Saxon and very dull, his successor, Richard of St Victor, was a Scot and very brilliant, and that the scholastics down the ages, running true to form, had concentrated all their attention upon the dull Hugh and not the brilliant Richard, whose brilliance he then went on to illustrate by quoting several pungent definitions. He conveyed all this by means of two or three cleverly turned sentences which gave the impression of being the considered condensation of a lifetime of study. It came as something of a shock to one reader, to discover shortly afterwards that Hugh of St Victor was not so dull after all, having supplied his successors with those very definitions which Pound thought were so brilliant in Richard; and further, that far from being neglected, Richard had a definite and considered position in the realm of mystical theology.

The deficiencies of Pound's earlier prose are of a relatively simple kind; they are not fundamental nor do they alter the general meaning of what he is saying. Nor does he shirk the troublesome business of thinking out exactly what he means to convey to his reader. It is annoying to read in 'The Serious Artist', first published in the *New Freewoman* of October and November 1913, a false analogy which moves from the nationality of literature to the nationality of music, without mentioning the fact that while both may be national, literature is tied to nationality through language in a way that music is not; it is annoying, but it does not really affect the meaning of what he is saying. Similarly, we may be surprised in his 'Notes on the Elizabethan Classicists', first published in the *Egoist* from September 1917 through into January 1918, when he tells us casually that: 'I think I have seen a mis-statement about the date of the earliest blank verse in English. These eight lines [from Tuberville] should prevent its being set too late,' saying nothing more about the mis-statement. Either the various relevant dates were worth setting down in some detail beside the mis-statement, or it should not have been mentioned at all. This does not, however, affect the truth of his assertions about the interesting movement discernible in Tuberville's lines.

The later prose turns into something altogether different. Its errors are often inherent in the style, in what he is saying, in every turn of the sentence. If you make precise and unqualified pronouncements involving and interlocking in the space of one or two sentences the arts, economics and religion, if you do this and make a mistake in the process, the whole edifice comes tumbling down. If you write a sentence, caring more for 'precision' and 'concentration' than the meaning of what you are saying, and the loose ends which in prose you must tie up, then you will arrive at such statements as: 'Not the idea but the degree of its definition determines its aptitude for reaching to music', or 'Clean the word, clearly define its borders and health pervades the whole human congeries', which look exact and profound on first reading, but begin to look ambiguous on closer examination. Without Pound's detailed explanation of what they mean, we have no way of knowing how profound or exact they really are. Some of his statements or assumptions would require a volume of explanation before the reader could possibly judge them. 'Gibbon's History of Rome is a meaningless jumble until a man has read Douglas.' This asks ten thousand questions in the space of fourteen words, and answers nothing. Nor is there any sentence in the rest of the essay from which it is taken, nor in any other work by Pound, which helps us to relate Gibbon to Douglas. What Pound says may be true, but there must be very few who are conversant with both authors and capable of understanding what Pound is saying, if indeed he is saying anything at all. 'Any general statement is like a cheque drawn on a bank. Its value depends on what there is to meet it.' A little thought, and this proposition begins to sag. The bank flicks a few pages and knows in a matter of seconds *exactly* what your cheque means. If you have no money in your account, and the bank allows you credit, the transaction is even further removed from the case of human knowledge, since it is the bank which has a fund and gives, not the person who writes the cheque. Human knowledge on the other hand requires continuous and active thought on the part of all concerned in its transmission, and bears no relation, except very loosely perhaps, with the business of banking. The precision of these sentences is more apparent than real. This sort of precision reaches its limit in *A Visiting Card* in such statements as: 'Criticism may be written by a string of names: Confucius, Ovid, and Homer. Villon, Corbière, Gautier', or 'Towards order in the state: the definition of the word'. In the essay 'Mang Tze: The Ethics of Mencius', first published in the

K

Criterion of July 1938, Pound remarks that the Mencian ideogram for 'raise the will' or 'exalt the aim' is 'definitely Dante's *directio voluntatis*'. But it is only by whittling meaning away to the point almost of extinction that a Mencian idea, bathed in Confucian philosophy and Chinese history, can be equated in this way with the terminology of Catholic philosophy. There may be points of similarity, but in the case of terminologies deriving from such different conceptions of the world, you must do more than merely *say* there is identity of meaning between them. This is, quite apart from his inconsistency in the same essay, his use of one measure—a very lenient one—for Chinese philosophy, and a quite different and bigoted measure for Christianity, the Jewish religion, and Marx and Hegel.

The havoc wrought by this prose style on Pound's literary judgements may be traced in the history of his treatment of Dryden. At no time did Pound ever like Dryden, as a poet or critic, but in the opening lines of his 'Notes on the Elizabethan Classicists' he gives a reasonable summary of the return to 'regularity' in English verse:

> The reactions and 'movements' of literature are scarcely, if ever, movements against good work or good custom. Dryden and the precursors of Dryden did not react against *Hamlet*. If the eighteenth-century movement towards regularity is among the least sympathetic to the public of our moment, it is 'historically justifiable', even though the katachrestical vigours of Marlowe's *Hero and Leander* may not be enough to explain the 'existence' of a Pope. A single faulty work showing great powers would hardly be enough to start a 'reaction'; only the mediocrity of a given time can drive the more intelligent men of that time to 'break with tradition'.

Fifteen years later his dislike of Dryden had developed into a phobia. In his *ABC of Reading*, designed to serve as a textbook, he recommends Crabbe and Pope for those who want to understand satiric couplets, but does not make any mention of Dryden. The idea of trying to study English satiric couplets without studying Dryden would be amusing if it did not illustrate the lengths to which Pound could go—though not always—once he had developed a prejudice. Even so, the blemish, although serious, is in a sense local and easily spotted and contained. The really pernicious error occurs when Pound's method takes over, relates things which are not related, and then submits this 'relationship' to tight formulation in his cryptic prose. The result—in a note on Eliot's essay on Dryden—is this:

> Dryden gives T.S.E. a good club wherewith to smack Milton. But with a modicum of familiarity or even a passing acquaintance with Dante, the club would hardly be needed.

Pound is not engaged here in literary criticism. He has not read Eliot's essay on Dryden, or if he has, not carefully, and he is certainly not writing a considered reply to it. The calling-in of Dante proves he did not understand that the essay, in its reference to Milton and Dryden, is about two different ways of using the English language. And the essay is so closely tied up with the character of English that Dante does not, and cannot, enter into it, even though, as Eliot had already pointed out in detail elsewhere, there is a sense in which more can be learnt about how to write poetry from Dante than from any English poet. In other words, Pound was not listening to what anybody else was saying. Certain stimuli—in this case the names 'Dryden' and 'Milton'—set him to formulating sentences, and the formulation was accomplished with bare-bones precision and condensation. With such a style at his disposal, the author was not troubled by the fact that he did not have anything about which to be precise. Nor is this an isolated case; such sentences, firmly chiselled out of nothing, abound in his later prose.

At what point we should begin to blame Ernest Fenollosa for Pound's later prose and method is hard to say, for although he wrote about Fenollosa and the 'ideogramic' method on a number of occasions, he did not explain what he meant by it. Or rather, he wrote three or four explanations which look simple enough at first sight, but are not always easy to interpret when one comes to consider them in detail. Fenollosa, if he did not actually cause Pound's style and method, seems at any rate to have confirmed him in the employment of certain ideas which led in this direction. As I pointed out in my discussion of Fenollosa's influence on the poems of the *Lustra* period, Fenollosa's widow gave Pound her husband's papers in 1913. Among them was a long essay called 'The Chinese Written Character as a Medium for Poetry', which, according to Pound, was 'practically finished' by its author. 'I have done little more', he wrote in 1918, 'than remove a few repetitions and shape a few sentences.' Pound published the essay first in serial form in the *Little Review* during 1919, in his own prose book *Instigations* (1920), and later as a separate booklet in 1936.

Beyond any doubt it enables us to look again with a fresh eye at certain aspects of the language of poetry. Whatever questionable things he may have said, about Shakespeare rarely using the word 'is', for instance, he does occasionally stir our reason and imagination by virtue of his insight into the relation between the language of poetry and the energies and forces which pulse, dart, flow, uncoil and merge in the world about us. He does not define this relation carefully, for he is intent mainly on the physical world as something mechanical, and also on proving a theory; but there are precious insights—old problems perceived from a new angle—for anyone who is willing to look for them. With all that he says or suggests about images and freshness of language, it is not hard to see why he appealed to the Pound of the *Lustra* period, and his influence at this stage was all to the good, confirming Pound in what he had been aiming at for several years before he saw the Fenollosa papers, and at the same time acting as a stimulant, and introducing Pound to the world of Chinese poetry.

Our concern is not with the essay as an independent document, but as an influence on Pound's method and style, so we will begin with what he had to say about it over a period of about twenty years. First the brief introduction he wrote in 1918:

We have here not a bare philological discussion, but a study of the fundamentals of all aesthetics. In his search through unknown art Fenollosa, coming upon unknown motives and principles unrecognized in the West, was already led into many modes of thought since fruitful in 'new' Western painting and poetry. He was a forerunner without knowing it and without being known as such.

He discerned principles of writing which he had scarcely time to put into practice. . . .

The accent is still on Fenollosa's relation to art, but already he is beginning to think of him as something more than a mere essayist. The work is 'a study of the fundamentals of all aesthetics'; it deals with new 'modes of thought': the man whose notebooks a few years before had introduced Pound to Chinese poetry, and caused him to write *Cathay*, is now beginning to take on the aspect of a philosopher. By 1933 he *is* a philosopher, one who had outlined the difference between 'the ideogramic method and the medieval or "logical" method'. Here is how Pound explains the 'ideogramic' method in *ABC of Reading*:

Fenollosa's essay was perhaps too far ahead of his time to be easily comprehended. He did not proclaim his method as a method. He was trying to explain the Chinese ideograph as a means of transmission and registration of thought. He got to the root of the matter, to the root of the difference between what is valid in Chinese thinking and invalid or misleading in a great deal of European thinking and language.

The simplest statement I can make of his meaning is as follows:

In Europe, if you ask a man to define anything, his definition always moves away from the simple things that he knows perfectly well, it recedes into an unknown region, that is a region of remoter and progressively remoter abstraction.

Thus, if you ask him what red is, he says it is a 'colour'.

If you ask him what a colour is, he tells you it is a vibration or a refraction of light, or a division of the spectrum. . . .

By contrast to the method of abstraction, or of defining things in more and still more general terms, Fenollosa emphasizes the method of science, 'which is the method of poetry', as distinct from that of 'philosophic discussion', and is the way the Chinese go about it in their ideograph or abbreviated picture writing. . . .

But when the Chinaman wanted to make a picture of something more complicated, or of a general idea, how did he go about it?

He is to define red. How can he do it in a picture that isn't painted in red paint?

He puts (or his ancestor put) together the abbreviated pictures of

ROSE	CHERRY
IRON RUST	FLAMINGO

That, you see, is very much the kind of thing a biologist does (in a very much more complicated way) when he gets together a few hundred or thousand slides, and picks out what is necessary for his general statement. Something that fits the case, that applies in all of the cases.

The Chinese 'word' or ideogram for red is based on something everyone KNOWS.[1]

In attempting to explain the method further in an article written about 1936, he spoke of 'The clamping of the word to the individual object', which was his aim, or one of his aims, with *Imagisme* in 1912, and then of 'The clamping of word to groups of objects; not necessarily of the same species, that is to say the ideogramic method (for the purpose of poetry)'. And a year later writing *Guide to Kulchur* he renewed his attack on western thought, as distinct from the method of the material sciences. These latter, according to Fenollosa (with whom Pound agreed), 'examined collections of fact, phenomena, specimens, and gathered general equations of real knowledge from them, even though the observed data had no syllogistic connection one with another'. The false knowledge derived from the despised western way of thinking Pound likened to the memorizing of a list of names and maxims from Fiorentino's *History of Philosophy*, and the real knowledge derived by means of the 'ideogramic' method to that of an experienced lover of painting who can tell a picture by Goya from one by Velasquez, and a Velasquez from an Ambrogio Praedis.

To say that this method, as outlined by both Fenollosa and Pound, is built upon a number of misapprehensions is putting it mildly. When Fenollosa wrote of the 'tyranny of medieval logic' from which science had had to break free, and Pound of the great contrast between the 'method of abstraction' and the 'method of science', they were as far almost from the truth as it is possible to

---

[1] It would appear that Pound never actually made enquiries to find out whether the sign for 'red' was in fact made in this way, but believed he had seen it mentioned in Fenollosa. But Fenollosa does not say—not in the essay on the 'Chinese Written Character' at any rate—that the Chinese made the sign for 'red' by putting together the pictures for 'rose, cherry, iron rust, flamingo'. He simply uses the words 'cherry, rose, sunset, iron rust, flamingo' in an explanation of abstract thought, saying nothing at all about Chinese signs.

get. Both men harboured the idealistic nineteenth-century view of 'science'. It had a method and if you followed this you got results. Actually this method is composed of at least three separate procedures which play varying parts in the progress of the sciences. There is first the collection of data and accurate labelling; secondly the attempt at describing the behaviour of a selected group of phenomena—this is what people usually mean when they speak of 'scientific method'; and thirdly, the use of imagination, when the scientist, confronted by a problem, some difficulty in current explanations of phenomena, tries to look at it from different angles; and connected with this aspect is the hunch, the guess, the leap ahead, which play a major role in the advancement of science.

Pound and Fenollosa failed to see that science had made such great progress in the western world precisely because it was based upon the European Middle Ages. Galileo, Newton and Einstein all worked from a base built by countless scholars and philosophers of the twelfth, thirteenth, and fourteenth centuries. The idea that the men of the Middle Ages did not examine or even look at phenomena is a sad relic of the Enlightenment; the fact is that they carried out an essential collection and labelling of phenomena upon which our modern science rests. This work was primitive by our present standards, but as A. C. Crombie, lecturer in the History of Science at Oxford, points out in *Augustine to Galileo*, the methods first used with complete maturity by Galileo were expounded in the thirteenth century. There was an essential continuity in the western scientific tradition, from Greek times to the seventeenth century. 'With the recovery of the full tradition of Greek and Arabic science in the twelfth and early thirteenth centuries, and particularly of the works of Aristotle and Euclid, there was born, from the marriage of the empiricism of technics with the rationalism of philosophy and mathematics, a new conscious empirical science seeking to discover the rational structure of nature.' The development of ideas on scientific method, and criticism of the fundamental principles of the thirteenth century system made from the end of the thirteenth to the end of the fifteenth century, prepared the way for the more radical changes of the sixteenth and seventeenth centuries. To a person not trained in modern science, the complexity of medieval science, in its attention to phenomena and precision of method, is quite bewildering, even today.

Working from Fenollosa's mistaken ideas about the history of science, Pound became convinced that modern science had progressed by being in opposition to 'abstract thought', whereas abstract thought is one of the main ingredients in scientific progress. It is because scientists shape and reshape abstractions derived from data that they arrive at new explanations of how phenomena operate. Far from being the process which Pound imagines, modern science moves ahead in its own field because, among other things, scientists have 'logical' thoughts about the material in front of them, no matter how primitive such thoughts may be in comparison with the highly developed thought systems of the Middle Ages. 'In Europe,' says Pound, 'if you ask a man to define anything, his definition always moves away from the simple things that he knows perfectly well, it recedes into an unknown region, that is a region of remoter and progressively remoter abstraction.' Exactly, and it was by juggling with this process that western man created the modern technological world. It was only by working with concepts derived from their data, by going into 'unknown regions', that scientists found new explanations for the processes of limited groups of phenomena. Science, all science, is based upon the assumption that there is 'regularity' in nature and that these regularities may be described in definite terms which will cover all occurrences of the same group of phenomena. It is by abstraction that the scientist draws from some complexity of phenomena a formulation designed to explain how it works. Even Pound's explanation of 'red' depends upon the abstraction of this colour from 'cherry, rose, iron rust, flamingo'. How Pound got the idea that scientists simply heap up information, facts, specimens, and somehow derive knowledge from this material without abstract thought I do not know, but probably it was by his own extension of Fenollosa's ideas in the 'Chinese Written Character'. Unrelated facts or specimens are of no more use to the scientist than to anyone else. What counts is the discovery of relationships and concepts which have a meaning for the scientist, and this implies thought, abstract thought of one kind or another. When Pound speaks of the biologist getting together a hundred or thousand slides and picking out what is necessary for his general statement, he is not, as he seems to think, describing the method of modern science, but only one part of the material technique belonging to one science. Though even this process, as described by Pound, seems to me to imply abstract thought of the western variety, otherwise how is the biologist to arrive at his general statement?

If you think yourself into a position of believing that knowledge, 'real knowledge' to use Pound's term, comes from the mere gathering and examination of objects or facts 'not necessarily of the same species', their examination without 'logical' thought, the final result, if you are a poet or a prose writer, will be the placing together of unrelated things and calling them related for no other reason than that you have placed them together.

Pound's error, I think, was in imagining that the scientist and philosopher indulge in different kinds of thought. Despite the vast differences in the aims and ends of the two disciplines, both use thought, both use 'logical' thought, it is just that the philosopher is much more highly skilled in this department than the other. The progress of the sciences has come mainly through the refinement of techniques, not through any great development of thinking by scientists, but thought is indispensable nevertheless. The reason probably why the two are so often treated as completely different is that people confuse one single aspect of scientific thought—that when the scientist is aware that the facts have outgrown the theory in which they were clothed and is straining to visualize and formulate a new one—with the whole process from beginning to end. The fact is that all human beings who reason do so by means of a process or processes too rapid and subtle for exact description. But to be of any value, reasoning must relate the world of concrete reality with that of abstract notions. As Newman says:

To apprehend notionally is to have breadth of mind, but to be shallow; to apprehend really is to be deep, but to be narrow-minded.

The latter is the conservative principle of knowledge, and the former the principle of its advancement. Without the apprehension of notions, we should forever pace round one small circle of knowledge; without a firm hold upon things, we shall waste ourselves in vague speculations.

Even when reasoning about concrete matters the mind does not merely observe and judge:

It is plain that formal logical sequence is not in fact the method by which we are enabled to become certain of what is concrete; and it is equally plain what the real and necessary method is. It is the cumulation of probabilities, independent of each other, arising out of the nature and circumstances of the particular case which is under review; probabilities too fine to avail separately, too subtle and circuitous to be convertible into syllogisms, too numerous and various for such conversion, even were they convertible.

The result of Fenollosa's essay was that in the end Pound almost gave up thought altogether, and instead concerned himself with arranging isolated gists, phrases and facts; 'possibly small,' he wrote in 1942, 'but gristly and resilient, that can't be squashed, that insist on being taken into consideration'. And at the end of this trail: the *Thrones* Cantos. There we have isolated phrases, fragments of speech, quotations, facts 'gristly and resilient', all drawn together and related—their only relationship much of the time being that they appear in the same pages together.

CHAPTER X

Sense of Responsibility

IT IS not to be supposed that a man of Ezra Pound's temperament and ability should broadcast for the Italian radio during the Second World War through either simple-minded idiosyncrasy or a calm and carefully worked out decision based upon knowledge of the contemporary world. It was in fact a mixture of both. He was in some ways well informed, better than most, with a wealth of information on some aspects of current affairs and a knack of putting his finger on things which others might have missed; but this was only one side of him. It had to compete against a fanatical impulse towards unreality, a disposition towards seeing the world as something simple and mechanical, which often got the better of his calmer and more discerning self. Pound with his insight sometimes saw this and, in his article on William Carlos Williams in the *Dial* of November 1928, described the position with disarming candour. Williams, with his exotic West Indian background and father in the rum trade, was able to look out on the United States as something interesting but exterior:

He was able to observe national phenomena without necessity for constant vigilance over himself, there was no instinctive fear that if he forgot himself he might be like some really unpleasant Ralph Waldo; neither is he, apparently, filled with any vivid desire to murder the indescribable dastards who betray the work of the national founders, who spread the fish-hooks of bureaucracy in our once, perhaps, pleasant bypaths. . . .

. . . I cannot, on the other hand, observe the nation befouled by Volsteads and Bryans, without anger; I cannot see liberties that have lasted for a century thrown away for nothing, for worse than nothing, for slop; frontiers tied up by an imbecile bureaucracy exceeding 'anything known in Russia under the Czars' without indignation.

And by just this susceptibility on my part Williams, as author, has the no small advantage. If he wants to 'do' anything about what he sees, this desire for action does not rise until he has meditated in full and at leisure. Where I see scoundrels and vandals, he sees a spectacle or an ineluctable process of nature. Where I want to kill at once, he ruminates, and if this rumination leads to anger it is an almost inarticulate anger, that may but lend colour to style, but which stays almost wholly in the realm of his art. I mean it is a qualificative, contemplative, does not drive him to some ultra-artistic or non-artistic activity.

That was in 1928. During the 1930's, under the impact of economic collapse and the increasing chaos of international affairs, Pound's difficulty increased. The more information he collected and the closer he got to understanding any problem, the greater his desire for action became, and his temperament was such that he simply could not believe what his own faculties told him, namely that the world was full of contradiction and chaos. He wanted action, some simple solution that would do away with the horror of a world that was not capable, given the conditions of twentieth century existence, of the relatively simple and ordered life of the American founders. It would probably be true to say that his desire for action drove him in search of information; he could not rest until he found out this or that about current affairs, and the information thus obtained only aggravated his desire for action. At the same time this self-nourishing process tended to weaken his sense of proportion until he came to think of himself as the key factor in the intellectual 'battle' of the century. Wherever Pound happened to be, there also was the intellectual front-line; any book he read and was taken with, especially if it was unknown or neglected, became an important document in man's mental struggle. I exaggerate perhaps, but it is not too far from the mark to be useful in assessing this part of Pound's career.

As the title of this chapter I have used the words 'sense of responsibility', which is, I admit, rather dangerous; different artists have different ways of being responsible: E. E. Cummings, for instance, said his piece in verse and refused to enter arguments, 'both sides' being for him but sides of one coin. Remy de Gourmont, I think it was, believed that the artist's (or perhaps the gentleman's) first duty was to keep himself out of the hands of the law. Pound on the other hand, with his mind full of economic theory, and his 'mechanical' approach to action, entered directly into the world of national and international affairs, where the participants are not always ready to listen to a distinction, no matter how clearly drawn, between politics and the 'science' of economics; he entered this world, with results well known. This attitude of his is deserving of the name responsibility; Pound in his own way felt responsible for the world around him. But it must not be thought that it was an excess of responsibility which caused his downfall, it was rather the absence of prudence and humility.

Pound had always been a believer in the importance of the individual genius in the history of mankind, but his belief was greatly strengthened about 1913 when he began reading the works of Allen Upward. Reviewing Upward's book *The Divine Mystery* in the *New Freewoman* of 15 November 1913, he quoted a long passage from the opening page which explains clearly the idea of genius which he himself held from at least that time onwards. This is the passage:

I was sitting like Abraham in my tent door in the heat of the day, outside a Pagan city of Africa, when the lord of the thunder appeared before me, going on his way into the town to call down thunder from heaven upon it.

He had on his wizard's robe, hung round with magical shells that rattled as he moved; and there walked behind him a young man carrying a lute. I gave the musician a piece of silver, and he danced before me the dance that draws down the thunder. After which he went his way into the town; and the people were gathered together in the courtyard of the king's house; and he danced before them all. Then it thundered for the first time in many days; and the king gave the thunder-maker a black goat—the immemorial reward of the performing god.

So begins the history of the Divine Man, and such is his rude nativity. The secret of genius is sensitiveness. The Genius of the Thunder who revealed himself to me could not call the thunder, but he could be called by it. He was more quick than other men to feel the changes of the atmosphere; perhaps he had rendered his nervous system more sensitive still by fasting or mental abstraction; and he had learned to read his own symptoms as we read a barometer. So, when he felt the storm gathering round his head, he put on his symbolical vestment, and marched forth to be its Word, the archetype of all Heroes in all Mysteries.

The genius then is one who can see the meaning of data, not just assemble or memorize it. Working from this idea, which in any case had already been in his mind as early as 1911 when he spoke of seeking out 'luminous detail' as distinct from that which is unimportant, Pound came to think of it as the duty of the poet and the writer generally to work in this fashion, to assemble data and penetrate its meaning. Towards the close of the First World War he began, slowly at first, but with increasing concern and activity, to collect data on the process of contemporary history with a view to ascertaining its meaning. His files, which contain the carbons of tens of thousands of letters he wrote between about 1928 and 1942, the letters of his correspondents, cuttings from various parts of the world, and such items as U.S. Treasury Reports, form a monument to his sense of duty if not to his sense of the possible, and for all the crankiness therein, is impressive testimony of his efforts to open up independent channels of communication; to get answers from people in a position to know the answers, and to communicate them to his literary colleagues, U.S. senators, members of the House of Commons—to anyone who might be likely to pass such information around or to act on it. A man who sees something to be restored, a balance to be righted, and sets out to rectify such matters, especially a man with the energy and approach of Pound, may well appear strident or off balance to those who do not understand what it is he is about; but he is not necessarily so, not certainly to the extent an outsider might imagine. A great deal of Pound's work as a literary critic and a critic of contemporary affairs assumes its proper significance only when seen as a movement against a contemporary current. In May 1938, for instance, he wrote to Claude G. Bowers, U.S. Ambassador to Spain and the author of *Jefferson and Hamilton*, a book much recommended by Pound, and complained that Lenin, Marx, Trotsky and Stalin were available in the United States 'in editions of 100,000 at 10 and 25 cents', whereas the works of Jefferson, Adams and Van Buren were 'unobtainable, or at 15 dollars'. He was neither condemning the Communists outright nor praising the American presidents unconditionally, he was attempting to restore a sane perspective which seemed to him to be missing from the America of 1938; and Bowers, as an historian of the early United States, and at the same time a man with some sort of sway apparently in the Federal administration, seemed to Pound to be just the man to buttonhole on such a matter. Pound's letters, even those to ambassadors or Secretaries of the Treasury, always give the impression of a man standing on the footpath gripping the lapels of some innocent bystander and in a loud voice telling him things for the good of his soul. Such behaviour may be termed eccentric, but let it not be forgotten that as far as Pound was concerned the future of European and American civilization, as he had known it, was at stake, and drastic action was called for on the part of those who understood this.

As Pound advanced in his study of Confucius and Mencius, so his concern for concrete data increased. Confucius, according to Pound, taught that a man who wishes to rectify his heart, seeks precise verbal definitions, and wishing to obtain precise verbal definitions must extend his knowledge to the utmost. Confucian knowledge, in Pound's translation, is not knowledge as it might be understood by a student of St Thomas's *Commentary on the Metaphysics of Aristotle*, but simply the sorting of things into what he calls 'organic categories'. It is not surprising then that a man, whose natural tendency and early beliefs had always been in the direction of concrete data, should have given more and more time to this when he seemed to be encouraged to do so by the Chinese philosophy in which he had absolute faith. The letters he wrote in pursuit of information, during the 1930's especially, vary greatly in quality, and many of them are of little or no importance except perhaps as indications of his zeal. Great numbers of them appear to have been simply 'opening shots' written with the intention of getting into correspondence with people in authority or important position, and thousands more are very hard to place, telling us little now except about their author's apparent bad temper.

One of the most enlightening exchanges of letters was with H. L. Mencken, enlightening in the sense that the two correspondents were of completely different temperament and wrote for more than twenty years at cross-purposes. Both were jovial to one another and at the same time serious; but whereas Mencken's 'cynicism' and humour were often based upon hard reality, Pound's humour was largely camouflage for his missionary zeal. In 1927, Pound urges Mencken to action to improve the state of the nation's Congress; Mencken in reply urges Pound to come on home and see the circus, it is really 'twenty times as bad as you suspect'. Writing to Pound on 2 November 1928, Mencken rejoices that Hoover will win the presidential election. After all, he remarks, a ninth-rate country deserves a ninth-rate president. Pound kept hammering at Mencken on the subject of monetary reform as a matter of primary importance. Mencken agreed that the present system was 'insane' but was not convinced that any of the new ones would be much better. He wrote in a letter dated 15 April 1940 that after the war all sorts of experiments would be tried, and you could be sure that the silliest would have the right of way. It is interesting to note that from at least 4 October 1939 Mencken was assuring Pound that President Roosevelt would find some way of drawing America into the war.

This subject of war was an important one to Pound, to which he had devoted much of his energy. He looked into the history of Krupp and Zaharoff during the 1920's, and his article 'Peace', which he published in his own magazine, *The Exile*, in the Autumn of 1928, repeated the core of a letter composed in June of that year by Pound and Count Albert Mensdorff and sent by Mensdorff, then an agent for the Carnegie Foundation in Europe, to Nicholas Murray Butler, chairman of the executive committee of the Carnegie Endowment for Peace. Here is that part of the letter in which Pound's influence is clearly visible:

On Page 67 of your Year Book of 1927 the wish is expressed for suggestions and collaboration of thought. This gave me the idea that I might venture to suggest certain points as worth while some study, considering the causes of war, which it might be perhaps more useful to go into carefully than to investigate the effects of war.

1) Intense production and sale of munitions; the whole of the trade in munitions and armaments might be subjugated to contemporary, not retrospective investigation via trade channels.

2) Overproduction and dumping, leading to trade rivalries and irritation.

3) The intrigues of interested cliques.

All these are general and constantly active forces toward war.

During the 1930's Pound not only wrote a number of articles dealing directly with war and peace, but touched on the subjects dozens of times in passing. Reviewing three books on the causes of war in 1933 he stated that an 'economic system which pays you more to blow your fellow man to hell than perform useful labour is less civilized than a system by which men are properly paid', and five years later he was still at it with the same vigour: 'Your American periodicals are now full of peace advertisements, one before me says war costs 25,000 dollars per corpse. I want to know WHO gets the 25,000 dollars.' One thing he seems to have been very definite about in his letters, from 1938 onwards, was that war in Europe would mostly be to the benefit of Russia. Writing to Congressman J. Voorhis on 24 October 1939 Pound said: 'European sanity meant a four-power pact and no more war west of the Vistula.' He believed, rightly or wrongly, that the diplomatic aim at that time should have been a four-power pact between Britain, France, Italy and Germany, with the first three powers warning Germany that she must not move to the west.

Much of what he wrote on this subject during these years was based upon information gathered by way of his wide correspondence; but what he does not seem to have realized is the possibility that many of the people who wrote to him were merely being polite and that some at least of their statements were not necessarily beliefs they held with any great conviction. So far as I have been able to make out, Pound never applied any very strict test to the information he received from his correspondents, nor went out of his way to check it, but used it according to his enthusiasm of the moment and whether or not it fitted in with what he already believed to be true.

Pound was certainly right in distrusting the news which emanated from London and Washington; where he went wrong was in supposing that he could put the necessary two and two together himself from the news he received by way of cuttings,

L

correspondence, and newsletters and periodicals of various kinds. He had spoken of this very danger in the *New English Weekly* of 25 July 1935 in which he said that 'By sheer dint of repetition we have all of us imbibed, absorbed prejudice, if not about the matters we were specifically intent on, certainly on periphery matter.' But as happened so often with Pound he was carried forward by a zeal unattended by even rudimentary caution and forgot his own warning.

The danger of 'blank cheque' terminology like 'fascism' and 'communism' is especially obvious when dealing with an individual like Pound. He wrote for communist newspapers and magazines, 'left wing' publications, fascist papers, 'right wing' journals, Italian technical reviews like *Rassegna Monetaria*, and any number of other publications belonging to various 'sects': *Delphian Quarterly*, *Aryan Path*, and so forth. Often he was not so much interested in what was 'wrong' with these groups but in what was 'right' with them, and if they gave him any—even the slightest—cause for belief that they might take notice of the things he had to tell, he did not hesitate to communicate with them. Thus he tried to 'educate' communists, fascists, the Japanese, the democracies, the American negro, social creditors, or anybody else who looked as if he, she or they might perform some function which Pound considered useful. In the middle and late twenties, he wrote for the communist *New Masses*; in the early thirties he was instructing expatriate America by way of Putnam's *New Review*; and about the same time he was attempting to explain to communist intellectuals that there was a difference between Russia and the United States, as in his 'Open Letter to Tretyakow' in *Front* of February 1931. Certain things might or might not be good for Russia, but it seemed highly unlikely that those same things could usefully be introduced into the United States. You cannot, he patiently explained, introduce a village tractor into a community where each farmer already has a tractor of his own. Nor did he see any need for a revolution in the mere forms and mechanism of the American government when Americans were too lazy and ignorant to use the mechanism they already had to better advantage.

From his earliest period as a poet Pound seems to have harboured great hopes for the future of the United States, and from at least 1912 to have entertained the hope of starting a 'cultural vortex' there. In *Patria Mia* which was first published in the *New Age* in 1912, he said: 'The thesis I defend is: that America has a chance for Renaissance and that certain absurdities in the manners of American action are, after all, things of the surface and not of necessity the symptoms of sterility or even of fatal disease.' And this hope remained with him, though in a more sophisticated form, during the 1930's when he was willing to write to anyone and everyone in order to get the 'vortex' moving: he wrote to Mrs Roosevelt, to members of the Roosevelt cabinet, to heads of departments in Washington, and to bankers like James Paul Warburg. He wrote to poets, novelists, professors, to fellow members of the National Institute of Art and Letters, and to many 'crank' groups. During 1934 his curiosity was aroused when he was informed officially that circulars being sent to bankers by the Senate Banking and Currency Committee were not available for public distribution. He finally obtained a copy through one of his correspondents, W. E. Woodward the historian, who was a member of the Roosevelt administration.

This was the sort of correspondence he carried on week after week for more than ten years, devoting something like one half of it to the various monetary reform groups in attempts to 'educate' them in history, to get them to see that often the things they proclaimed with such fury had been thought of before and in some cases put into practice. He tried to make them see that study of the idea in action in the past might be of assistance in the present. However, as he wrote to Archibald MacLeish in 1938, 'I take no responsibility for vagaries of the cranks in various "movements". Butchart's *Money*[1] the first solid publication of the new econ/ in English.' Butchart's book he regarded as a serious and balanced work and not the product of a sect.

Probably the thing he drove at most in his correspondence with the reform groups was the importance of terminology. Writing

[1] *Money*, Selected Passages Presenting the Concepts of Money in the English Tradition, compiled by Montgomery Butchart. London, 1935.

to C. H. Douglas in 1936 on the possibility of improving the *New English Weekly*, he said:

> But you could assist me there by suggesting that they get onto the campaign for clear terminology, distinction between meanings of different words. Capital is not same as property. Partaggio not same as usura. Money not same as credit. Money a measured claim. Claim is one thing, measure is another. These damn blurrs make econ. unreadable, and help the enemy. All very simple but someone has got to keep at it.

It was after a bout of letters like this that Douglas wrote to Pound on 7 January 1936:

> Pending engaging a whole-time secretary to correspond with you, I suggest that you concentrate on the subject of taxation as a form of modern highway robbery combined with iniquitous interference with the freedom of the individual.

One method Pound used to gather economic information and opinions was to send out a sheet headed 'Volitionist Economics' containing eight printed questions with space for replies. It ran as follows:

> Which of the following statements do you agree with?
> 1. It is an outrage that the state shd. run into debt to individuals by the act and in the act of creating real wealth.
> 2. Several nations recognize the necessity of distributing purchasing power. They do actually distribute it. The question is whether it shd. be distributed as favour to corporations; as reward for not having a job; or impartially and per capita.
> 3. A country CAN have one currency for internal use, and another good both for home and foreign use.
> 4. If money is regarded as certificate of work done, taxes are no longer necessary.
> 5. It is possible to concentrate all taxation onto the actual paper money of a country (or onto one sort of its money).
> 6. You can issue valid paper money against any commodity UP TO the amount of that commodity that people want.
> 7. Some of the commonest failures of clarity among economists are due to using one word to signify two or more different concepts: such

as, DEMAND, meaning sometimes WANT, and sometimes power to buy; authoritative, meaning also responsible.

8. It is an outrage that the owner of one commodity cannot exchange it with someone possessing another, without being impeded or taxed by a third party holding a monopoly over some third substance or controlling some convention, regardless of what it be called.

Replies came in from people with a number of different opinions, ranging from A. R. Orage who was then editing the *New English Weekly*, and the belligerently independent poet Basil Bunting, to the New York banker and administrator, James P. Warburg. Some of those to whom he sent it had ideas very similar to his own and answered accordingly, but others disagreed, argued, ridiculed, or suggested that the questions were loaded in favour of Pound's own theories.

Another way Pound collected information was through the little papers and pamphlets put out by various political and economic movements, mainly in England, France and the United States. This is no place to make a survey of such literature, but I would like to correct a common misunderstanding among people who have not studied it, a misunderstanding unfortunately which is sometimes encouraged rather than alleviated by those who are strongly opposed to such material, namely that it is all a pack of lies. Actually this is not so. A good part of it, including some so-called 'anti-semitic' literature, is accurate enough as far as 'facts' are concerned, but that is not the point. The real danger with such material lies in the selection of 'facts' towards a narrow end, but even more in the constant repetition of a particular theme which finally blinds both reader and writer to all but a very small part of human affairs, a part which has one 'meaning' when taken by itself and quite a different meaning when placed in the larger perspective. By reading this kind of material constantly during the 1930's Pound's own mind was affected, but in conjunction with his other sources of information this minority press was often the means by which he obtained accurate news not available elsewhere. It is just as well to keep this in mind when Pound's views on current affairs are under discussion.

Early in 1938 Pound wrote to a number of American authors,

including Archibald MacLeish, Van Wyck Brooks, and Claude Bowers, in an attempt to enliven the work of the National Institute of Art and Letters. He urged MacLeish, who apart from being a poet and critic was a member of the Roosevelt administration, to help him form a group inside the Institute to work for:

A. admission of decent writers.

2. some sort of bulletin for communication between members.

I mean we have got to recognize the Inst as an organization, and communicate inside it.

The institute should lead in a demand for making better stuff available. First need is reprint at say $1.00 of the best of the writings of the american founders/ Jefferson, J. Adams, Van Buren. . . .

. . . Inst should criticize the sabotage of endowments, I.E. utter failure to do what they are endowed for.

To Henry Seidel Canby, secretary of the Institute, he made the same suggestion regarding reprints of the writings of the early presidents and reminded him about the need for a bulletin of communication among members:

A job, and I think the first job for a serious Institute is the publication in convenient form of the thought of John Adams, Jefferson, and Van Buren. That kind of thing is particularly the sort of thing an institute could and should do.

Creative genius can not be made obligatory of members.

But intellectual responsibility can, and in fact when it is not, the Inst. is a mere sham.

The disgusting torpidity of American universities is a subject for Institute's attention.

Note again my demand for a bulletin, even if only four pages monthly wherein each member when so inclined shall have right to print 10 lines in parliamentary language.

Pound never lost an opportunity to praise the American founders and to urge the publication of their writings in accessible editions. Even when a London book club wrote for his advice in 1939 and asked him to become a patron, he suggested immediately that there was a need for, and as much interest 'in selections from the men who created the American system as for those who made the bolshevik revolution'.

One thing I became very much aware of, while examining Pound's files, was his ability, or the ability of one part of him, as it were, to stand aloof and weigh things calmly, even while another part was engaged in violent argument. It has sometimes been assumed that the two attitudes are incompatible, that Ezra Pound angry cannot at the same time or on the same day be Ezra Pound the painfully slow digester of data and weigher of evidence; and yet, some of the calmest and most intelligent of the Cantos, those taken from the writings of John Adams for instance, were composed at a time when, as his correspondence and stray articles show, he was so disturbed by world affairs as to be sometimes almost incapable of putting down a reasoned discourse.[1] Or again, soon after the start of war in 1939 one finds him engaged simultaneously in a campaign to keep the United States out of the war and another to assist English agriculture, which he believed was essential to that country's future. If he was 'anti-English' in one sense, he was certainly not so in the sense of proposing what he thought to be harmful to the best interests of the English people. He was hostile to England as a force trying to drag America into the war; but at the same time he saw local English agriculture as important to England if she was to remain strong.

Always, however, he returned to the state of America, its health, economic and intellectual, and sometimes his thrusts had considerable point to them, as when he wrote in March 1940 to an officer assisting a Congressional investigating committee, suggesting that the Carnegie Endowment for Peace was not doing the work it had been founded for, and drawing attention to the 'enlightenment' obtainable from the Endowment's annual report for 1939:

Page 6/ The time has passed for the discussion of so-called national problems. There are no longer any such problems of outstanding consequence.

[1] For an extreme example of the way in which one and the same mind may be a rubbish dump for all manner of unpleasant or distorted notions and ideas and almost simultaneously the creator of splendid poetry, compare Pound's Italian prose book *Orientamenti* (Venice: Casa Editrice delle Edizione Popolari, 1944) with the *Pisan Cantos* written shortly afterwards. Many of the same ideas appear in both, sometimes disfiguring the poetry as well as the prose. But the difference is startlingly clear.

Page 7/ Dr. Harlow . . . had a delightful 2 weeks in Syria. Prince L. accepted invitations to dinner or luncheon at 18 group houses . . . And in all it is difficult to see how a visitor under the auspices of the endowment cd. have made a better impression. (p. 8)

Page 13/ reprint of report of 1933, 'strengthening the League of Nations'.

Page 63/ $355,149.77 (seventy-seven cents) spent on going to Bogota and other places where you could neither start a world war nor stop one.

During 1939 and '40, he not only kept up a stream of letters to politicians like Borah and Taft who were against America getting involved in the war in Europe, but continued his more serious enquiries into American history, writing to historians, for example Charles Beard and D. R. Dewey; to Beard on one occasion urging him to begin a series of pamphlets on American economic history, leading off with the chapter on John Taylor of Caroline (Chapter XII) in Beard's *Economic Origins of Jeffersonian Democracy*, and to Dewey, author of *Financial History of the United States*, seeking further information about various matters mentioned in that work. One of the last articles on economics which he published in the United States before being cut off by the war, was one on gold called 'The Inedible' which appeared in the Jesuit paper *America* of 2 March 1940. It was early in this same year that Pound achieved life membership in the American Academy of Political and Social Science, and no sooner had he entered than he was trying to 'organize' it, just as he had done several years earlier with the National Institute of Art and Letters.

He explained to the President of the Academy, Ernest Minor Patterson, in a letter dated 6 February 1940 that the president, secretary and a few fellow members could look forward to some excess activity from him during the first few months of his membership at least; and instantly launched into the suggestion:

If the Academy feels any responsibility for the state of the country, or the American mind or the rising and wilting generation, some of its members must feel as I do the apalling lack of handy compendia of the thought and aims of the American founders . . . If this is off the Academy's line, one could at least stimulate a demand. . . .

A month later he was telling Dr Patterson:

A definition is not a one man job. To be useful for a science it must be matured, it must be a consensus, it must be both valid and accepted by at least the group using it. Bales of printed paper go to waste for lack of defining the basic words before writing 'about' the subject.

I offer my own definitions only in the hope of getting them polished and perfected. I have improved them since the May issue of the *Rassegna Monetaria*, 1937, and expect to keep on working at them. But they can't do the work until some authoritative body either adopts them or adopts something better.

These definitions, which were on the subject of money, were similar to those he published in the pamphlet *What is Money For?* in 1939. In an article published in the *Delphian Quarterly* of July 1940, called 'The American System: Why Not Revive It?' Pound wrote:

May I begin patiently with the suggestion that you cannot understand what is going on today either in America or in Europe unless you have got some idea of how things got to where they are? If you don't like news from Europe, wouldn't it be advisable to begin with a little real American history?

This sounded all right perhaps, but the trouble was that all Pound could offer as 'real American history' on occasions like this, was a handful of books like Van Buren's *Autobiography*, Willis A. Overholser's *A Short Review and Analysis of the History of Money in the United States*, and Bowers' *Jefferson and Hamilton*, which remained isolated works and could not be correlated, unless the reader undertook a study of his own at once more detailed and comprehensive than that offered by the historians whom Pound recommended. What Pound did not understand was that the mere pronouncement of the words that certain books needed to be correlated did not of itself achieve this end, and that such a correlation in any case would require a lifetime of careful examination far beyond anything he himself had been willing to give to the study of history.

A letter written early in the war which gives some idea of Pound's ability to think seriously about the structure of the American system of government while at the same time keeping his mind on current affairs and seeking information about gold sales by the U.S. Treasury, was one he sent to E. E. Cummings on 8 June 1940:

Waal as to old Ez his rightness. Do we perceive a tenDENCy to perceive that the choice is between a republican (in the old sense) with strong executive form of govt. (at least as strong exec. as Tommy Jeff) WITH an organic insides wherein every bloke is represented by a bloke of his own trade or profession.

AND on the other an bloody 'and, a dictatorship by and for usura, run by figureheads . . .? Also a bit of classy curiosity re/ purchase of gold by the gummyment seems to me timely.

His ability in the midst of turmoil to think, and to urge others to think, on fundamentals rather than on lines suggested by propaganda is clear in this letter to William Carlos Williams, dated 14 July 1941:

What no one seems to remember is the damage done to England during the Napoleonic wars by simply being cut off from ALL contemporary thought. Same goes for the U.S. now. I note it in *Hika* and other magazines. Not only gross ignorance of thought on the Axis side of the line. . . . BUT gross ignorance of Irish thought and of English thought.

They have heard of Douglas because I told 'em 23 years ago or 21 or 20 or whenever. BUT they are bone ignorant of 20 years English thought on guilds that preceded it.

Whole masses of geo-political thought ignored. The Acad. of Soc. and Pol. Sci. is ham ignorant. Even Bolchevism was not discussed, basic fact that no one was really communist, not in Europe or the U.S., but the capitalists did not open their papers to serious analysis of communism.

The whole occident wants homesteads or an equivalent, plus defence of purchasing power of labour, especially agricultural.

What is the sense of *Hika* giving only one side?

The opposition that you indicate is TIME LAG, or at least you better figure out how far there is any real opposition and how far it is time lag and nowt but time lag.

In this chapter I have shown that this particular aspect of Pound's career, in which he tried to discover the process of modern history, was by no means clear cut, but full of contradictions. The person who would understand Pound in this capacity must not make the mistake of looking for a single 'answer' but be prepared to accept the fact that there is none, and that Pound was quite capable of formulating a clear warning against some error and simultaneously of committing it himself. How many times during the 1930's did he not warn people, as in his long essay in the *North American Review* of December 1937, on the Jefferson-Adams Correspondence, against thinking that they had been the first to discover the moon or the sea? And yet he was forever doing just that himself, especially in economic history where his lack of knowledge had sad consequences for his later Cantos as well as for some of his prose. It was quite normal for Pound to write, on one and the same day, an angry and simpleminded article calling down punishment on those who would drive the world to war rather than submit to monetary reform, and, to an historian of religion, a letter seeking information about an extended text of Scotus Erigena. By facing this fact we are better placed to enquire into the process by which the poet of clear speech was transformed into the author of 'political' broadcasts some of which are dense to the point of being almost unintelligible.

CHAPTER XI

Pound and Politics

POLITICS, in the sense of following any one party, Pound had none. He did not care what party was in power, nor for that matter what form of government was being practised, so long as the result was 'good' government. In theory a good government for Pound was one which 'impinges least upon the peripheries of its citizens', its proper function being 'to facilitate the traffic, i.e., the circulation of goods, air, water, heat, coal (black or white), power and even thought; and to prevent the citizens from impinging on each other'. Looked at in terms of nineteenth-century America, the America of Pound's childhood, this meant as little government as possible, and what there was of it, for the convenience of the populace and not the other way round.

Outside the very limited functions of government, a man was expected to look after himself, 'to stand unabashed', Pound wrote, 'in the face of the largest national luminaries, to reduce the objections of doorkeepers and minor functionaries, to pass the "ropes", etc., designed for restricting democratic ingress'. This was the United States Pound was brought up in and continued to admire and be influenced by long after he had gone to live in Europe. What led him from this aloof American view of the state as 'public convenience' into taking an active part in political brawls on an international scale was primarily his passion for monetary reform. The idea of the state as an organization 'to prevent the citizens from impinging on each other' was one thing in the context of nineteenth-century America, quite another when it was linked to the idea that citizens of the banker class 'impinge' upon the rest of the community by controlling, and sometimes manipulating, money to their own ends. Once Pound had admitted the right of the state to take control of a nation's money, he was entered on something far more complicated than he ever realized, which turned him, almost without his knowing it, into a supporter of the absolute state.

It may be that in the end all statements are political, no matter what they are about; at any rate it is within the power of an opponent to make many statements appear so, if he desires, and to turn what the writer did not intend as political into support for this or that political view. However for convenience in communication we agree that some statements are less political than others and more apt to be discussed in terms of some other aspect of their contents than politics. Pound's evolution, from a critic making legitimate comment on the world around him into something very close to an out-and-out political writer, is well worth the trouble in tracing, firstly for the way it enables us to locate and cast away material which obstructs our view of the essential work, and secondly for the light it throws on one of the flaws in his method.

In Pound's early prose there are one or two items which might be said to have a political slant, though a rather vague one. Writing about Rabindranath Tagore in *Poetry* for December 1912, he said:

The Greek gave us humanism; a belief in *mens sana in corpore sano*, a belief in proportion and balance. The Greek shows us man as the sport of gods; the sworn foe of fate and the natural forces. The Bengali brings to us the pledge of calm which we need overmuch in an age of steel and mechanics. It brings a quiet proclamation of the fellowship between man and the gods; between man and nature.

It is all very well to object that this is not the first time we have had this fellowship proclaimed, but in the arts alone can we find the inner heart of a people. There is a deeper calm and a deeper conviction in this eastern expression than we have yet attained. It is by the arts alone that one people learns to meet another far distant people in friendship and respect.

I speak with all gravity when I say that world-fellowship is nearer for the visit of Rabindranath Tagore to London.

This review of some of Tagore's poems was written at a time when Pound and Yeats were pushing Tagore's work to the utmost, in opposition to London's slowness in accepting the Bengali poet. Whether the barrier to acceptance was political or sprung from reasons of 'colour', I do not know, but Pound and Yeats between them seem to have broken it.

We see here and there in the prose of the London years that Pound was susceptible to politics long before he took a direct interest in them. Although he was well aware of the necessity, in a high civilization, of leisure and calm thought untroubled by the spectre of its immediate applicability to the world of action, he had a very strong nonconformist trend in his personality and he was not comfortable, I suspect, unless he could hear a typewriter going, or a group of people planning 'direct action'. His primary concern was with the life of the mind, but close on its heels came the desire to harness the mind to action. This extract from the article 'Allen Upward Serious' published in the *New Age* of 23 April 1914 will show what I mean:

> I must needs make a partial summary of certain things that he stands for, or that he appears to me to stand for; certain conclusions which I draw more or less from his books.
> 1. That a nation is civilized in so far as it recognizes the special faculties of the individual, and makes use thereof. You do not weigh coals with the assayer's balance.
> 1a. Corollary. Syndicalism. A social order is well balanced when the community recognizes the special aptitudes of groups of men and applies them.
> 2. That Mr Upward's propaganda is for a syndicat of intelligence; of thinkers and authors and artists.
> 2a. That such a guild is perfectly in accord with Syndicalist doctrines. That it would take its place with the guilds of more highly skilled craftsmen.

The ideas are from Upward, but it will be seen how neatly and completely Pound was able to fit inside the other man's thought when it was concerned with 'going into action'. Certain things needed doing in order to make the world a better place for the arts to exist in, and only the dullness, or the mendacity, of some leaders and vested interests stood in the way. Whatever his reason may have told him to the contrary, Pound was burdened with a tendency to regard human affairs as mechanical, and in this light it was the sheer inefficiency of the processes he observed which upset him. 'Why not clean up the mess and do it properly?' was the way he looked at political affairs, not seeing that such a question was based upon a serious misunderstanding of the problem it sought to elucidate. Not that Pound could not sometimes write clearly on matters touching on politics, and indeed add to our understanding of them, but the reader must always be on guard against a distortion resulting from his inability to resist anything which looked like a simple straightforward solution to an educational, political or economic problem. Throughout the period we have been discussing, art or 'the intelligence' was the driving force behind most of Pound's pronouncements bearing on the ordering of human affairs. Pound had given careful thought to his attack upon war in the preface to his *Gaudier-Brzeska*, and meant what he said, but it was the sculptor's death in battle that caused him to crystallize his thoughts on the subject:

We may take it as an axiom of ethics that no nation has any longer the right to make war of offence against any other. We can even conceive a time when it would be considered as much an outrage and a nuisance for one European nation to attack another, as it would for Kent to make war upon Wessex. . . .

The idea is by no means new, for Dante sets forth a scheme for an international court in his treatise on Monarchy, and Burkhardt, who was presumably a German, marks the highest degree of civilization attained by the Renaissance as the moment when Venice refused to make war on Milan, 'holding that a war between buyer and seller could be profitable to neither'. . . .

A weakness in defence of the world's peace is as ignominious as is the rupture of that peace in the first place.[1]

Pound's general comment on the war in a letter to Harriet Monroe in November 1914 is intelligent and guarded—just the sort of letter one might expect a person to write who knew something of what was going on, but knew also that he did not know everything and was disposed to wonder rather than make too many definite statements.

[1] This preface unfortunately was removed from the 1960 edition of *Gaudier-Brzeska*, published at Hessle, East Yorkshire.

This war is possibly a conflict between two forces almost equally detestable. Atavism and the lothsome spirit of mediocrity cloaked in graft. One does not know; the thing is too involved. I wonder if England will spend the next ten years in internal squabble *after* Germany is beaten. It's all very well to see the troops flocking from the four corners of Empire. It is a very fine sight. But, but, but, civilization, after the battle is over and everybody begins to call each other thieves and liars *inside* the Empire. They took ten years after the Boer War to come to. One wonders if the war is only a stop gap. Only a symptom of the real disease.

Four years later, in a letter to John Quinn, he suggested that the war and the international situation may have been 'in no small measure due to the English and American habit of keeping their ostrich heads carefully down their little silk-lined sand-holes', and then went on to discuss centralization of power:

Certainly, for execution of war measures, power ought to be centralized, and you know that I am as much opposed as anyone can be to any impediments to that. But this question of having a whole nation's reading held up by one man has NOTHING whatever to do with winning the war. It is a permanent state, for peace as much as for war.

A. R. Orage, editor of the *New Age*, did more than anyone to bring Pound into contact with the world of politics. He published large quantities of Pound's journalism between 1911 and 1922. In his article 'In the Wounds: Memoriam A. R. Orage' published in the *Criterion* of April 1935, Pound wrote:

Orage sat in Cursitor Street in the old *New Age* days with a Diogenes lantern of a new pattern, it showed up many curious profiles. Pickthall came in with facts. The young Turks knew somebody was lunching with the high, the HIGH, oh very, and so forth. Whatever one lost in those days in nickle plush and Ritz dinners, one gained in zest for knowledge.

Orage was a Guild Socialist who began to support Major C. H. Douglas, the founder of Social Credit, when he met him during the First World War. Douglas, at this stage, was not the leader of a movement nor even the founder of Social Credit, for all that was still in the future. He was by profession an engineer and had spent some time in India as manager of the British Westinghouse Company in the East. Later he was employed by the Government in constructing a railway for the Post Office under London and during the First World War was sent to the Royal Aircraft Establishment at Farnborough. Out of this experience he formed the idea that there was something essentially wrong with the modern accounting system, in that it did not seem to mirror faithfully the facts of production. Holbrook Jackson printed several articles by Douglas on this subject in *The Organiser* during 1917, and about a year later Douglas was introduced to Orage. It was in Orage's office in the year 1918 that Pound first met Douglas and became interested in money and credit. 'Those of us who saw the Major's point in the first weeks of his first declarations,' he wrote in his *Criterion* article on Orage from which I have already quoted, 'find it rather difficult to unsee it, or to put ourselves in the role of non-perceivers.' Douglas's first real expression of his ideas in print was published in the *English Review* of December 1918. Gradually, after his talks with Orage and the other writers who gathered in Orage's office, Douglas drew his thoughts together and came to the conclusion that the modern production system produced prices faster than it distributed the power to buy, and out of this he developed his ideas for the control of banking and credit and the provision of 'national dividends'.

Looking at all this as it must have appeared to Pound, we see that it happened just at the time when he was up in arms against the publishing system and looking for the reason why modern capitalism seemed to be so careless of good art and letters. Fifteen years after his first meeting with Douglas he wrote an article for the *Criterion* called 'Murder by Capital' which goes some way towards explaining the feeling that must have been stirring in him during the First World War. By the time this article was published in the issue of July 1933, Social Credit was an established idea with a growing following in various parts of the world. Here is what Pound said about some of the happenings which turned his mind towards economics and the ordering of human affairs:

Twenty years ago, before 'one', 'we', 'the present writer' or his acquaintances had begun to think about 'cold subjects like economics' one

M

began to notice that the social order hated *any* art of maximum intensity and preferred dilutations. The best artists were unemployed, they were unemployed long before, or at any rate appreciably before, the unemployment crises began to make the front page in the newspapers.

Capitalist society, or whatever you choose to call the social organization of 1905 to 1915 was *not* getting the most out of its available artistic 'plant'.

'I give *myself* work,' said Epstein when he was asked if he had any.

The best writers of my generation got into print or into books mainly via small organizations initiated for that purpose and in defiance of the established publishing business of their time. This is true of Joyce, Eliot, Wyndham Lewis and the present writer, from the moment his intention of breaking with the immediate past was apparent. My one modern volume issued by Mathews[1] was sent to the ineffable printer before dear old Elkin had read it. He wanted a 'book by' me. In the case of *Quia Pauper Amavi*, he again wanted a book by me and suggested that I omit the *Propertius* and the *Mœurs Contemporaines*.[2]

The story of getting *Lustra* into print is beyond the scope of this essay, it belongs to stage comedy not even to memoirs. If a new England or a new generation is being born, it can only know the wholly incredible island of those years *if* some genius who remembers them can be persuaded to devote himself wholly and exclusively to developing a comic technique.

You might put the question in the following form: What drives, or what can drive a man interested almost exclusively in the arts, into social theory or into a study of the 'gross material aspects' videlicet economic aspects of the present?

This turning towards politics was not, however, a matter of Douglas's theories or the arts only. There were other forces at work. Throughout these years Pound was not only a contributor to the *New Age* but also one of its readers, and he placed great faith in Orage's own notes on current affairs, which formed the backbone of the paper. To understand Pound's development at this stage one must consult these notes. Their general tone may be gauged from the following comment on the Treaty of Versailles, taken from his 'Notes of the Week' in the issue of 22 May 1919:

[1] *Lustra*, first published 1916.
[2] *Quia Pauper Amavi* was published by the Egoist Ltd, in 1919.

There can be no doubt whatever that war is contemplated not only as a possibility, but as a high probability in the peace that is just about to be signed. Hatred and distrust and fear of Germany are to be found in almost every line of the terms; and since upon a peace of hate it is impossible to build a peace of justice, the pillars of the present peace are certain to moulder and crumble away and to bring down war upon the world once more.

The articles Pound was writing in the *New Age* at this time, although they are still linked to the arts, disclose a definite trend towards politics. In the issue of 21 August 1919, he wrote, 'It is the curse of our contemporary "mentality" that its general concepts have so little anchor in particular and known objects; that, for example, in a legislative body (read House of Commons) trying to make laws about coal, there is only one man who knows how coal lies in the rock'. He went on to say, 'Spain lost its democracy, the *cortes* their liberties, in the time of Charles V. Liberties as easily acquired have been as easily lost—always for a bribe or a fanaticism. The American people have sold theirs for a mess of soda water and walnut sundaes; each race as it likes, and always in the name of salvation.' In the issue of 11 September, he wrote, 'the man of goodwill may find himself first on one side and then on the other of any given dilemma, first for concentration, then for freedom or for decentralization'.

Orage's influence on Pound is quite clear in this comment on the League of Nations, published in the *New Age* of 8 January 1920: 'A League of Nations backed up by force is a danger; its chief danger is that every local dispute may produce a world conflict. A League of Nations with the power in the hands of a small committee appointed by Governmental inner cliques in each nation is a peril; on the basis of the *New Age*'s demonstration of the recession of power from the people.' However, the most important indication of the turn his thought was now taking is contained in an article called 'Credit and the Fine Arts' which appeared in the *New Age* of 30 March 1922. 'One recognizes', he says, 'that there is no functioning co-ordinated civilization in Europe; democracy has signally failed to provide for its best writers; aristocratic patronage exists neither in noun nor in adjective.' The system, he had decided, was no longer working properly, it needed to be set right; but as I have already suggested, the task of setting something right in the realm of human affairs was usually conceived of by Pound as mechanical; as simply a matter of finding the right switch and switching it on. Within a year or so of meeting Douglas, Pound began to think of Douglas's plan for monetary reform as the 'right switch' and set about, as he thought, the process of switching it on. Thus we find him reviewing Douglas's *Economic Democracy* in the *Little Review* of April 1920, and writing six pages on 'Le major C. H. Douglas et la situation en Angleterre' for the French journal *Les écrits nouveaux* of August-September 1921.

It was probably during 1919 while he was moving closer to politics that Pound drafted his 'Hell' Cantos, which are concerned almost entirely with politics, economics, the press and public affairs. Pound's hell is full of politicians, 'Profiteers drinking blood', and those 'who had lied for hire'. Although it has been compared with Dante's hell, to which it is outwardly similar in places, and to which it refers for some of its meaning, Pound's hell is not the graded hell of Catholicism, but a very limited hell catering only for certain types of people involved in twentieth-century politics, 'big business', literature and journalism. In fact, it is not really a hell at all, but Pound's description of certain aspects of post-war London—an earthly 'hell', not a spiritual one:

> and the fabians crying for the petrification of putrefaction,
> for a new dung-flow cut in lozenges,
> the conservatives chatting,
>   distinguished by gaiters of slumflesh,
> and the back-scratchers in a great circle,
>   complaining of insufficient attention,
> the search without end, counterclaim for the missing scratch . . .

A narticle on W. H. Hudson called 'Poet Strayed into Science', which Pound wrote during his last year in London, gives us some idea of the attempt he was then making to find some sort of balance between the new world of politics into which he had recently been drawn, and the world of poetry. It was published in the *Little Review* of May and June 1920:

In an age of pestilence like our own there is little but the great art of the past to convince one that the human species deserves to continue; there can be no quarrel between the archeologist who wishes to hear the 'music of the lost dynasty', or the gracious tunes of the Albigeois, and the man who is so filled with a passion of the splendour of wild things. . . .

A bloated usury, a cowardly and snivelling politics, a disgusting financial system, the sadistic curse of Christianity work together, not only that an hundred species of wild fowl and beast shall give way before the advance of industry, i.e. that the plains be covered with uniform and verminous sheep, bleating in perfect social monotony; but in our alleged 'society' the same tendencies and the same urge that the bright plumed and the fine voiced species of the genus anthropos, the favoured of the gods, the only part of humanity worth saving is attacked. The milkable human cows, the shearable human sheep are invited by the exploiters, and all others regarded as caput lupinum, dangerous: lest the truth *should* shine out in art, which ceases to be art and degenerates into religion and cant and superstition as soon as it has tax-gathering priests: lest works comparable to the Cretan vases and Assyrian lions *should* be reproduced or superseded. . . .

'Finance', which is nothing but a concatenation of usuries, hardly subtle, but subtle enough to gull the sheep and cow humans. . . .

That is enough to show how in a matter of two or three years, Pound's own observations of the state of the arts and society, the weekly writings of Orage on current affairs, and the early teachings of Douglas, all combined to produce in him a new awareness of the political world, and a new desire for human society to be 'put right', starting off with monetary reform as the first essential step. We are now ready to follow his excursion into politics proper; but first, however, there is one point which needs to be made clear: it was about this time, while he was writing the early Cantos, that Pound began to try to draw the various segments of knowledge together and make them into one single whole. The result was that seldom did he address himself to politics in isolation; he linked it with other subjects, e.g. Canon Law, Platonism, music, Aristotle on economics, and so forth. This method, as a method, I have already discussed; I bring it up here in order to point out one of the difficulties facing the commentator who would distinguish Pound's politics from his other work. That he mixed in politics—of this there is no doubt; but because of his method of bringing all things together into a single whole, and despite the fact that he was always hankering after 'direct action', his politics are liable to be mixed up with other topics perhaps far removed from the practical politics of his own day, such as maritime insurance under the Roman Empire. The 'left wing' intelligentzia which Pound was in a habit of attacking during the 1930's especially, for being out of touch with reality, was, even in its theorizing, much closer to the heart of practical affairs than Pound ever was. So we are dealing with one who *thought* he was playing a part in the practical politics of the nations, when in fact he had absolutely no gift whatever for understanding the process by which ideas go into action, and little or no effect upon the politics of his time. Contrary to what Pound himself believed, he was an incurable theorist, whose clamour about 'ideas going into action' was nothing more than theorizing upon theories, and it is this which makes his politics so hard to analyse and to treat fairly. I will show what I mean by taking two quotations from political articles in his magazine *Exile*. In the issue for Spring 1927 he wrote, 'Both Fascio and the Russian revolution are interesting phenomena'. In the Autumn issue of the following year he said, 'The job of America for the next twenty years will be to drive back the government into its proper place, i.e. to force it to occupy itself solely with things which are the proper functions of government'. Now it will be seen that whereas the second of these statements has a definite active political flavour about it and could quickly be turned into a party slogan, the first is much more aloof. It is the statement of a man who is not interested in politics as such, but merely as interesting phenomena to be weighed by the disinterested observer along with Boccherini, Roman Law, and the literary style of modern American presidents. Nowhere, let it be noted, does Pound make this distinction, which I have just made, between two quite different approaches to political material. The fact that there might be a danger here does not seem to have occurred to him, with the result that he is constantly slipping from the position of disinterested observer into direct political praise or blame of living politicians, and because of his theory of knowledge as a 'unity', constantly treating these two separate activities as one.

For one who was often well-informed, Pound's failure to grasp how human affairs are conducted is sometimes almost unbelievable. When he writes for instance, 'Good economics are as sound for Russia as for the U.S.A.', we grant the grain of truth in this statement, but the ignorance it implies of human nature, and the realities of the world he was living in, is breathtaking in its enormity.

One of the longest and clearest statements he ever made on this subject is contained in Chapter I, Part IV of his *ABC of Economics*, published in London in April 1933. It explains I think better than anything else he ever wrote how economics and politics led him into such trouble, almost without his realizing what was happening. I quote from the statement at some length:

Science or no science an economic system or lack-of-system is bound to be affected by the political system in which or beside which it exists, and more especially by the preconceptions or prejudices or predispositions and attitudes implied in the political system.

The preconception of democracy, let us say at its best, democracy as it existed in the minds of Jefferson and Van Buren, is that the best men, kaloikagathoi, etc., will take the trouble to place their ideas and policies before the majority with such clarity and persuasiveness that the majority will accept their guidance, *i.e.* 'be right'.

The preconception of let us say the Adamses, or aristodemocratic parties is that privilege, a little of it, will breed a sense of responsibility.

The further Toryism is that the best should be served.

In practice it is claimed that the best get tired or fail to exert themselves to the necessary degree.

It seems fairly proved that privilege does not breed a sense of responsibility. Individuals, let us say exceptional individuals in privileged classes, maintain the sense of responsibility, but the general ruck, namely 95% of all privileged classes, seem to believe that the main use of privileges is to be exempt from responsibility, from responsibilities of every kind.

This is as true of financial privilege as of political privilege.

The apparent exception seems to occur at the birth of any new privileged class, which amounts to saying that any new governing class is bound to be composed of exceptional men, or at any rate of men having more energy and being therefore more fit (apt) to govern than their fellows.

The dross of the intelligentzia, lacking the force to govern, constantly try to spread the belief that they are the 'best', the agathoi, etc.

Obviously no best, no even good, governing class can be spineless; this applies even to an administrative class, or people administering economics. The term 'good' in either case must include a capacity for action; some sense of relation between action and mere thought or talk.

A lot of rot is talked and written on the assumption of political and economic laws existing *in vacuo*. . . .

A democracy, the majority which 'decides' in a democracy functioning as such, would presumably choose sound economics shortly after it had learned to distinguish the sound from the unsound. Subjects of an autocrat would obey, and continue obeying the economic decisions of their ruler or rulers as long as the orders were economically sound, and for a considerable period after those orders were unsound. Various durations of patience in intermediate forms of government . . .

The point is that the orders of an omniscient despot and of an intelligent democracy would be very much alike in so far as they affected the main body of the country's economics. Whether as independent citizens, individuals, etc., or as pack animals, the nutrition of the population would have its importance.

For any particular country, the most immediate road thereto has a good deal to be said in its favour, and that road would start from the conditions in which the said country finds itself at the moment.

For a person with this method of looking at the world, saying everything and explaining nothing, it is only a matter of time before he moves from 'general principles' into the political arena, and is commenting on controversial figures in world politics in exactly the same fashion, believing while he does it that he still retains his aloofness. In Chapter III, Part V of the same book, Pound delivers himself of the opinion that:

Popular fancy and Ludwigian cheap-jackery show the dictator as man of the hour, force of will, favoured of fortune. The phase 'intelligence' is more interesting. Mussolini as intelligent man is more interesting than Mussolini as the Big Stick. The Duce's aphorisms and perceptions can be studied apart from his means of getting them into action.

In other words, he wants to praise a political figure for his politics, which means taking part in politics, but at the same time to remain aloof and to do so on a set of terms drawn up by himself and to which he expects his readers to adhere. It is not a question of whether Pound was right or wrong in his attitude to Mussolini, but of his ignorance of the fact that in politics you cannot, as in literary criticism, define your terminology and apply it to what you like. In politics the individual is like a sailor in a small sailing craft on the ocean. He may, by learning to make use of wind and wave, travel where he will, but only by patiently co-operating with the elements, not by opposing them.

Pound could be violently partisan, praising Mussolini and heaping abuse on the United States and England, while at the same time on a related topic, showing himself quite disinterested. In an article called 'Abject and Utter Farce' first published in *Harkness Hoot* in November 1933, he praised the work of the Union of Democratic Control for instance, an English organization devoted to the study of 'peace' and the armaments industry, which was decidedly 'left wing' when Pound wrote his article. He also recommended *The Bloody Traffic*, a book on the armaments industry by the British 'left wing' writer Fenner Brockway. During the Spanish civil war, he refused to take sides. When in 1937 his friend Nancy Cunard sent him an anti-Franco questionnaire on Spain, which was addressed to the 'Writers and Poets of England, Scotland, Ireland and Wales', Pound wrote to her that he was not going to get involved in an argument about communism or any other sort of 'ism'. 'Personally,' he said, 'I am against taking sides in a sham conflict.' What he meant was that the war was not really the result of the beliefs of the participants but of manipulation by international finance and the armaments industry. The following year a pro-Franco organization called the Friends of National Spain, formed in London in 1937 to 'combat the flood of propaganda from Valencia and Moscow', wrote to Pound for his support, but once again he declined to take sides, giving as his reason that the Friends of National Spain refused to face up to the economic realities underlying the struggle.

It ought now to be apparent that simply to accuse Pound of

'Fascism', as many have done, is meaningless. Yes, he was a supporter of Italian Fascism, or some aspects of it, during the 1930's and early 1940's, and he went on expecting great things from Mussolini in the way of monetary reform, long after it should have been clear to him that Mussolini's government was in as big a mess as anybody else's; but at the same time he was the supporter of half a dozen other ideas which were, if anything, in complete opposition to the Fascist system. There is ample evidence scattered through Pound's writings during the 1930's to support his statement in *Jefferson and/or Mussolini* (1935) that he did not advocate Fascism for the United States. He believed that Fascism was the right form of government for Italy, under the circumstances then prevailing, but not for the U.S. To make this clearer, here is what he said about the American system in an article called 'Our Own Form of Government' which he wrote about 1936. It shows two things: (1) that he had very definite nineteenth-century ideas about the American system long after he had become actively interested in Fascism in Italy, and (2) that the only form of government he wanted to see working in the U.S.A. was old-fashioned American democracy, but he wanted to see it working properly:

Our own form of government was our own. No single man did more to destroy it than, to my mind, Woodrow Wilson. With its defects, if any, with its virtues bred in the race of our founders we can at any rate conserve a clear idea of what it was and what they intended.

The office of president was first given and intended to be in futurity given to a ripe man, to a man of judgement and experience. The initiation of such little national legislation as was wanted was set in the representative body. One House to reflect the will and even the emotions of the people, the other to bring maturity of experience and knowledge of tradition.

The ideological riots could and should have occurred in the Lower House. That is what it was made for. There is not the shadow of a doubt that the 'House' was intended as the high debating club for the nation.

There is not the shadow of a doubt that the impulsiveness and instability of the people was there given a chance to enjoy itself in all proper exuberance.

There is not the shadow of a doubt that we were founded by ideological war. No mere essurience brought the Mayflower and the Lyon and the other early ships to New England. No mere sense of business or desire to get into fat land erected our constitutional documents . . .

The racial intelligence of the New England stock formulated a system of government. Ideological warfare eliminated hereditary privilege and retained most of the racial institutions. In fact it retained all of them save for a list of exceptions. British Common Law was assumed wherever there was not expressed law to the contrary. One chamber for debate, with emotion. That is, to reflect the feeling and immediate will of the people, to initiate, to start legislation. Another chamber of mature men, to keep the keel level. One still more mature magistrate to have the final words in such matters, and to decide in times of emergency on immediate actions *in the frame* of the national principles and legislative decisions.

And one body to decide when these decisions were coherent and concordant with the root principles of the constitution.

The president when elected was supposed to have got over the power lust of adolescence. He was not there to initiate legislation. He was there to use a ripe judgement. . . .

Obviously the House and every other department and bureau in Washington will be overloaded if the central government assume all or 98% of all activity intended by the Fathers for local treatment and properly governable by local treatment.[1]

In another article about two years later he wrote, 'The total democracy bilge, by which I mean the clichés, the assumptions, the current cant about "the people" arose from sheer misunderstanding or perversion.' What Jefferson meant by equality, according to Pound, was not that all human beings were equal, but 'Equality before the law courts, equality in the sense of there being no insurmountable obstacles imposed by arbitrary classification and arbitrary limits of categories'.

If it is agreed that these are reasonable, even if arguable, statements about the American system, it will probably be agreed also that taken generally Pound's politics are a bundle

[1] This extract is taken from Ezra Pound, *Impact*, Chicago, 1960: edited by Noel Stock. I found the article originally in 1959 in typescript among Pound's letters for the year 1936, but have not so far been able to find it in print at the time it was written.

of contradictions. Certainly it would be a brave person who would undertake to prove otherwise.

One of the reasons why he became such an ardent champion of Italy during the 1930's was because of the attacks upon that country by outsiders who according to Pound had no first-hand knowledge of what was really going on there. And this was also one of the reasons why he wrote *Jefferson and/or Mussolini*, which was his idea of setting the record straight. Had he gone carefully through overseas propaganda against Italy, comparing it with facts properly gathered and tested in Italy, and then written a well-mannered book intended to persuade people in America and England that they were being supplied with false information, this might have been a legitimate, almost non-political work, and it might have done some good. But instead of that, he wrote an interesting, eccentric and extremely naïve account of Fascism as he had observed it in passing, together with his own interpretation of Jeffersonian democracy, which, from the very title onwards, reads as if it were calculated to be offensive to as many as possible of the people who really mattered politically in the United States and England. As a personal and private memo to people who understood many of the things he was talking about and would be willing to make allowances for his beliefs and prose style, the book might be considered a valuable work; but as informative and persuasive reading matter for the busy man of affairs, the journalist and the reading public, it can only be described as nearly useless. What could such people be expected to make of Pound's claim, for instance, that Mussolini in his ruling of Italy was a creator and an artist? 'Take him as anything save the artist,' he wrote, 'and you will get muddled with contradictions.' *Jefferson and/or Mussolini*, for all the valuable material it contains, was the product of that Pound who was completely out of his depth in the world of international political journalism. As a public document, the book is about as naïve as Pound's statement in the 1937 essay 'Immediate Need of Confucius' that holders of high office in the Occident at that time dare not be left alone in a lighted room with the *Ta Hio* of Confucius. 'They cannot face the forty-six characters in the solitude of their library,' he said. 'Men suffer

malnutrition by millions because their overlords dare not read the
Ta Hio.' A man who writes like that cannot expect to be taken
seriously either as a commentator on Confucius or as a fighter
against malnutrition. What looks at first sight like a profound
statement, linking the world of philosophy with the world of
action, dwindles away under examination to a pseudo-statement
which does not really mean anything.

I suggested at the beginning of this chapter that what turned
Pound from a supporter of the old American idea of as little
government as possible into a supporter of the absolute state, was
his belief, which began to develop after his first meetings with
C. H. Douglas in 1918, that usury was a corrosive force working
against social order and the arts, and that international bankers
used money, credit and usury as tools with which to maintain
power over the rest of mankind. Mankind had to be protected,
and goods properly distributed; and when England and the
United States seemed to be failing to carry out these tasks, Pound
placed more and more of his hope in Italy, and to a lesser extent,
in Germany. As one who was fascinated by aphorisms, Pound
drew comfort from occasional statements by Mussolini, such as
'Production is done by machines but consumption is still performed by human beings', and others by Dr Schacht of Germany,
which seemed to indicate that at last some genuine monetary reform was on the way. What has to be admitted is that whereas
Pound had endless patience with the form of socialism indulged in
by Italy, he had no patience at all with the United States, and used
quite different systems of measurement when assessing the merits
of the two countries. What made him favour Italy to such an extent were indications, or what he believed to be indications, that
Mussolini was an 'artist', that he really meant business, and that as
far as Italy was concerned monetary reform was just around the
corner. Like most members of the human race, but with far more
energy and enthusiasm, Pound had a tendency in political matters
to see only what he wanted to see, which was further exaggerated
by his method of dealing in 'gists' and cutting them away from
their living context. Some of the indications of monetary reform
in Italy which kept Pound in a state of enthusiasm for ten years or

more, are summarized in the following sentences. On 17 March 1932, for example, the *Popolo d'Italia* published an article attributed to Mussolini which stated that international finance was becoming more and more hostile to Italy owing to his policy of opposing international loans. Pound in a letter to C. H. Douglas, dated 13 November 1937, pointed out that a series of articles against international finance by a writer called Zappa had just appeared in *La Stampa*. 'What other country', he asked, 'could have run 'em in a daily paper?' On 6 May the following year he wrote to Joseph Brewer of Olivet College, Michigan, who had offered him a special literary position, that he did not want to give up the freedom he had in Italy. Fifteen thousand dollars a year would be insufficient bribe, he said, if he could not lecture to his students about Chinese history or the monetary writings of Jefferson, Van Buren or John Adams. These were topics which he was permitted to lecture on in Milan, he wrote, and which were reported in the press at a time when they were supposed to be in complete opposition to the views of the government in Rome. About a month later, in reply to J. Leo Coupe, who had asked him for an article for *Hamilton Life*, Hamilton College, Pound said that Dr Schacht had recently emitted a truth far more 'liberal' than any emitted by any republican Secretary of the Treasury since the assassination of Lincoln, and the Italian paper *La Stampa Sera*, on its front page two days before, had called attention to the grain harvest in relation to the purchasing power of forty million Italians. Isolated at Rapallo, as much by his own prejudices as by geography, Pound saw these things as offering the hope of a new world after his own desires, and the more the United States moved into opposition to Italy and Germany, the closer Pound drew to these two countries. As we know from everyday experience, once a process of that kind begins, belief and ideas in the strict sense cease to play a dominant part in a person's judgement and are replaced by prejudice and stubbornness. Trapped by his misconception of political realities, which after the alignment of the various powers led him into stubborn mishandling of his own precarious position, Pound continued to think of himself as having political importance for Europe and America, refused to be silent, and inevitably slid more and more into conformity with Italian propaganda.

In the early days of the war he wrote the following footnote which appears on page 136 of *Italy's Policy of Social Economics*, a book by the Hungarian-Italian economist Odon Por, translated by Pound into English and published at Bergamo in 1941:

The family allowances provisions approach steadily nearer and nearer to C. H. Douglas's Social Credit principles. They do not constitute, obviously, a national dividend per capita as Douglas proposes, but they are definitely consumer credit. On Feb. 11, 1941, they were extended far beyond the working class and made to include college graduates, sons and daughters of professional men, who weren't yet earning their own livings.

Pound translated this book in the hope of distributing it in America and keeping the peace between that country and Italy.

The similarity between some of the broadcasts Pound made in 1942 over Rome Radio, and the articles on international finance and the war to be found, for instance, in the Italian periodical *Rassegna D'Oltremare* for the same year, is such that they might almost have been written by the same hand. Constantly surrounded by propaganda which attacked gold, international finance, Wall Street, Churchill and Roosevelt, it is not surprising that Pound, having by this time lost all sense of reality, and no longer able to distinguish clearly between reality and his own hopes and desires, attacked the president of the United States and various aspects of American policy in broadcasts delivered after the United States and Italy were at war. He also did the same in pamphlets written in Italian and published in Italy during the same period. In summing up, I would say that Pound as a political writer is almost the extreme example of the theorist and extreme individualist exhausting himself against the rock of reality.[1]

---

[1] Pound spent the war years in Italy. He was arrested by the Americans in 1945 and later charged with treason, but the charge was never heard. He was committed to St. Elizabeth's Hospital, a government institution for the insane in Washington, D.C., where he remained for about twelve years: reading, writing, receiving visitors, and carrying on an enormous correspondence. He was released as unfit to stand trial, and the charge dropped on 18 April 1958.

CHAPTER XII

Economics

POUND having given a good part of his life, during a period of forty years, to the study of economics and the incorporation of the results into his poetry and prose, it is a subject we must consider carefully if we are to see his life's work as a whole. To clear up a common misunderstanding, I would point out that there was nothing unusual about a poet venturing into this field. Both Wordsworth and Coleridge had been there before him, to mention only two. It was not Pound's interest in the subject which was an error, but his speaking as an authority, as if he had mastered it, in all its aspects, which he had not. Wordsworth, when he wrote about the spread of manufacturing industries, the increasing disproportion between wages and the necessities of life, and suggested means for a wider and better distribution of material wealth, was writing from a reasonable practical base, as was Coleridge also when he said:

It is not uncommon for 100,000 *operatives* . . . to be out of employment at once in the cotton districts, and, thrown upon parochial relief, to be dependent upon hard-hearted taskmasters for food . . . It is this accursed practice of ever considering *only* what seems *expedient* for the occasion, disjoined from all principles or enlarged systems of action, of never listening to the true and unerring impulses of our better nature, which has led the colder-hearted men to the study of political economy, which has turned our Parliament into a real committee of public safety. In it is all power vested; and in a few years we shall either be governed by an aristocracy, or, what is still more likely, by a contemptible democratical oligarchy of glib economists, compared to which the worst form of aristocracy would be a blessing.

Unlike his predecessors, Pound did not stay within the bounds of reasonable opinion, where he might have done considerable good and left a competent following, but on the basis of enquiry into certain aspects of monetary history, and monetary principles, he launched out as a sort of coordinator of all economic knowledge. On the other hand, when he did speak within his knowledge he left a number of definitions and clarifications which are an addition to the subject.

Pound's economics also need study to counter the serious mistreatment his views have suffered at the hands of friend and foe alike. This mistreatment is sometimes very simple. One recent biographer treated the economics as a joke and a source of some colourful detail, thus saving himself the necessity of discovering what it was all about. A more serious critic, in a note on Pound's use of Greek in the *Cantos*, published the astounding conclusion that Pound had made a careful study of Aristotle's *Politics* in relation to the economic theory of the Middle Ages, stating that 'Pound has gone back from medieval economic scripture to the source'. There is nothing in Pound's writings, either published or unpublished, that I know of, which supports such a conclusion. A third type of writer, a biographer fiercely in favour of most of Pound's economics, and accepting almost anything that he has said upon the subject, leaves behind a longer and perhaps more serious trail of error than the other two, because he says a great deal more and, to many who have not studied the matter, might appear to prove his point. The general impression he gives is that Pound was an omniscient, precise and systematic student of economic history who had the whole subject at his fingertips. It is not only by what he says that this biographer does damage, but by what he omits or does not know. Actually Pound's method of study was not systematic, but haphazard; he took up books on economic history, or thrust them away, not after careful comparison with accepted works and a good part of the accumulated knowledge of that particular field—which he had not, in any case, mastered—but largely according to his prejudices and enthusiasms of the moment. Sometimes he struck a rich vein by this method, but he missed more than he found, as I shall have occasion to show in my chapter on Pound as an historian.

His main assumptions were that he could abstract the true nature of the process of economic history from a very limited study of occasional and incomplete episodes in the history of

N

money and banking, and secondly that usury and bankers were at the root of the worst of the world's troubles. As a result, his method of enquiry leaves much to be desired. In the case of the Sienese bank known as the Monte dei Paschi, for example, he worked from early records; in the case of some other aspects of Italian economic history during the Renaissance, and of the economic history of nineteenth-century America and the industrialized countries generally during the twentieth century, he did no more than select the 'facts' he wanted from a wide and weird assortment of books, pamphlets and cuttings of widely varying quality. These ranged from serious attempts to carry academic history to a wider audience, such as Claude G. Bowers' *Jefferson and Hamilton*, to the often unreliable and sometimes positively false selections made by monetary reformers. Pound looked upon himself as a co-ordinator of essential monetary history, no matter where it had come from, but unfortunately his method was not strict enough. Even in the case of the Monte dei Paschi he did not examine the records as an historian; he did not question them against other records and the writings of other historians, to establish their validity and their meaning in relation to the world around them in all its variety. He went to the records, discovered what he regarded as a 'good' bank, and took what information and quotations he needed to prove his point. He enquired into American history in a similar way. He took what he wanted from a few works like Jefferson's letters and Van Buren's autobiography, and linked these, according to his original assumptions, with 'facts' and opinions taken from a miscellaneous assortment of other books, pamphlets and cuttings; but at no time did he submit this material to any careful test. He did not, for instance, check Jefferson's statements against contemporary records, to see if what he said was true, or exaggerated, or false, he simply accepted those parts which fitted in with his assumption about the part played in history by usury and the bankers. While academic historians may use this method at times, through inattention, or because they believe, from experience, that it is safe to take the risk, few of them make it the basis of their work. Here is an example of how Pound drew general ideas on the process of history from what two or three record-clerks and archivists wrote about two Italian banks. This extract is from his pamphlet *Social Credit: An Impact* published in 1935:

Two kinds of banks have existed: the Monte dei Paschi and the devils. Banks differ in their intention. Two kinds of banks stand in history: banks built for beneficence, for reconstruction; and banks created to prey on people.

Three centuries of Medici wisdom went into the Monte dei Paschi, the only bank that has stood from 1600 till our time.

Siena was flat on her back, without money after the Florentine conquest. Cosimo, first duke of Tuscany, had all the Medici banking experience behind him. He guaranteed the capital of the Monte, taking as security the one living property of Siena, and a certain amount of somewhat unhandy collateral.

That is to say, Siena had grazing lands down toward Grosseto, and the grazing rights worth 10,000 ducats a year. On this basis taking it for his main security, Cosimo underwrote a capital of 200,000 ducats, to pay 5 per cent to the shareholders, and to be lent at $5\frac{1}{2}$ per cent; overhead kept down to a minimum; salaries at a minimum and all excess profit over that to go to hospitals and works for the benefit of the people of Siena. That was in the first years of the 17th century, and that bank is open today. It outlasted Napoleon. You can open an account there tomorrow.

And the lesson is the very basis of solid banking. Credit rests *in ultimate* on the abundance of nature, on the growing grass that can nourish the living sheep.

And the moral is in the intention. It was not for the conqueror's immediate short-sighted profit, but to restart the life and productivity of Siena, that this bank was contrived.

The hell banks have, from as far as the record takes us, started as gangs of creditors, associated to strangle the last ounce of profit out of their debtors. This they have done with splendour, boasts and parade. They have stood for exactitude in accounting. Once the dice have been loaded, they have counted up every point, every decimal. Chief and most glorified was the Banca S. Giorgio, the pitiless company of Genoese creditors, the model bank among bankers, against which I am, for all I know, the first to utter detraction.

'About the year 1200 there existed in Genoa, divers societies. . . .

'In 1252 they united. . . .

'In 1451, 9th April. The commune of Genoa vested in perpetuity its dogana (that is the collection of all import tax), in the Banca S.Giorgio.' That means that the bank got all the proceeds.

'1539. The Doge, governors and procurators confirmed and anew conceded and assigned to the protectors of S.Giorgio all the proceeds of the salt tax . . . approving the addition of the taxes on oil and grain, meat, wine, etc . . . with the right to sell the same if they chose.

'1749 the bank got the right to tax church property also, but at a fourth less than the secular.

'The revolution of 1797 disorganized its collection of taxes, the provisional government leaving the bank (of S.Giorgio) provisionally its internal administration and the collection of customs, took from its directors their *absolute civil and criminal jurisdiction* as incompatible with unity of the republic, and the sovereignty of the people.'—*Memorie sulla banca di S.Giorgio*, Genoa, 1832. Compiled by their keeper of archives, Antonio Lobero.

Lobero seems rather indignant at this infringement of bankers' omnipotence, his spirit appears reincarnate in our day in Paul Einzig.

This shows what bankers will placidly do if you let 'em. The great company of St. George could be both plaintiff and judge in a civil or criminal suit against its interests.

The arts did not flourish in Genoa, she took almost no part in the intellectual activity of the renaissance. Cities a tenth her size have left more durable treasure.

Working in this manner Pound was able to collect a large number of 'facts' and opinions which appeared to justify his original assumptions. These 'facts' and opinions—often separated entirely from their original context—he regarded as the key to all other history, and as such incorporated them into his *Cantos* and prose. While some of what Pound discovered finds support in the works of some of the most careful of economic historians, many of his conclusions bear no relation whatever to the present state of our knowledge of economic history. To take but two examples: his idea of what economic life was like in the Middle Ages and his account of the 'war' between Andrew Jackson and the Second Bank of the United States in the 1830's are both hopelessly out of touch with a vast amount of important scholarship carried out during the past fifty years. Our idea here, however, is to trace the general ideas about the process of history which Pound obtained by his study of money and banking. By the mid-1930's when he wrote Canto 45, the 'usury' canto around which the poem revolves, he had decided that usury was the fundamental corrosive which ate into and undermined civilization and the good life:

> no picture is made to endure nor to live with
> but it is made to sell and sell quickly
> with usura, sin against nature,
> is thy bread ever more of stale rags . . .

At this stage he had not defined usury and regarded it simply as excessive interest, without having any clear idea of how to determine what was excessive. His way of approaching the problem was through an idea he found in the Middle Ages. On one side he placed the man who puts money into a venture and shares proportionately in the profits and losses; on the other side, the man who shares in the profits if it succeeds, and if it fails has a hold over the remaining assets of his partners. This is how Pound explained it in the Social Credit magazine *Fig Tree* of September 1936:

We share the cost of a ship: we share in the cost of the cargo; and we take returns in proportion—this is good sport and good fellowship: partaggio.

But; we share in the expenses; I take a profit if there be one; but if the ship sinks I take your house.

That is a different arrangement: usura.

By the time he wrote *A Visiting Card*, first published in Italian in 1942, he had decided that 'capital' might be defined as a 'productive undertaking' or the securities of such an undertaking, meaning 'securities that presuppose a material basis which yields a product that can be divided periodically, paying interest (share interest in monetary form) without creating inflation, which is superfluity of paper money in relation to available goods'. This sort of 'capital' and 'interest', based upon a definite material product, he regarded as perfectly just. Two years later in *Gold and Work*, also first published in Italian, he stated that 'the distinction between production and corrosion has been lost; and so has the distinction between the sharing-out of the fruits of work done in collaboration (a true and just dividend, called *partaggio* in the Middle Ages) and the corrosive interest that represents no increase in useful and material production of any sort'. Usury then was a rate of interest which exceeded the productive increase of the undertaking for which the money had originally been lent. Finally, in the 1950's, Pound defined usury as a charge for the use of purchasing-power, levied without regard to production, sometimes without regard even to the possibilities of production.

Although usury as a corrosive was the central point in his thinking, to which all else to do with civilization was referred, he did not look upon it as part of a complicated historical process, to be taken in conjunction with that process, but as the tool of the 'usurocracy', that is of a certain type of banker who was intent on maintaining his power over the rest of mankind. History as seen by Pound was a continuous struggle between the producer, essential to civilization, and various types of usurer and monopolist who inserted a false system of book-keeping between the producer and his just recompense. The insidiousness of the usurer, according to Pound, always followed the same road. Here is what he wrote in *An Introduction to the Economic Nature of the United States*, first published in Italian in 1944:

abundance, any kind of abundance, tends to create optimism. This optimism is exaggerated, usually with the help of propaganda. Sales increase. Prices of land, or of shares, rise beyond the possibility of material revenue. The banks that favour exaggerated loans, in order to manœuvre the increase, restrict, recall their loans, and presently panic overtakes the people.

One reason the usurers do this is to make a profit on debts contracted during a period when money is plentiful and cheap, debts which have then to be repaid during a period when it is scarce and expensive. Sometimes the money lent by the usurer is coin, but at other times it is paper-money or cheque-money which he has created 'out of nothing' at his own pleasure. One of Pound's main generalizations about the role of the 'usurocracy' in history first appeared in *Gold and Work* and was repeated several times in different forms in the *Pisan Cantos*. Here first is the prose version:

The economic facts behind the American 'Civil' War are extremely interesting. After the Napoleonic wars, after the 'Civil' one, after Versailles, the same phenomena may be observed.

Usurocracy makes wars in succession. It makes them according to a pre-established plan for the purpose of creating debts.

For every debt incurred when a bushel of grain is worth a certain sum of money, repayment is demanded when it requires five bushels or more to raise the same sum.[1] This is accompanied by much talk of devaluation, inflation, revaluation, deflation, and a return to gold. By returning to gold, Mr Churchill forced the Indian peasant to pay two bushels of grain in taxes and interest which a short time before he had been able to pay with one only.

In Canto 74 he tells it in this way:

so the total interest sweated out of the Indian farmers
      rose in Churchillian grandeur
as when, and plus when, he returned to the putrid gold standard
as was about 1925 . . .

This is repeated in Canto 77, in a slightly different form:

'And with the return to the gold standard' wrote Sir Montagu
'every peasant had to pay twice as much grain
      to cover his taxes and interest' . . .

The 'Sir Montagu' mentioned here was Sir Montagu Webb, a British businessman who lived for many years in India and wrote *India's Plight* (1934) and other works on the impact of the Gold Standard on that country's economy and people. According to Pound's way of looking at history the First World War served as a mechanism by which the 'usurocracy' brought about an expansion of purchasing-power and the creation of debts during a period when money was plentiful. The return to gold by Winston Churchill after the war was the mechanism by which it

[1] These ideas were taken mainly from the works of Arthur Kitson, author of *The Bankers' Conspiracy*, London, 1933. Inventor, engineer, and businessman, Kitson was already well known in the United States and England as a monetary reformer when he published *The Money Question* in London in 1903. He discussed banking privately on a number of occasions with the important London banker Sir Edward Holden, and contributed a series on the subject to the *Times Trade Supplement* in 1918.

reduced the amount of purchasing-power in circulation, so that debts created during or shortly after the war, when the pound sterling was plentiful and had declined in its power to purchase goods, had to be repaid at a time when its power to purchase had increased considerably. There is no denying that bankers have sometimes done very well for themselves out of political events like war or the return to the Gold Standard; but what Pound failed or refused to see is that these men are only part of a vast system of mercantilism in which everybody is involved who uses, even in the slightest degree, the accumulation of civilization now at our disposal. Pound wanted a simple and comfortable answer, and what could be more simple and comfortable than to be able to blame a small class of wealthy men whose business is, of necessity, carried out mainly in secret? Bankers play an important part in world affairs, this is true, but instead of trying to discover what that part was, in relation to the day-to-day business of the world in general, Pound admitted little or no evidence except frag-mentary and isolated items which 'proved' that the 'usurocracy' was the enemy of mankind and civilization. Facts tending to sup-port the view that while some bankers may have gained out of some political wangle, others appeared to have lost, or evidence suggesting that the struggle between bankers on matters of the utmost importance was often fierce and genuine, he always dis-missed as propaganda to keep people occupied while the real theft was in progress. He believed that by following the trail of the 'money power' it was possible, without any straining of fact or logic, to travel new routes in history, to cut through or bypass masses of dead detail and verbiage, and to arrive at an under-standing of the nature of the historic process.

It is only in the light of his ideas about the part played in history by bankers, banking and money that Pound's economic clarifi-cations and definitions take on their full significance as a small but definite addition to a difficult subject. Ideally this addition should be accessible without reference to numerous details of monetary history; but the trouble is that most people, including millions who imagine themselves to be completely innocent of economics, have in fact imbibed the teachings of 'orthodox economics'. It is not that Pound's teachings are difficult, but that most people, knowingly or unknowingly, are already heavily armoured against his darts.

It is Pound's view that the 'controllers' of money have been able to obtain great power over mankind because of mankind's failure to understand the nature of money, with the result that it is treated as a commodity to be bought and sold under 'market conditions'. In reality, however, it is, or should be: (1) a means of exchange; (2) a measure of price; and (3) a guarantee of future exchange that will retain its purchasing power until next week or next year if you do not feel inclined to spend it instantly it comes into your hand. The reader will have noticed that this definition leaves out entirely any suggestion of the idea that money is somehow a creative force which assists in the actual production of goods and services. Such an idea is, for Pound, a perversion. A ship, an aircraft, or a building consists of raw materials (provided by nature) which have been brought to a certain focus or form by material force guided by the intelligence of man. For Pound the plea 'we can't build this house, we haven't enough money' is a dangerous quarter-truth, a departure from right order with just enough truth in it to make it effectively poisonous.

And it is here that the webs of confusion are often spun, some of them so subtle as to entangle clear minds; certainly Pound himself did not bring out as he should have that: money is an instrument, an instrument of man's policies, not in itself a store or source of energy, but a magnificently efficient instrument for the directing and channelling of energy—in some degree, of all man's energies once he begins the process of exchange by money and to exercise his energies within a community. And here again we must make a dissociation of the highest importance, between the essential nature of money and money as men choose to accept it. That is, we must try to distinguish between the concept of money as defined by Pound and money as it is accepted and understood (or misunderstood) by those who use it, with all its accumulation of conventional layers and auras. For money, brought into existence by the will of man to further exchange and social life, has been granted its tremendous power because of its usefulness and because of man's own ignorance and laziness, and a host of other complicated and complicating factors—one might almost say social aromas, matters of prestige and the like. Gold because it is rare and beautiful; bank buildings because they are solid and impressive; all these things have played a part in placing money in its present unquestioned position. It is important to remember, however, that these conventional trappings, important though they now may be, have no life of their own, strictly speaking, but owe their existence to the basic work performed by money's essential nature. Pound has never suggested that money is not important, far from it, but what he has insisted on is that money cannot play any part in actual production—cannot drive a nail or design a building—and this is probably a key dissociation for a monetary society if men are ever to escape from the nightmare of twentieth-century materialism, better described perhaps as 'controlled chaos'.

Money, unlike a shovel, say, or a weaving machine, is not a simple instrument directed more or less towards a single end, but is complicated rather by the fact that it has two quite distinct purposes: it is both a means of exchange and a measure of price; and according to Pound the 'controllers' of money have two instruments at their disposal, manipulating one while the public is concentrating on the other. When a man makes a table he does not at the same time make the money by which somebody else will be able to purchase this table from him; nor am I suggesting that such ought to be the case. I am merely drawing attention to it as something which is usually lost sight of. Pound takes the view that the man who plays no part in production and concentrates all his attention on money, the means of exchange and measure of price, and upon the fact that its 'value' can be altered according to the amount of it in circulation and by other factors, can gain an enormous advantage over other citizens and even over the government. This is how he described the power of the banking class in an article published in *Action* in 1938:

One of the prime means of extortion is that of insisting on payment in something which the payer has not, and which he can only obtain at a price unjustly high.

In present circumstances your taxes are to be paid in money. And the taxpayer is too illiterate in matters of money to ask what money is; who issues it; under what circumstances is it obtainable?

Pound claimed that by elevating money above goods and services and the men who make goods and services, mankind had elevated the 'controller' of money into a special position. I will illustrate what he had in mind by referring to documents relating to the Williams Brothers, merchants who operated from the American east coast during the last century. During a curtailment of the currency, beginning in 1837, money began to command a higher price in relation to goods than it had before the curtailment, as the following letters show:

Nobody wants lumber and everybody wants money. (26 September 1839.)
I can't turn anything into money—if I do it is at a ruinous rate. (16 October 1839.)
Money has become so extremely scarce that it has been almost impossible to sell produce and when sold to good men extremely difficult to collect. (26 January 1842.)[1]

The produce existed and men wanted to buy it who themselves in their turn had things wanted in the community, and yet sales could only take place by way of money, that is by way of a third party who from Pound's point of view had nothing to do with the transaction concerned. But by isolating the monetary aspect of this situation, instead of seeing it as a problem involving the whole mercantile system, sometimes with its origins far removed from banking, Pound oversimplified and once again was able to lay the blame on the 'usurocracy'. What he did not understand, or disregarded, was that in some periods of monetary stringency, like the one just quoted, bankers are often as short of money as anybody else, having expended it trying to avoid a collapse, and go out of business along with many merchants. Those bankers who survive do so by a commonsense shepherding of all their funds.

[1] Anita Shafer, 'The Williams Brothers, Shippers and Merchants, 1825–1850', *Bulletin of the Business Historical Society*, Harvard, June 1952.

Bound up with this aspect of money is credit, which Pound has referred to as the future tense of money. Credit is one man's belief that another will be able to produce certain goods or services within a certain time, although this has now been translated into a belief that he will be able to pay a certain sum of money within the specified time. 'Credit', says Pound, 'is a social product. It does not depend on the individual alone.' The confidence that one man has, that another to whom he has given credit will be able to pay him a thousand pounds in two years' time, depends on the state of society, a belief, among other things, in the efficacy of the police force in maintaining law and order—or as Pound says: 'in the probabilities and possibilities of the human congeries.'

After many years of study he came to the conclusion that monetary manipulation could be reduced to variations on the following 'rackets': (1) the lending of that which is made out of nothing; and (2) the alteration of the value of the monetary unit. The fact that banks create money 'out of nothing' is now admitted by some leading bankers. It was admitted during the 1920's by Reginald McKenna, chairman of the Midland Bank, by H. W. Whyte of the associated banks of New Zealand before the New Zealand Monetary Commission, 1955, and is praised as a public service by Mr Bray Hammond, a former Assistant-Secretary of the Federal Reserve Board of Governors in Washington, who in his book *Banks and Politics in America* says:

The funds they lend originate in the process of lending and disappear in the process of repayment. This creative faculty was far easier to observe a century and a half ago than it is now . . . Nowadays banks give the borrower deposit credit, not circulating notes, and the result is that their function is less obviously monetary than it used to be but in magnitude more so.

Pound recognized that in creating money in this way the banks were carrying on an essential function. He attacked them because he felt that somehow they were keeping to themselves a process which should be more closely related to the various realities of production and social life. 'There are', he wrote, 'useful and potentially honest functions for banks and bankers', but no man should have the right to manipulate the community's measure of price and means of exchange.

Pound's ideas on how to reform the present system, his writings on behalf of Social Credit and Gesell's stamp scrip, the best of these are available for the reader who wishes to delve further. The central idea around which his writings on economics revolve is his idea of usury: it was the corrosion, as he thought, of society and the arts by 'finance' which first drew him to the study of money and banking, and this study caused him to focus his attention on usury as the main cause of the destruction of civilization and the good life. Seen from this angle the history of human societies was a sad trail of empty husks, their insides eaten out by usury and its consequences.

It seems to me that at a number of points Pound is right, or if not right at least very close to being so. But the pressure of the times, and his own itch to get things done, combined in such a way as to blind him to the fact that he was accepting into his system facts and ideas that had the look of solidity about them but could not possibly pass any strict test—either as to their own validity, taken in themselves, or their relevance to the historical setting in which he saw them. Beyond this again there was also the question of whether these items enjoyed, in any real sense, the relationship to one another which Pound's method of thinking automatically imposed upon them.

CHAPTER XIII

Pound as Historian

WHEN DURING the First World War, or shortly afterwards, he set himself the task of explaining history, Pound took on more than he bargained for. History, to quote another poet, has many cunning passages and contrived corridors; unless you go carefully and find some way of ignoring or coming to terms with it, you will end up its prisoner. The philosopher Bradley, as Hugh Kenner remarked, provided T. S. Eliot with a liberating view of history. Pound had no such view. He rushed in with cutlass waving, against a foe who is everything at once, and in the end was bound fast. Having myself begun the study of history as a disciple of Pound, I will perhaps be pardoned if I discuss this aspect of his work in terms of my own experience. First through some of his published work, and later by way of a correspondence in which he wrote something like fifty thousand words in less than five years, I was introduced into the world of history as seen by Pound. Previously I had read a certain amount in this field, but only at random. After reading the *Cantos* and some other writings, I studied the subject more carefully, always with an eye on Pound, until finally, on entering into correspondence with him, I began to accept his version of the process, with only a few reservations. One doubt however crept in early; this concerned his treatment of Benjamin Nelson's book, *The Idea of Usury* (1949). He dismissed it as a work that might have been relevant once, say twenty years before the date of its publication, but was of no use now, in the 1950's. What exactly caused my suspicion, I do not know, but I looked the book up in the Melbourne Public Library and discovered that Nelson appeared to prove a number of things which threw doubt upon some of Pound's ideas about the Church's attitude to usury. At that time I took it for granted that Pound had enquired deeply into everything he wrote about, and that he had mastered the literature of economic history; any doubts I had therefore were soon overcome, and I continued my studies very largely, though not entirely, under his direction.

Pound's overriding idea was that since he had already discovered the true nature of the process of history, and drawn certain conclusions from his discoveries, there was no longer any need for anyone to be digging into economic history too far beyond the limits of his own earlier reading. It was simply a waste of time. He wanted monetary reform in the present, and economic history was only useful in so far as it proved his ideas right and assisted them into action. I will spare the reader a detailed account of my growing dissatisfaction with Pound's method and conclusions, and my realization that he did not study history so much as pounce upon the items he needed with rare enthusiasm, and, within the limitations of his assumptions, make a quick appreciation of the period under consideration. I will, however, show how my own studies first clashed head-on with Pound's, for it will enable me to illustrate in some detail how his method of enquiry worked and the shakiness of the foundations upon which it was possible for him to base far-reaching conclusions. I had always assumed that Pound's statements on monetary history were based upon an exhaustive examination of the evidence; that, for instance, when he wrote in unmistakable terms about the struggle between President Andrew Jackson and Nicholas Biddle's Second Bank of the United States, as in Canto 37, he was speaking from certain knowledge derived from a full enquiry into the history of the United States at that period. 'This difference between what is known, and what is merely faked or surmised,' he wrote in the essay 'Date Line' (1934), 'has at all times seemed to me worth discovering.' Nobody will deny the justness of this statement; the pity is that Pound himself did not follow it.

When I first began my own enquiry into the Jacksonian period, I went back to the presidential messages and other state papers of the presidents involved—John Quincy Adams, Jackson, Van Buren, and Tyler. Still under Pound's guidance, and accepting more or less at its face value most of what he had said about history, I found in these papers a great deal of material which added weight to what he had already written on the subject, and it was accepted by him as such. It passed through my mind that if the material I had sent was new to him, perhaps his enquiry had not been as thorough as I had supposed. After all, in investigating a public struggle involving the presidents of the Union, one of the first places to look, in order to get one's initial bearings, would be the public statements of the presidents concerned, not in brief extract, but at some length. In time, by comparing what I was learning with what Pound had written, I came to the unavoidable conclusion that the main source of his material on the struggle was the 'Autobiography of Martin Van Buren',[1] who was in many ways the 'brains' behind President Jackson. During the St Elizabeth's period he obtained further material from Thomas Hart Benton's *Thirty Years' View*.[2] Benton, like Van Buren, was one of the men behind Jackson, and what they said about the Second Bank, while it may have been true, could not be accepted without much further enquiry. Pound's incorporation of the Van Buren material into Canto 37, which was probably written during 1933, is excellent as an account and condensation of Van Buren's statement as to what Van Buren thought about the 'bank war'. But as either a record of Van Buren's real part in the struggle, or of the struggle in general, it might be seriously deficient. It is the same with the Benton material which Pound compressed brilliantly into Cantos 88 and 89. It is excellent as a record of those thoughts and facts which Benton chose to make public, but hardly to be accepted, without further investigation, as *the* story of what happened. What is more, it is very hard to avoid the conclusion that the reason Pound accepted Benton's version so readily in the 1950's was that it fitted in so well with what he had already decided and written on the subject as a result of his reading of Van Buren's Autobiography and a few other works. This sort of thing is not unknown, of course, among academic historians: the formulation of a definite opinion as to what happened, followed by the piling up of only that evidence which turns a guess into a

[1] Vol. II of the Annual Report of the American Historical Association for the year 1918, Govt. Print. Off., Washington, 1920.
[2] *Thirty Years' View: or A History of the Working of the American Government 1820 to 1850*, 2 vols., New York, 1854–6.

certified fact. Pound however gathered almost all his history in this manner.

Long after my enquiries into the Second Bank of the United States had extended far beyond Pound's, I still clung to his interpretation, taking the view that although he may have been wrong in some of his details and perspective, his intuition had enabled him to penetrate further below the surface than others, and that the 'bank war' was essentially a struggle between Jackson, Van Buren and Benton—who stood for financial independence—and bankers who wanted to involve the United States in the international mercantile system, which at that time, and for many years afterwards, revolved around London. I still believe there is probably some truth in this idea, but it cannot stand alone, as Pound has put it forward, as the history of the period. Taken in conjunction with a number of other detailed works, the book which did most to convince me that Pound had not really enquired into the Jacksonian era at all was Ralph Hidy's *The House of Baring in American Trade and Finance*.[1] This work, which rests largely on the day-to-day correspondence of the Barings in London with their American agent Thomas Wren Ward, helps to show that whatever blame it may be possible to lay on London for America's ills during the 1830's and early 1840's, the main cause was with the ordinary American merchant, the big men and the little men. They wanted the benefits of the international system, and they wanted quick profits, and when they got caught in the normal processes of mercantilism, many of them cried out against London as the source of their trouble or against Nicholas Biddle and Philadelphia. Van Buren's part in using this feeling against Biddle and the Second Bank is not at all clear. No one has done him justice as yet, one way or the other. What we do know, however, is that Van Buren's energy against Biddle was utilized by the bankers of New York—Van Buren's own state—to wrest

[1] Harvard, 1949. Other important works on this period are Walter B. Smith, *Economic Aspects of the Second Bank of the United States*, Harvard, 1953; Bray Hammond, *Banks and Politics in America*, Princeton, 1957; Thomas Payne Govan, *Nicholas Biddle*, Chicago, 1960; Lee Benson, *The Concept of Jacksonian Democracy*, Princeton, 1961.

financial supremacy from Biddle in Philadelphia and deposit it in Wall Street.

Another point in Pound's version of the story, which I began to find unsatisfactory, was his attitude to Nicholas Biddle, who was treated by Pound, as by Jackson and Van Buren, as the leading villain on American soil. For Pound, Biddle was always seen as somehow linked to the 'usurocracy' in London, but this is an oversimplification. Biddle built the Second Bank into an enormous institution, and tried to tie it to the Federal Government as controller of the money and credit which he knew would be needed for America's development. He did a large amount of business overseas, both directly with firms like the Barings and Rothschilds in London, and indirectly by way of Hong Kong and India. From Pound's point of view this would automatically prove that Biddle was hand-in-glove with the headquarters of the 'usurocracy'. There is however much evidence to show that Biddle, with his hold over money and credit inside the United States, was feared almost as much by London as he was by President Jackson. At any rate, the Barings, who were supreme in the financing of American development at that time, regarded him as a dangerous competitor, as well as an associate in Atlantic trade; dangerous for his competition in matters like foreign exchange operations, but dangerous also in the sense of being over-ambitious and likely to over-reach himself. This of course was what he finally did, helping to wreck the American economy and cause chaos in other countries for a number of years during the late 1830's and early 40's, and it was only because of their extreme carefulness that the Barings managed to survive the storm.

This leads to another of Pound's oversimplifications, his attitude generally to the American economy during the bank struggle, and his view that the financial crash and stringencies of the period were the work of the 'usurocracy'. As for the American economy, Americans in their desire for a certain type of life had tied themselves by trade to England and Europe and set in motion something which probably it was impossible to reverse once it gathered momentum. After studying the day-to-day papers of the Barings and other aspects of the American economy and banking at this time, I cannot but take the view that to blame the 'usurocracy', as Pound does, is to admit that you do not really understand some of the more obvious aspects of international trade. In one sense, everybody was to blame, or at any rate everybody in England and America who had taken advantage of the system in order to make big or quick profits. And what Pound did not know when he made his statements on the part played by the 'usurocracy' in the 'bank war' was that the Barings escaped from the crash not because they sat with the Rothschilds and a few other bankers in high isolation, controlling the puppets below, but because of arduous work, lasting over a period of years, during which time they listened carefully to what was going on and made sure that their money and many affairs were properly channelled and that, when the crash came, they were not over-extended. It was not wickedness, as far as I can see, that saved them, nor was it their position in the 'usurocracy', but sound banking practice which would apply at all times and places, at least within the context of mercantilism as it is accepted by our civilization.

Some of the books which caused me to change my mind about the Jacksonian period, including Hidy's *House of Baring*, were not available when Pound began writing on this subject during the 1930's. There were enough, however, that had he studied them, could have saved him from the false account he has left. One such book is Leland Jenks' *The Migration of British Capital to 1875*, which was published in New York by Alfred Knopf in 1927. I was surprised in 1960, when I showed it to Pound, that he had never seen it before. It is without doubt an important book and contains an overall account of the United States in the international system of the time that, had he examined it carefully, might have enabled him to avoid some of his most serious errors. The fact that he did not know this and a number of other works essential for an understanding of the American economy, seems to indicate that his continual cry about the destruction of economic knowledge by the 'usurocracy' was based, in part at least, on his ignorance of the essential literature of the subject.

It is unfortunately true that many of Pound's statements and hints regarding history go far beyond his knowledge. This is due partly to the careless method of collecting and assessing his raw material, which I have been describing, but also to his unsatisfactory prose method; his method of putting down crisp sentences which explain nothing, and sometimes, because they are beyond the writer's own knowledge, are incomplete and open to any one of half a dozen interpretations. I will give one example here. About 1950 Pound began to read the nineteenth-century American historian Alexander Del Mar, and in his letters, in periodical leaflets like *Mood* and *Four Pages*, and on the covers of booklets published by the Square Dollar Press of New York, and later of Washington, D.C., began to refer to him as America's greatest historian, the father of modern historiography etc., and to suggest that there was something sinister about the fact that he was unknown.[1] As a result of Pound's enthusiasm, two of his works, *A History of Monetary Crimes* (1899) and *Roman and Moslem Moneys*,[2] were reprinted by the Square Dollar Press, over which Pound exercised considerable influence.

Del Mar was certainly a very interesting historian of money. Whether he was always reliable is another matter, but he does sometimes throw new light on old problems. According to Arthur Nussbaum in his *History of the Dollar*, Del Mar was the first writer to use the word 'inflation' in the sense that it has now come to be used all over the world in various languages. Nussbaum describes him as 'an American monetary writer of ques-

[1] One of Pound's recent biographers, writing apparently from firsthand knowledge, says that Pound 'discovered' Del Mar in the Summer of 1950. It appears that he saw the title of Del Mar's *History of Monetary Systems*, in the 'yellowed back pages of an early work by Louis Agassiz'. It should be pointed out, however, that there was a large extract from Del Mar in *Money*, edited by Montgomery Butchart and published in London in 1935, a book which Pound advertised more in his correspondence and published work than almost any other he was interested in during the 1930's. But not only that, *Money* also included a bibliographical note by the editor drawing special attention to the *History of Monetary Systems* and Pound was still advertising Butchart's book in his letters twenty years later. Assuming that the biographer is accurate in what he says, it may be that Pound did not read it thoroughly in the first place, or had forgotten the reference to Del Mar by the time he came upon the name again in 1950.

[2] This latter consists of three chapters from the *History of Monetary Systems*, the first American ed. of which was published in Chicago in 1896.

tionable merit', which may not do him justice. Del Mar was born
in New York city in 1836, educated as a civil and mining engineer,
and in the early 1860's began to write on such topics as 'Gold
Money and Paper Money'. In 1865, the year in which he published his *Essays on the Treasury*, he was appointed Director of the
Bureau of Statistics. In 1872, he represented the United States at
the International Statistical Congress in Russia and in 1876 was
appointed Mining Commissioner to the United States Monetary
Commission. In addition to those already mentioned, his works
include a *History of the Precious Metals, Money and Civilization,
History of Money in America*, and dozens of articles and pamphlets
on money, gold, silver, and insurance. Most of his works were
published in both London and the United States. It will be seen
then that whatever theories he held about the past, Del Mar had
plenty behind him when he spoke on money. Pound's attitude
after he read some of his works in 1950 was very simple: Del Mar
was a great historian, why had he been neglected by the colleges
and universities? The answer of course was the 'usurocracy'. All
he did was to state that Del Mar was a great historian and that
young people ought to read him without delay. Nowhere did he
explain *why* he was a great historian, other than to say that his
writings 'may be taken as preface to whatever anyone may henceforth write on such subjects'. He did not try to explain his actual
place among the historians of his time. But the value of a writer
like Del Mar depends on his being presented by someone who
understands where he was wrong, where he needs modifying or
careful watching, and is able to explain his contribution to his
subject. Del Mar's main subject was numismatics and the precious
metals, about which Pound knew little or nothing, so that his
dogmatic statements about Del Mar's importance, and his saying
that he made great progress from Mommsen, have no real meaning. When he wrote that Del Mar's writings 'may be taken
as preface to whatever anyone may henceforth write on such
subjects', he was not speaking from knowledge, from a careful
examination of Del Mar against the extensive literature of numismatics and the contents of the world's main coin collections,
but giving us his own interpretation without reference to outside

authorities or very many outside facts. We have his own confession or boast in the essay 'We Have Had No Battles', published in *Polite Essays*, that he depended for correction of his historical facts and ideas on four authors belonging to the monetary reform side of historical writing:

> only from concurrents do I receive any real correction. Butchart, Angold, Jeffry Mark, McNair Wilson help me correct my deflections. Time and again I have to rectify my angles of error, or put in the missing components. But from the liary of the 'other side' these corrections are not forthcoming.

All four of the men mentioned here were active in monetary reform circles before the Second World War. Butchart was editor of *Money* and *Tomorrow's Money*, Angold a poet who also wrote on economics for the *New English Weekly*, Jeffry Mark a writer on usury and reform (as well as a musician), and McNair Wilson a man of many parts—a heart specialist, war correspondent, medical correspondent for the London *Times*, and an economic historian. They were among the more intelligent reformers, and McNair Wilson's writings on Napoleon contain much useful information, but for Pound to admit, as late as 1936 or '37, that it was from these 'concurrents' only that he received correction, was as good as admitting that he had no conception of what was contained in the bulk of the economic history writing of his time. Had he studied books like Kathryn Behrens' *Paper Money in Maryland 1727–1789*, published by the Johns Hopkins Press in 1923, he might have received considerably more correction about the dangers of paper money than was available from his four reformers.

In matters like this Pound had little sense of reality and was able to mislead himself, as much as others, by his short sharp sentences which seemed to be full of meaning and yet were often meaningless. Many years earlier, it was Pound who insisted upon the importance of style in writing, only to be trapped later by his own style into a pernicious way of thought which was not really a way of thought at all, but ideas with little or no logical link between them.

To return to Del Mar, much of his work, including part of *A*

History of Monetary Crimes, does not depend on numismatics but on his knowledge of American history in the 1860's and of Federal politics, through which he held, for a time, the position of Director of the Bureau of Statistics. There is little doubt that some of this material belongs to the essential history of the period, but it is not the whole story, by any means, and hardly the basis for calling Del Mar America's great historian. It needed an expert, for example Harold Mattingly, the English numismatist, or R. A. G. Carson of the British Museum, properly to assess Del Mar's position as an historian. Pound's assessment of him as a great and unfairly neglected historian, simply on the strength of his own judgement, and bemused by his own prose, carries no conviction.

This would not matter greatly except that about 1955 Pound chose to construct Canto 97 from Del Mar's *History of Monetary Crimes* and to place several of his theories in other Cantos, not as theories but established facts. Let us examine the result. Pound's performance in Canto 97 is something of a puzzle. The whole of it is interesting and in places, the way he handles the language, reminiscent of Pound at his best; but what we are supposed to see in the Canto as a whole, I am at a loss to know. It appears to be a condensation of monetary history, from Roman times to the end of the nineteenth century; the words are mostly Del Mar's, the selection and arrangement Pound's. Looking at the Canto by itself, without reference to the work by Del Mar from which it is taken, it can mean everything, or nothing. If the reader likes to apply himself to the various cryptic passages and fill in the gaps—sometimes rather extensive—with his own knowledge of history, he can draw some sort of meaning from it. But it must be his own knowledge he brings to bear on it; there is nothing in Pound's prose or the earlier Cantos which explains it. The reader might conclude, for instance, that it tells about the importance of money in history, or that the same monetary swindles have been committed in every age for several thousand years, or that numismatics is the key to history generally. The work has no general meaning; it is simply a series of disjointed statements, some of which make sense on their own, some of which do not. If on the other hand we take the Canto in conjunction with Del Mar's

History of Monetary Systems, then it is even more puzzling, or rather dissolves into chaos. It may be, of course, that I miss the point. But I have checked Canto 97 phrase by phrase against Del Mar's text and I cannot see what Pound is getting at. Occasionally yes, but for the most part the extracts are either meaningless or misleading whether in or out of context. When we refer some line in the Canto to Del Mar's text, we find that Pound has used part of a footnote which is not important and quite incidental to the book generally. This is quite apart from his apparent errors in transcribing the text or his apparent misinterpretations of Del Mar's meaning. Part of this failure is due to the unsatisfactory method of the *Cantos*, but the main fault, I think, lies with Pound's belief that he had wrestled with economic history and mastered it, and therefore could make it obey his call—in this case, could make two thousand years of it curl up obediently within the space of seven pages.

Pound's most serious historical errors occur in his handling of the Middle Ages; or more precisely, perhaps, this is the field in which he has done most harm. Some serious and indeed highly intelligent students of literature, including some who have been careful about Pound's views on history generally, have been misled into thinking that he is something of an authority on this period and as a result have taken away an entirely false impression of the economic life of the Middle Ages and the Church's attitude to usury and the Just Price. Pound actually knew a great deal about the Middle Ages, so long as we take this to mean knowledge that has not been drawn together with care and thought. He had gleaned much information through his reading over the years, and had also learnt to penetrate the period, in some of his verse, in a way that goes much further than historical knowledge; but if one is dealing with history, as history, there is no substitute for the systematic examination of the academic historian. Pound saw that 'For over a thousand years the acute intellectual labour of Europe was done *inside* the Catholic Church', but fell into the error of thinking that he knew what this 'intellectual labour' was, which is a different matter altogether. He made it look very easy when he wrote: 'The steady building up of social and economic criteria,

ever with a tendency to control, via Constantine, Justinian,
Charlemagne is still there in the records. It is still there as thought
and discrimination for anyone who chooses to look at it.' Anyone
reading this who at the same time knew about Pound's knowledge
of some other aspects of the Middle Ages, such as the poetry of
Cavalcanti, or the architecture of Italy and France, might perhaps
be pardoned for assuming that the poet was writing from precise
knowledge, a firm grasp of 'the records', having studied them,
weighed them, and extracted the essence. 'The definition of
money did not advance for 2000 years,' he wrote in his comment
on Aristotle in *Guide to Kulchur*, 'though the canonists did spade-
work on the Just Price, with usury as a sub-section.' The confidence in the tone, the use of 'spade-work' and 'sub-section', all
point to a man who is on familiar territory. Elsewhere in the
same book he tells us that if we look at European thought from
one angle it will appear to burrow into scholasticism and say farewell to reality:

If, on the other hand, you follow the good father Cairoli you will
find another, and a far more vigorous current going down into the
details of action.

The fibre holds strong from St Ambrose (340–397) to St Antonino
da Firenze (1389–1459).

The 'new' historic sense in our time demands this tradition, as it
demands whole slabs of the record in latin of such men as Claudius
Salmasius (and at this moment neither I nor Prof. X. Q. nor anyone
else really knows their names or their number).

The fibre here mentioned is condemnation of monopoly and
usury and attempts at establishing the Just Price. He was not content, however, to speak of the economics of the Middle Ages and
the art of the period as two distinct subjects, which we might, in
time, learn to connect, but drew them together boldly, as in this,
another extract from *Guide to Kulchur*:

Of [Sordello's] age, that just before Dante's, we have concurrently a
fineness in argument, we have the thought of Grosseteste, and of
Albertus. We have a few fragments of enamel, and a great deal of
stone-work.

A PAIDEUMA carried on, out of Byzantium, or, at least as I see it, the romanesque building and the arab building in Sicily, was Byzantine or late Roman *structure*, the difference being merely in expensiveness. With the break down of Constantine's and Justinian's economic system, no one cd. cover church walls with gold mosaic . . .

Modena, San Zeno (Verona), St Trophime (when did cloisters become an habit?) the churches in Sicily and the other Veronese structures add nothing that wasn't there in St Apollinaire (Classe, Ravenna).

Mohammed was against usury. There is the like fineness of outline in Cordova (the Mosque) in AlHambra, and AlCazar (Sevilla). Plus the honey-comb plaster.

For European architecture a development occurs in St Hilaire (Poitiers) and the Hall of Justice of Poitiers. Here the architect has invented. The cunning contrivance of lighting and the building of chimneys is, at least for the layman, something there invented . . .

This total PAIDEUMA is anti-usura. A tolerance of gombeen men and stealers of harvest by money, by distortion and dirtiness, runs concurrent with a fattening in all art forms.

I have not deflected a hair's breadth from my lists of beautiful objects, made in my own head and held before I ever thought of usura as a murrain and a marasmus.

And finally, in *A Visiting Card*, he stated that 'an expert, looking at a painting (by Memmi, Goya, or any other), should be able to determine the degree of tolerance of usury in the society in which it was painted'. This was the structure Pound built up in relation to the Middle Ages especially. Let us see what we can discover about the composition of his materials and the solidity of his foundations.

It will be seen that he gives two authorities in the passages I have just quoted: the modern Catholic author Father L. P. Cairoli and the seventeenth-century Calvinist, Claudius Salmasius; the truth is that apart from oddments picked up here and there in his other reading, and from monetary reform writers, these two historians were the main source of his knowledge of the economic history of the ancient world and the Middle Ages. He read some of Rostovtzeff also, it is true, but this did not greatly affect his thinking. The main two books he worked from were Cairoli's *Il Giusto*

Prezzo nel Medio Aevo and Salmasius' *De Modo Usurarum*. When first he obtained the Salmasius for his library, I am unable to discover, but he mentioned it as a source of information on the 'known beginnings of usury' in his article 'The Individual in His Milieu', published in the *Criterion* of October 1935. When and how he obtained the Cairoli I am perhaps in a better position to establish, as he mentioned it in his correspondence. In a letter which I found among Pound's papers, written in 1936 to a priest in London, he says that the Archbishop of Costanza, Mons. Pisani ('And if, say, we had a pope, like Pisani?'—Canto 97), has just sent him a very beautiful book. This adjective 'beautiful', he writes, may surprise some people who do not expect to find it applied to a treatise on economics; but Cairoli has treated the Just Price in the Middle Ages with such lucidity of spirit, that he, a pagan, can find no other adjective for it. There are many other letters during 1936 and early 1937 in which Pound mentions the Cairoli book or discusses the Church and the Just Price with people like Edwin Muir, Christopher Hollis and others interested in monetary reform, in such a way as to indicate that some, at least, of the matter was new to him and a recent enthusiasm.

These two works by Cairoli and Salmasius, supplemented, not by systematic study but by oddments from McNair Wilson, Christopher Hollis, the Rev. Henry Swabey and other writers, were the main source of his knowledge of the history of the Just Price and the teachings of the theologians on usury. The main reason, I believe, why Pound was so delighted with Cairoli's book, was that its thesis about the strong 'fibre' stretching from St Ambrose in the fourth century to St Antonino in the fifteenth, fitted in perfectly with his idea that good art and anti-usury doctrine go together. But he arrived at this conclusion without the systematic study and knowledge of the sources essential to good historical judgement. The untangling of the teachings of the theologians on economics and usury, against the background of the actual economic practices of the time, is actually as difficult a subject as it is possible to conceive; so difficult, in fact, that Domingo de Soto, one of the leading theologians of the School of Salamanca, admitted in 1553 that 'this matter of [foreign] exchange, although sufficiently abstruse by itself, becomes each day more complicated because of the new tricks invented by the merchants and more obscure because of the conflicting opinions advanced by the doctors'.

Pound may be right in seeing a connection between usury and the state of the arts and society. His idea is, I believe, based upon a deep intuition, and this intuition may well be correct. What I am objecting to is the way he hastily attached his intuition to a shaky assortment of 'facts' which bear little relation to the Middle Ages, or at any rate the economy of the Middle Ages, as it emerges from modern scholarship. Far from being an economically simple period the Middle Ages were extremely complicated, due not only to the highly sophisticated business methods of the time, especially in Italy, but to the fact that the business community had to understand and take count in their operations of the teachings of the theologians. They had to obey the theologians or else pretend to do so while hiding their real operations. The rise of Italy, followed by the rest of Europe, began about the middle of the eleventh century and reached its peak towards the end of the thirteenth century, with increased trade accompanied by many inventions and improvements in commerce and finance. Techniques such as partnerships, joint liability, book-keeping, letters of credit, insurance, bills of exchange etc., which are still generally thought of as belonging only to a much later period, all flourished during the Middle Ages. Raymond de Roover even goes so far as to say that 'Contrary to a widespread belief, the Middle Ages were not static, but as dynamic as modern times',[1] and in a survey of the history of accounting, writes: 'In response to the needs of rising capitalism, the Italian merchants [of the thirteenth, fourteenth and fifteenth centuries] created double-entry book-keeping and developed it to a point of perfection which was not to be surpassed for several centuries.'[2] Pound, in his anxiety to build some foundation upon which he could stand his deep feeling about usury, was too hasty,

---

[1] 'The Story of the Alberti Company of Florence, 1302–1348, As Revealed in Its Account Books', *Business History Review*, Harvard, Spring 1958.

[2] 'New Perspectives on the History of Accounting', *The Accounting Review*, July 1955.

did not fully know what he was doing, and linked his intuition to an arbitrary, incomplete and at times downright false set of facts. With regard to a possible connection between, for instance, certain architecture, for example the Cathedral at Modena and 'the degree of tolerance of usury' in the society in which it was built, it is not possible to examine Pound's idea in detail, against the fact, since nowhere does he commit himself to a definite statement of what he means by 'tolerance'. But it would be possible to show that most or possibly all the great art works mentioned by Pound were created at times when interest rates were exceedingly high, the ideas of the business community and the theologians in a state of interesting tension and conflict, and the general feeling in the community probably against usury as a matter of principle, though unconnected to any very clear idea about the conduct of business.

It might be concluded, therefore, that Pound was not really an historian at all, but a writer who wanted to use history, who wanted to know the nature of the historic process, without studying history as such, or finding some method by which he might use it without getting dragged into the maelstrom of historical 'facts'. He did approach it by way of 'facts', but not having the necessary training or the patience to wait until he had acquired it, lost his bearings and all sense of proportion. If any of his work concerning history survives, it is because he saw through and beyond his own jerry-built constructions, to things that were definitely there, and left us, if not satisfactory definitions of what he saw, at least an inkling of what to look for.[1]

[1] If we are to understand how far Pound was wrong on questions like the medieval idea of the Just Price we must first appreciate the fact that this and related matters first reached the modern world in completely garbled fashion and that Pound and other monetary reformers simply accepted the prevailing ideas. They knew what they were looking for before they found it, and so found what they were looking for: a lever to use against the contemporary world. But had Pound consulted the various references to the Just Price in Albertus and Aquinas, and seen how these had been interpreted by the most important of the orthodox commentators, Cajetan, he might have found his way into a world far different from that invented or assumed by historians like Weber, Sombart and Tawney and reformers like A. J. Penty. Some of the more recent publications dealing with this aspect of economics in the Middle Ages are listed in the bibliography.

CHAPTER XIV

An American Tradition

IN THE opening chapter we saw how Pound grew up in an atmosphere that was in every respect American. At no time, even after his departure from the United States, did he regard himself as anything but an American; but the 'Americanism' which he had breathed from birth was something he took for granted. He understood that he had roots, but was not much interested in examining them in detail. During his London years, however, he began to read Jefferson and gradually his interest in his American background increased until America began to take a central place beside Confucius in his thought and work. My first chapter was limited to those American elements which had formed Pound's immediate background; I will treat now of the wider American background as Pound himself discovered it in his reading into history. I am purposely bringing the reader to face the fact that, although our idea of Pound is very much influenced by our knowledge that he is an American, yet our actual understanding of the America which produced Pound is very vague indeed. Most of us, knowing his nationality, have made certain assumptions based upon the United States of 1920 and onwards, careless of any greater exactitude. The truth is that Pound's America, of the second half of the nineteenth century, with family roots, temperament and part of his philosophy going back much further, was something very different from the United States of today.

'I do not think I have ever abandoned the frontier,' he wrote to an official of the American government on 8 November 1937, and to a certain extent this was true. He did not believe that he had lost his frontier heredity or that it had caused him to react into an opposite extreme. His pride in the America which produced Whistler and Lincoln is quite obvious in the poem 'To Whistler—American' published in the first issue of *Poetry* in October 1912. Similar manifestations are to be found throughout the prose of his

London years. He even believed in the possibility of an American
'awakening', on the basis of the tradition created by Lincoln,
Whistler and Whitman, which would make the Italian Renaissance 'look like a tempest in a teapot'. There is pride in his description of the New York he had known as a child:

> The New York 'wharves', which H.J. records as heaped with water-
> melons and bushel-baskets of peaches, must have been not too unlike
> the old fruit market and other seemingly endless 'Covent Gardens' on
> the west side 'down town', to which I was taken by my Great Uncle,
> and, after his death, by my Great Aunt in the search for advantageous
> provisions. I remember a man throwing a large jack-knife some fifty
> feet after a fleeing male figure. The incident was unique so far as I was
> concerned, but seemed to arouse no curiosity among the bystanders. . . .
>   And at the end of the street jingled the small horse bells of the
> Madison Avenue horse-cars, bobbing down towards the white-washed
> tunnel, and beyond the car line was the Express Company, and beyond
> that the tracks from the 'Grand Central', invisible because of the wall
> and the Express Company; and beyond that was 596, Lexington
> Avenue—with the cable cars.

This same New York is lovingly recorded in the *Pisan Cantos*, in
verse that is perfectly suited to the mood of quiet regret for something once known, that is now gone, and yet somehow seems to
live on:

>   and the remains of the old South
>   tidewashed to Manhattan and brown-stone
>   or (later) the outer front stair
> leading to Mouquin's
>   or old Train (Francis) on the pavement in his plain wooden chair
> or a fellow throwing a knife in the market
> past baskets and bushels of peaches
>   at $1. the bushel
> and the cool of the 42nd St. tunnel   (periplum)
> white-wash and horse cars, the Lexington Avenue cable
> refinement, pride of tradition . . .

There is even a certain amount of pride in his description (1918) of
the 'America of tomorrow':

Unfortunately the turmoil of Letts, Finns, Esthonians, Cravats, Niberians, Nubians, Algerians, sweeping along Eighth Avenue in the splendour of vigorous unwashed animality will not help us. They are the America of tomorrow.

There was another aspect of the American past which he did not know about or really appreciate until 1928 when his father arrived in Rapallo with a bundle of old newspaper clippings telling of the family's interest in monetary reform, or monetary problems, half a century earlier. This was important for Pound; he was no longer a lone American calling for reform, or member of a clique, but began to see himself as part of a solid American tradition:

It was only when my father brought some old newspaper clippings to Rapallo in 1928 that I discovered that T.C.P. had already in 1878 been writing about, or urging among his fellow congressman, the same essentials of monetary and statal economics that I am writing about today (1942).

The 'T.C.P.' mentioned here was his grandfather Thaddeus Coleman Pound, a congressman who in frontier country had issued his own paper money backed by lumber. In one of these clippings, Thaddeus Pound explained that an amendment he had tabled to a bill about silver coinage had been an attempt to keep some of the nation's non-interest-bearing debt in circulation as currency. In a letter written in August 1957, Pound said:

Family tradition is that Blaine kept me grandpop out of Garfield's cabinet and that T.C.P. kept Blaine out of the White House, neither making comeback. If job was promised T.C.P. / that wd indicate Garfield had clean velleities, presumably re non-interest bearing debt to be kept as currency.

What Pound lamented was that although people like his grandfather had apparently been saying these things in the second half of the century, and historians like Brooks Adams writing books on the place of money in history, none of this seemed to seep through into the education system: 'My generation (that born in the 1880's) was dragged up in black ignorance of economics.'

Reading into American history he discovered, or so he believed, that the 'tradition' to which his grandfather belonged was rooted in American life as far back as the framing of the Constitution. While such a 'tradition' did indeed exist—it lasted until the Free Silver campaign near the turn of the century—Pound takes too many short-cuts. The narrowness of his view of American economic history in the nineteenth century may be gauged from this statement made in 1944:

> The true history of the economy of the United States, as I see it, is to be found in the correspondence between Adams and Jefferson, in the writings of Van Buren, and in quotations from the intimate letters of the Fathers of the Republic. The elements remain the same: debts, altering the value of the monetary units, and the attempts, and triumphs of usury, due to monopolies, or to a 'Corner'.

Broadly speaking this American 'tradition' to which Pound subscribed, consisted of opposition to the idea of a national debt held by a few private stockholders, especially foreigners, opposition to the control of the national currency by private bankers, and, on the positive side, support for the idea that the Federal government should be independent of the banking system in its money dealings, and where necessary be able to issue its own currency and credit without having to borrow from outsiders. Some extracts from the writings which exemplify the 'tradition' have been quoted by Pound—some of them over and over again—in articles which are available. A good example is this from a letter by Jefferson to John Adams, which Pound used in his article on the Jefferson-Adams correspondence:

> By comparing the first and the last of these articles (this follows a table of figures) 'we see that if the United States were in possession of the circulating medium, as they ought to be, they cd. redeem what they cd. borrow from that, dollar for dollar, and in ten annual installments; whereas usurpation of that fund by bank paper, obliging them to borrow elsewhere at $7\frac{1}{2}\%$, two dollars are required to reimburse one.'

Other aspects of this 'tradition' are not sufficiently known, however, and not available in any of Pound's works, nor in any of the books which he recommends, so it will bridge an inconvenient gap if I give extracts from some of the writings of the Presidents. The Second Bank of the United States, said President

P

Jackson in his Farewell Message of March 1837, 'asserted, and it undoubtedly possessed, the power to make money plenty or scarce at its pleasure; at any time and in any quarter of the Union, by controlling the issues of other banks'. The similarity between this and some of Pound's statements on banking is obvious and needs no comment. According to Martin Van Buren, who followed Jackson as President, this control by the Second Bank, or the banks, did not stop at New York or Philadelphia, but was centred in London. Here is an extract from his Annual Message of December 1839:

> The dependence of our whole banking system on the institutions in a few large cities is not found in the laws of their organization, but in those of trade and exchange. But this chain of dependence . . . does not terminate at Philadelphia or New York. It reaches across the ocean and ends in London, the centre of the credit system.
>
> The same laws of trade which give to the banks of our principle cities power over the whole banking system of the United States, subject the former in their turn to the money power in Great Britain. It is not denied that the suspension of the New York banks in 1837, which was followed in quick succession throughout the Union, was produced by an application of that power. . . .
>
> From this influence our banks cannot now entirely escape, for it has its origin in the credit currencies of the two countries; it is strengthened by the current of trade and exchange which centres in London, and is rendered almost irresistible by the large debts contracted there by our merchants, our banks and our States.
>
> It is thus that an introduction of a new bank into the most distant of our villages places the business of that village within the influence of the money power in England: it is thus that every new debt which we contract in that country seriously affects our own currency and extends over the pursuits of our citizens its powerful influence.
>
> We cannot escape from this by making new banks, great or small, State or national. Endangered in the first place by their own mismanagement . . . they are yet subjected beyond all this to the effect of whatever measures policy, necessity, or caprice may induce those who control the credits of England to resort to. . . .
>
> . . . it is peculiarly in the nature of such abuses as we are now encountering to seek to perpetuate their power by means of the influence they have been permitted to acquire. It is their result, if not their

object, to gain for the few an ascendancy over the many by securing to them a monopoly of the currency, the medium through which most of the wants of mankind are supplied. . . .

It will readily be seen from this Message why Pound developed such admiration for Van Buren. Drawing upon statements like these he came to believe that the controllers of American money and credit did not use it in the interests of the people as a whole, they did not provide a stable measure of price and means of exchange, they falsified this measure by the 'classic' manœuvre of altering the value of the monetary unit to their own advantage. What Pound believed to be the first step in this process, the creation of debt, especially debt that comes from the issuing of paper beyond any possibility of repayment in material terms, was described by Van Buren as: 'the creation of debts, to an almost countless amount, for real estate in existing or anticipated cities and villages, equally unproductive, and at prices now seen to have been disproportionate to their real value.' The error then, according to Pound, was to force up the land market as if unworked land far from railways could yield—yield in the sense of producing wanted goods at the place of need. The analogy in the 1930's, he says in *ABC of Economics*, 'is that the American fool has repeated himself, putting "industry" in the place of land, i.e. stocks, shares in industrial companies which either were not in shape to produce or had no possible market anywhere within dreamable range of the selling price of stocks in New York'. Or again, let us compare Van Buren on the difference between genuine bills of exchange and 'bills of exchange not drawn to transfer actual capital nor on the credit of property transmitted, but to create fictitious capital', with Pound on a similar matter:

Should the circulation of capital be automatic? We must distinguish between capital and purchasing power. Striving for a clear terminology one might limit the term capital to the sense of 'productive undertaking', or the securities of such an undertaking, i.e., securities that presuppose a material basis which yields a product that can be divided periodically, paying interest (share interest in monetary form) without creating inflation, which is superfluity of paper money in relation to available goods.

The controller of money and credit, says Pound, can alter the value of the monetary unit to his own advantage, and he quotes this passage from the *Law of Civilization and Decay* by his fellow American Brooks Adams, first published in English in 1896:

Perhaps no financier has ever lived abler than Samuel Lloyd. Certainly he understood as few men, even of later generations, have understood, the mighty engine of the single standard. He comprehended that, with expanding trade, an inelastic currency must rise in value; he saw that, with sufficient resources at command, his class might be able to establish such a rise, almost at pleasure; certainly that they could manipulate it when it came, by taking advantage of foreign exchange. He perceived moreover that, once established, a contraction of the currency might be forced to an extreme, and that when money rose beyond price, as in 1825, debtors would have to surrender their property on such terms as creditors might dictate.

Van Buren, who as Governor of New York introduced the Safety Fund system with the intention of preventing bank crashes, as President brought in the Constitutional Treasury in an attempt, Pound believed, to hold down the power of the banks over national purchasing power. Later, President Tyler vetoed attempts to charter a new Federal bank, after the Second Bank of the United States had collapsed, and both he and President Polk are placed on Pound's 'honour roll' in Canto 87. A system where the controller of purchasing power alters the value of the monetary unit is bad enough, Pound would say, but on top of that they seek, as Van Buren put it, 'to perpetuate their power by means of the influence they have been permitted to acquire': they begin to use money as 'an instrument of policy', as Pound says in Canto 87, quoting C. H. Douglas.

President Jackson, according to Pound, not only put a stop to the Second Bank's encroachment on the Federal government, but removed another weapon for control of policy from outside, by paying off the national debt. Pound writes: 'Upon examining the receipts and expenditures of the government between 1816 and 1833, even Dewey[1] admits that the great decrease of expendi-

---

[1] D. R. Dewey, *Financial History of the United States*, N.Y., 1903. Pound used the 12th edition published some years later.

ture was due to the reduction and, finally, to the elimination of the payments of interest on public debt.' The debt was paid off in 1834-5 and in 1836 the United States Treasury had an active balance which was distributed to the various states. Pound's correspondence in April 1940 was full of references to this elimination of the debt and distribution of the surplus, details of which he had just discovered in Dewey. 'Another bung knocked out of the anti-dividend buggars,' he wrote to C. H. Douglas on 3 April, which is a reference to Douglas's plan for the distribution of 'national dividends'. He also included an account of Jackson's accomplishment, together with figures showing receipts and expenditures of the Federal government and the gradual elimination of interest payments, in his 1944 booklet, *Introduction to the Economic Nature of the United States.*

For Pound the high point of Lincoln's presidency was crystallized in the President's statement: 'and gave to the people of this republic the greatest blessing they ever had—their own paper to pay their own debts'. This is from one of Lincoln's letters, a reference apparently to the paper money called 'greenbacks', issued during the Civil War and bearing no interest. There is also an interesting resemblance of ideas concerning a wide distribution of the national debt. In a letter written on 11 May 1940 Pound suggested that it would be useful to have a national debt that was also a means of distributing purchasing power widely over the community at so much per person. Compare Lincoln's statement in his Fourth Annual Message of December 1864, on the same subject: 'For obvious reasons the more nearly this property can be distributed among all the people the better. To favor such general distribution, greater inducements to become owners might . . . be presented to persons of limited means.' Lincoln's successor, Johnson, whom Pound knew of mainly through W. E. Woodward's *New American History* and Claude G. Bowers' *The Tragic Era*, had this to say about debt and outside financial control in his Fourth Annual Message of 9 December 1868:

. . . $64,000,000 was the amount owed by the government in 1860, just prior to the outbreak . . . when, in the Spring of 1865 the nation successfully emerged from the conflict, the obligations of the government had reached the immense sum of $2,873,992,909 . . . Our foreign debt is already computed by the Secretary of the Treasury at $850,000,000 . . .

This vast debt if permitted to become permanent and increasing must eventually be gathered into the hands of a few, and enable them to exert a dangerous and controlling power in the affairs of the government. The borrowers would become servants of the lenders, the lenders the masters of the people. We now pride ourselves upon having given freedom to four million of the coloured race; it will then be our shame that forty million of people, by their own toleration of usurpation and profligacy, have suffered themselves to become enslaved, and merely changed slave owners for the new taskmasters in the shape of bond-holders and taxgatherers.

This 'tradition' with its obvious appeal to the monetary reformer took up perhaps a disproportionate amount of Pound's time after 1932, but it must not be thought that he lost touch with the broader history of nineteenth-century America. It was as a Yankee that he spoke in 1944 when he said:

No man could be a director of Salem Museum who had not sailed round both the Cape of Good Hope and the 'Horn'. The construction of fast clippers was New England's glory a century ago. These clippers had brought the kind of wealth that follows exchange of goods with the orient and the entire world.

And there is a similar note of pride when he tells about the basis of American humour, the false gold bricks, made of lead with surface layer of gold, and the nutmeg trick perpetrated at the St. Louis Exposition by a 'true son of Connecticut'. Of his own family's part in the making of that America, he wrote:

Let us take a 'typical American family'. Two Wadsworth brothers, or two men of that name, arrived in Massachusetts in 1632. In 1882 their descendants had a family reunion and published the history of the family. In the eight generations we find all sorts and conditions—rich and poor. One, at the age of sixteen, sold his hair for a shilling, and 'this was the first money he ever did see'. Another fitted out a ship with his own money, during the Civil War. On the 250th Anniversary the participants presented equal variety and extremes among them— members of the Stock Exchange, salesmen, doctors, a telegraph operator and two old women for whom a collection was taken up. Under these conditions class warfare, in the true sense of the word, does not exist, even though the differences in wealth and position are undeniably visible . . .

Let us compare a score of personal cases in order to understand the foundation of American economic history. In the docket of a great-grandfather, Justice of the Peace in New York State, the fines run from $1.30 to about $25.00, and the tribunal's expenses from 8c. to $1.30.

His daughter, at least once in her life, went to work in a factory, married a man who became a Congressman, supervised the kitchen, not as a spectator, but in order to prepare meals for about forty lumbermen. At the time of her separation she had $100,000.00 in the bank, but the bank failed. My father, the first white man to be born in that part of Wisconsin, was looked after by a male redskin instead of a nurse. He inspected mines in Idaho, and got a job in the Land Office. One week he had his kindling wood sawed by a certain man for a dollar. Ten days later he asked the man if he wanted to saw a little more wood. 'Saw wood? Saw wood? Say Homer do you want to go East and sell a mine? I got $10,000.00 in the bank.'

In 1919 I met in Paris a quiet little man, Ambassador at the time, whom my father remembered thirty-five years before in the act of reaching for a revolver to help out his partner. American distances are different from the European, and the statistics do not record all the nuances.

In some ways Pound broke away from his background, not in order to deny it, for this he never did, but because of the limitations it seemed to impose on his work as a poet and student of civilizations. In his disposition however and much of his thinking, he remained always a product of nineteenth-century America before those fateful years at the turn of the century, when American industrialism broke through into leadership and remade the world. What may be surprising to many is that his advocacy of Confucius was not in any way at odds with the mechanistic tendency of his American heritage; as they existed in Pound, Confucius and this tendency were very close to being one and the same.

CHAPTER XV

Confucius and Nineteenth Century Science

Pencilled firmly in the margin of Pound's copy of Henry Adams' *Degradation of the Democratic Dogma*, against a statement by Brooks Adams in his introduction, that human beings are greedy, avaricious and cruel, and need to be restrained by law, is a large and emphatic 'NO'. And beside where Brooks wrote that it is to restrain and regulate competition that laws are devised, are the words 'NO: EDUCATION'.

This taken by itself would mean nothing, but it is backed by Pound's considered words in a number of places, and is in fact an accurate record of his philosophy. For Pound, virtue is the same thing as the right kind of knowledge. Brooks Adams, in his hour of despair, having lost faith in America, democracy, and history, and not yet returned to religion, was drawing attention—though with the unbalance and overemphasis of the heretic—to a truth about the world:

and the flesh is, in a general way, incarnated in the principle of competition, which, rooted in the passions of greed, avarice, and cruelty is apt to prevail to an unendurable degree unless restrained by law. And it is to regulate and restrain competition that human laws have been and are still devised.

But for Pound, a Jeffersonian and offspring of the Enlightenment, human cruelty and greed could be cured by an application of knowledge. Get your facts right and everything else will fall into place, is a crude way of putting it, but is, nevertheless, a just summary of this philosophy. The marginal comments in the Henry Adams book were not made while Pound was still in the process of 'forming' his philosophy—not, for instance, during the 1920's when T. S. Eliot, aware of Pound's roots in Rousseau and the perfectibility of man, was prompted to ask: 'what does Mr Pound believe?'—not then, but sometime between the middle of 1940 and the middle of 1943, after he had translated Confucius, studied Mencius, and adopted Fenollosa, Confucius and Mencius as his 'classics'. The two currents of thought which came together to produce Pound's philosophy were the nineteenth-century idea of science, and Confucius. These currents, although at first sight they may appear to have little in common, both stem from the same way of looking at the world; from the same beliefs and assumptions. The relevance of these two influences on Pound's attitude to virtue and knowledge is seen as soon as we enquire into the difference between science and theology, and examine the link between his roots in nineteenth-century science and his adoption of Confucius.

The beginning and end of physical science is the world of matter. It deals with the 'mechanical' working of finite things, as distinct from their nature. Theology on the other hand, and from a different point of view, says that the nature of things is not self-explanatory and is from God, who is the cause and source of all things, including the 'laws of nature', which he is at liberty to maintain or alter as he pleases. Physical science starts with sensible facts; theology with God; and ideally, with each one about its own business, are incapable of collision.

Where science examines, catalogues, compares and arranges sensible facts, and attempts to explain the workings of the natural world, theology is concerned with the Creator, souls, such matters as conscience and duty, and all the dealings between God and his creatures. Or in other words, theology deals not with the 'mechanics' of the universe, but is the 'science' of a universe into which moral evil has been introduced; and the Church, from this point of view, is God's instrument to remedy this situation.

What occurred during the seventeenth and eighteenth centuries was that man became obsessed with the physical and 'mechanical' side of creation. The universe began to take on more and more the aspect of a machine, with God as Inventor, so that moral evil and Original Sin tended to disappear, and were replaced by the idea that evil is really a fault in the workings, and that, as knowledge increases, it will gradually fade away. The man of the Enlightenment worked out a new 'natural' theology, not like the Catholic, starting from God, but by viewing the natural world as a graduated scale, a staircase leading up to the Inventor or Chief Engineer. The Divine Plan was in the working of the 'mechanical' Universe. There were, and are, of course, numerous versions of thought along this line, but generally speaking this view of the world, in so far as it can be treated in this summary fashion, was pursued along two different courses: there were those who saw every increase in scientific knowledge as vindication of the Divine Plan; such a one was the nineteenth-century naturalist Louis Agassiz whom Pound greatly admires; and those who became so fascinated with physical facts, the complexity of the universe, and their own power over it, that they were quite happy to forget the Chief Engineer. Pound belongs to the first group, those who see the Divine Plan in the natural world. But when I say 'belongs' I mean only that it had a major influence on his thought, not that he pursued this line either as a scientist or philosopher. At no time did he draw his thinking into a real system, with the result that the gods of ancient Greece sit side by side with nineteenth-century science in a way that may or may not be consistent. There is no way of telling really, as Pound has not committed himself to any revealing statement of his philosophic position—not even in the *Cantos*.

His immersion in old-fashioned science was so deep, owing as much to his American background as to his reading, that we are not surprised when we find that his ideas about the types of human mind, for example, closely resemble those offered by a line of famous investigators stretching from Turgot in 1750 to Andrew Lang more than a century later. Turgot in his *Plan de deux discours sur l'histoire universelle* presents the history of mankind according to cultural stages, from the hunting stage through pastoral life to the rise of agriculture, and finally the introduction of government. A century later Sir Edward Tylor, in his two works *Researches into the Early History of Mankind* (1865) and *Primitive Culture* (1871), tried to discover the characteristics of primitive modes of thought by means of psychological analysis of primitive cultures. A few years later, Andrew Lang (*Custom and Myth*, 1884) set out to study 'the mental condition of savages' and the 'common simple ideas of humanity'. Compare this search for underlying psychological unities with Pound's attempt to determine the 'basic psychologies', all the way from his statement about 'the milkable human cows, the shearable human sheep' in 1920, to the references to the hunting tribes and the 'butchers of lesser cattle' in the *Rock-Drill* and *Thrones* Cantos, and his formulation, by way of Frobenius, about 1957, of four 'basic psychologies or types of mind': 'the hunters, the agriculturists, the butchers of lesser cattle, and the creators'. Ethics, he wrote in a comment on his translation of Confucius' *Unwobbling Pivot*, 'are born from agriculture; the nomad gets no further than the concept of my sheep and thy sheep'.

Another line of thought from the Enlightenment which Pound accepted into his philosophy was the attempt to classify phenomena according to the idea of nature as a graduated scale. The first great work of modern classification was carried out by the Swedish naturalist Linnaeus in *Systema Naturae* (1735) and *Species Plantarum* (1753). Around the beginning of the nineteenth century Lamarck said it would be possible by observing nature carefully to descend by imperceptible steps from a 'perfect' creature like man to formless matter. Under the impact of men like Lyell and Hutton in geology, and Darwin in biology, these classifications and ideas led on to 'evolution' and modern biology. I have not been able to discover any indication that Pound ever did any serious reading on the subject of Darwin or 'evolution' but he did express himself sharply on several occasions to the effect that he did not believe that mind had developed out of mud. For this reason the naturalist who appealed to him was the nineteenth-century Swiss-American, Louis Agassiz of Harvard, one of the greatest teachers of his day. Agassiz opposed 'evolution' but was a strong proponent of the idea that the mind of God is everywhere visible in the ordering of nature, as this is visible to the scientist. Pound called this 'the intelligence working in nature—a tradition that runs from Mencius, through Dante, to Agassiz, needing no particular theories to keep it alive'. But it is hard to see how he was able to move, except by arbitrary leap, from the classifications of a nineteenth-century scientist, to the philosophy implied in the first canto of the *Paradiso*:

> La gloria di colui che tutto move
> per l'universo penetra, e risplende
> in una parte più, e meno altrove.

(The All-mover's glory penetrates through the universe, and re-gloweth in one region, and less in another.)

For Dante, God is the 'somma luce', the supreme light who penetrates into the nature of all things, this light being reflected, but only reflected, in their concrete being. Which might be difficult to relate to scientific enquiry into the 'mechanics' of sensible fact; nor does Pound anywhere attempt to explain this relationship: he states simply that it exists.

He seems to have read some Agassiz, or perhaps only heard about him, in the early 1930's, but does not seem to have read him seriously until after the Second World War. 'Agassiz, apart from his brilliant achievements in natural science,' he wrote in the 1950's, 'ranks as a writer of prose, precise knowledge of his subject leading to great exactitude of expression.' Both Linnaeus and Agassiz are given a place in the *Rock-Drill* and *Thrones* Cantos.

The connection between science and the other major influence on Pound's philosophy, namely Confucius, or Pound's interpretation of Confucius, is clear as soon as we turn to his translation of the *Unwobbling Pivot* and *Great Digest*. Thus in the *Pivot*:

He who can totally sweep clean the chalice of himself can carry the inborn nature of others to its fulfillment; getting to the bottom of the natures of men, one can thence understand the nature of material things, and this understanding of the nature of things can aid the transforming and nutritive powers of earth and heaven [ameliorate the quality of the grain, for example] and raise man up to be a sort of third partner with heaven and earth.

And again:

He who defines his words with precision will perfect himself and the process of this perfecting is in the process [that is, in the process par excellence . . . the total process of nature].

The clearest indication of the connection, however, is to be found in the *Digest*, where virtue and knowledge turn out to be one and the same thing. What you have to do to be 'good' is first of all to sort things into 'organic categories'. The relation between this and what a scientist does when he classifies the phenomena of his science, will be seen immediately:

The men of old wanting to clarify and diffuse throughout the empire that light which comes from looking straight into the heart and then acting, first set up good government in their own states; wanting good government in their states, they first established order in their own families; wanting order in the home, they first disciplined themselves; desiring self-discipline, they rectified their own hearts; and wanting to rectify their hearts, they sought precise verbal definitions of their inarticulate thoughts [the tones given off by the heart]; wishing to attain precise verbal definitions, they set to extend their knowledge to the utmost. This completion of knowledge is rooted in sorting things into organic categories.

When things had been classified in organic categories, knowledge moved towards fulfillment; given the extreme knowable points, the inarticulate thoughts were defined with precision [the sun's lance coming to rest on the precise spot verbally]. Having attained this precise verbal definition [*aliter*, this sincerity], they then stabilized their hearts, they disciplined themselves; having attained self-discipline, they set their own houses in order; having order in their own homes, they brought good government to their own states: and when their states were well governed, the empire was brought into equilibrium.

In addition to these translations we have Pound's statement in his essay on the 'Ethics of Mencius' that 'When the aims of Shun and Wan were set together, though after a thousand years interval, they were as two halves of a tally stick . . . That things can be known a hundred generations distant, implied no supernatural powers, it did imply the durability of natural process which alone gives a possibility for science.' Unless the aims here mentioned were simply a list of public works, bridge building and gutter cleaning, this suggests that ethics is a science like physics, depending on the durability or regularity of nature as it is tackled by the physicist. It seems to ignore completely the depths and the glories of the human heart.

Pound read one or two of the 'standard' translations of ancient Chinese literature before he left America, or during his first years in London, and may have gained a little knowledge of Chinese poetry from Allen Upward about 1912; but it was not until he was given the Fenollosa papers towards the end of 1913 that he was introduced to Confucius. Among Fenollosa's books was the first text he had seen of the *Unwobbling Pivot*. While his knowledge of ancient Chinese may appear doubtful or eccentric to the professional scholar, his admiration for Confucius, his hanging on to his every word, these things are beyond doubt, and the influence of this philosophy over a period of forty years is basic to an understanding of Pound's thought. He used a quotation from Pauthier's French version of the *Pivot* in his *Gaudier-Brzeska* (1916), and about a year later asked Margaret Anderson whether he should do an article on Confucius for the *Little Review*. His first major excursion into Chinese philosophy was about 1923 when he devoted Canto 13 to Confucius. In 1928 he published his first translation of the *Great Digest* (*Ta Hio*), and five years later, speaking of students who knew only English, he declared: 'I have translated the *Ta Hio* so that they can learn where to start THINKING.' Writing the essay 'Date Line' early in 1934 he answered Eliot's earlier query: 'what does Mr Pound believe?' with the simple sentence: 'I believe the *Ta Hio*.' He published a condensation of the *Analects* of Confucius in 1937, an Italian version of the *Digest* in 1942, an Italian version of the *Pivot* in 1945, and at least four editions of the English version of this work between 1947 and 1951, including one with Chinese text. In addition to this he published his full translation of the *Analects* in the *Hudson Review* during 1950, the same work as a booklet a year later, and again, with an additional one and a half page note, in 1956. This latter is interesting because like similar notes attached to Canto 85 and the *Digest* it again indicates the close link between Confucian philosophy and the collection and arranging of natural facts or the facts of history: 'Likewise he [Confucius] collected the *Historic Documents*, asserting, quite truly, that he had invented nothing. Without Kung [Confucius] no one would discover that his teaching, or at any rate the root and the seed, are there in the "History Classic".' Pound continued with his Confucian studies through the 1950's and Canto 99, written about

1957, is almost a paraphrase of the *Sacred Edict*, an eighteenth-century Chinese document in the Confucian tradition. It is easy to see, incidentally, why Pound mentions the Stoic, Epictetus, whose emphasis on temperance and moderation is extremely Confucian. But there are a number of places where the resemblance goes even deeper. Where Pound's translation of the *Digest* has: 'affairs have scopes and beginnings. To know what precedes and what follows, is nearly as good as having a head and feet,' Epictetus says: 'In every act observe the things which come first, and those which follow it; and so proceed to the act.' The philosophy of Confucius—as it comes to us through Pound—is essentially naturalistic, conceived in terms of 'right action', meaning action in harmony with 'the total process of nature'. When a Confucian says: 'be at ease in *total* rectitude' (my italics), he may not be rejecting any Christian dogma, but he is certainly placing himself in opposition to Christian experience, whose wisdom warns against absolutes like 'total rectitude' or 'absolute sincerity'. According to this experience man is not strong enough to face absolutes in this way; never good enough to seek after absolute sincerity or try to plumb the depths of his own soul or motives. He is expected to seek sincerity, to examine his conscience—but not absolutely, for such knowledge, if not beyond his understanding, would be beyond his power to endure. And the danger is that assistance might readily be offered by the powers of evil. The Christian emphasis is on God's part, not on man's; on God's power to redeem man from the depths if only man will abandon his own will in God's. But for Pound, entrenched in a world that does not recognize the human heart, nor believe in the introduction of moral evil into the universe, goodness consists in discovering 'the total process of nature' and then acting on this discovery. Original Sin he believes is a hoax perpetrated by priestcraft. The priest is a shepherd, the people are 'milkable human cows' or 'shearable human sheep' who are looked after by the shepherd and then 'milked' or 'fleeced'; and Original Sin, as requiring the intervention of the priest between man and God for its remedy, was and is the priest's method of getting and keeping a grip on his 'flock'. The priestly mind, according to Pound, goes back to the 'butchers of lesser cattle', the nomads who in the dim past discovered that instead of killing and eating bulls, which were inclined to be ferocious, it was much easier to fatten the placid cow or ewe and kill it only when the need arose.

It is my own belief (not based on evidence) that Pound's whole attitude to religion, his lifelong misunderstanding of some aspects of Christianity, as well as his horror of Original Sin and the Jewish religion of the Old Testament, may have been due to his early training possibly in some form of American Bible-religion, against which he revolted in that religion's own spirit of private judgement; so that all his life his religion has been a dialogue with that original Bible class.

Like the nature to which it clings, the naturalistic philosophy of Confucius and the Enlightenment is essentially aphoristic—though not in all cases—and like nature (as we know her or experience her), given to bursts of brilliance, colour and energy. There is a pleasant hardness and some wisdom in this passage from the *Analects*:

> Love of manhood minus love of study: befuddlement into naiveté.
> Love of knowledge without love of study: runs wild into waste incorrelation.
> Love of keeping one's word, without study runs amok into doing harm.

But this is a philosophy, no matter how well expressed, bounded by physics, having no metaphysics. Although Pound emphasizes the importance of the will in Confucian philosophy, it is no more than finding the right channel for the release of energy and the proper working of nature. 'The earth belongs to the living,' wrote Pound, quoting Jefferson, and the Poundian philosophy is, in a sense, contained in this sentence, which is naturalistic and revolutionary. Despite occasional similarities it is a far cry from the belief in a universe of good and evil, in which the family, and if possible, the community, is a 'bond which embraces . . . a piety towards the dead, however obscure, and a solicitude for the unborn, however remote'. Pound has helped to conserve, but it is not really true to call him a conservative.

CHAPTER XVI

Conservation of the 'Better Tradition'

POUND the poet was in his element when he plunged into
London literary life in 1908 and set about conserving the
'better tradition' in literature. If his twenty years in Rapallo was
an unfortunate self-imposed exile, away from everything that
appealed and was important to him as a poet, critic and observer
of life in general, in London he was at home. An article he wrote
during the first half of 1913 conveys his feelings. He may not
like many of the things in the literary world around him, he may
be impatient with it for its slowness, but he is part of it, and
enjoying himself in writing for it, despite any protestations he
may make to the contrary:

For well over a year I have been trying to make a poem of a very
beautiful thing that befell me in the Paris Underground. I got out of a
train at, I think, La Concorde and in the jostle I saw a beautiful face,
and then, turning suddenly, another and another, and then a beautiful
child's face, and then another beautiful face. All that day I tried to find
words for what this made me feel. That night as I went home along
the rue Raynouard I was still trying. I could get nothing but spots of
colour. I remember thinking that if I had been a painter I might have
started a wholly new school of painting. I tried to write the poem
weeks afterwards in Italy, but found it useless. Then only the other night,
wondering how I should tell the adventure, it struck me that in Japan,
where a work of art is not estimated by its acreage and where sixteen
syllables are counted enough for a poem if you arrange and punctuate
them properly, one might make a very little poem which would be
translated about as follows:—

> The apparition of these faces in the crowd:
> Petals on a wet, black bough.

And there, or in some other very old, very quiet civilization, some one
else might understand the significance.[1]

[1] From 'How I Began', op. cit.

This was during the *Imagist* and *Vorticist* period when Pound was not only organizing one or more artistic 'revolutions', and fighting those elements among the 'old guard' which he considered harmful, but was at the same time enjoying a certain amount of fame as a poet and translator in the most respectable circles. The *Times Literary Supplement*, for instance, in its review of *Cathay* in the issue of 29 April 1915 was favourably impressed: 'Mr. Pound has kept to the reality of the original because he keeps his language simple and sharp and precise. We hope he will give us some more versions of Chinese poetry.' Pound was not, at this stage, working outside the system: he was an accepted literary rebel, and because of the beauty of so much of his work, tolerated by many of those whom he considered his enemies. It was Richard Aldington's opinion, some years later, that Pound could even have become 'literary dictator of London', had he gone about it with care and tact.

Working in these conditions, Pound in his fight to conserve the 'better tradition' made use of two weapons, related, and yet in another sense completely different and opposed. These were: (1) prose as an instrument of persuasion, clarification, and definition and (2) poetry as a means of continuing or extending the 'better tradition' and bringing it up to date. Pound's prose, like that of any major poet, is related to his poetry, but in Pound's case we have a strange anomaly: while his best poetry was often conservative in tendency, his prose was nearly always revolutionary. In a short piece called 'Breviora' in the *Little Review* of October 1918 he wrote:

The better tradition of English: 'Seafarer', lines in the 'Wanderer', parts of Layamon, Chaucer, Gavin Douglas, Golding, Marlowe (translations as well as original work), William Shakespeare (as certain other critics have noted), Ballads and Elizabethan songs (rigorously selected), Wyatt, Donne, Waller, Herrick, later a few catches of Dorset and Rochester, Crabbe, Landor (selected and sifted).

Against this place the following passage from *Mauberley* written less than two years later:

A pale gold, in the aforesaid pattern,
The unexpected palms
Destroying, certainly, the artist's urge,
Left him delighted with the imaginary
Audition of the phantasmal sea-surge,

Incapable of the least utterance or composition,
Emendation, conservation of the 'better tradition' . . .

The first, the prose formulation, is interesting perhaps as an example of Pound's weeding-out, but it is cranky and it is an attempt to revolutionize English literature, to throw out not just bad poetry, or the sort of poetry which has been done better in other languages, but poetry which is an essential part of the tradition, and to which our language, by its very nature, is tied. He fails to take note of the variety of English, leaving out a number of facets which are essential to it. But turn to the extract from *Mauberley* and we find just the opposite. The poet intent upon his job as a poet, with the sound of the spoken language as well as past literature echoing in his ear, conserves the 'better tradition', not by a list of names but by incorporating it into the newly created language of twentieth-century English poetry. The reason for this anomaly is fairly simple. In his prose Pound was at liberty to be as revolutionary as he liked, to attack or praise what he liked, and once he started writing for the *Little Review*, to do so more or less in any style he saw fit: a liberty which he often took advantage of. But in poetry he was not so at liberty, not if he wished to renew English poetry and conserve the 'better tradition' in verse that was closely related to the spoken language of his own day. He was limited by the English language, to which he had to conform if he was to travel the road he had chosen. Pound met this challenge and succeeded in renewing English poetry. The problem of the word, as he called it, consisted, in so far as it dealt with literature, of finding and arranging words that would light up the minds of contemporary readers and enable them to see their own world in terms of their own time, as distinct from the terms of Shakespeare's time, or Keats's. The literary word 'must rise afresh in each work of art and come down with renewed light'. Here is Pound's summary in 1942 of the renewal of English poetry in this century:

In one's youth one discusses style—or one should. The poetical re-form between 1910 and 1920 coincided with the scrutiny of the word, the cleaning-up of syntax. This should be tackled in addition to, almost apart from, the question of content: one should seek to define the image, to discover the truth, or a part of the truth, even before one has learned that it may not be the whole truth.

I repeat: the art of poetry is divisible into *phanopoeia*, *melopoeia*, and *logopoeia*. Verbal composition, that is to say, is formed of words which evoke or define visual phenomena, of words which register or suggest auditory phenomena (i.e., which register the various conventional sounds of the alphabet and produce, or suggest, a raising or a lowering of the tone which can sometimes be registered more accurately by musical notation), and, thirdly, of a play or 'dance' among the concomitant meanings, customs, usages, and implied contexts of the words themselves.

In this last category Eliot surpasses me; in the second I surpass him. Part of his *logopoeia* is incompatible with my main purpose.

We have collaborated in literary criticism, we have made decisions and taken measures against certain diseases of writing. The problem of the word cannot be exhausted in a single lifetime.

Pound was already feeling towards the 'modern cadence' in some of his earliest published poems deriving from Swinburne, Browning and the Nineties. It is instructive to compare:

> When her lips upon these eyelids
> One last poppied kiss have burned

published in 1905 by Bliss Carman, with these lines written by Pound about three years later:

> Upon these lids that lie over us
> Sodden and lead-heavy.

Already Pound was beginning to compose 'in the sequence of the musical phrase, and not in sequence of a metronome', and to put words to work again, instead of allowing them to fall into, and fill, convenient and accepted patterns of sound and meaning. If

most of the time in his poems written before 1911 he works within these accepted patterns:

> 'It is not, Raana, that my song rings highest
> Or more sweet in tone than any, but that I
> Am here a Poet, that doth drink of life
> As lesser men drink wine.'

turning them only slightly to his own uses:

> In us alone the element of calm.

or using archaic and nineteenth century language to produce a
delicate sound of his own:

> In wild-wood never fawn nor fallow fareth
> So silent light . . .

yet there are lines in which the poet is master of his words, lines
which for this reason look ahead to *Ripostes* and *Lustra*, and even
beyond these to *Propertius*, *Mauberley* and the *Cantos*:

> So that I might find you again,
> Alone.

What is interesting here is not only the conscious attempt at a
meaningful cadence, but the striving for a straightforward and
natural language. In the lines:

> . . . the impalpable
> Mirrors unstill of the eternal change?

and

> I have slipped
> Your grasp, I have eluded.

he has succeeded in combining forceful and direct language—as
forceful and direct as it was then possible for him to be in the
poetic language he was then using—with a conscious manipulation of sound. Already at this early stage, when his head was still
full of the soft sounds of the nineteenth century, when he had
recognized the virtues of hard melodic line in Villon, Dante,
Catullus and Martial, but had found no method of creating such

a line in English, he could dimly see, or feel, that as far as English was concerned the secret at that time lay in a 'music' of groups of syllables of varying sizes, fitted closely to simplicity of statement.

Summing up Pound's overall poetic 'method' after the appearance of *Homage to Sextus Propertius* in 1919, T. S. Eliot wrote:

As the present is no more than the present existence, the present significance of the entire past, Mr Pound proceeds by acquiring the entire past; and when the entire past is acquired, the constituents fall into place and the present is revealed. Such a method involves immense capacities of learning and of dominating one's learning, and the peculiarity of expressing oneself through historical masks. Mr. Pound has a unique gift for expression through some phase of past life. This is not archaeology or pedantry, but one method, and a very high method, of poetry.

These historical masks are the means by which Pound expresses or grasps the fleeting and precarious present, which will not stand still, as it were, like a sculptor's model, for constant observation, but must be grasped as it passes or not at all. As a result Pound's poetry is a poetry of 'gists and piths', a poetry without explanations or 'bridge passages' concerning the meaning of what has gone before and of what is to come. It is a recognition of the fact that poetry, whatever it is, is not prose or 'explanation'. That it is a mysterious something which does not 'say' this or that, but penetrates the mind of the reader by means of some process almost wholly unknown. We may make discoveries around the edges, a point here, a point there, on the circumference, but of the nature of this thing and the means by which it penetrates the mind, in a way that nothing else can, or does, we know next to nothing. All we do know about poetry is that it works; that the best of it, anyway, achieves what it sets out to do.

Nineteen-fifteen was for Pound an important year, which saw not only the publication of his own *Cathay* and of Eliot's 'Prufrock' in *Poetry*, but one of his attempts to see the role of poetry in the framework of civilization, an attempt which is mirrored in his prose of that year, and in the essay 'The Renaissance' in particular. Allen Upward, with his learning drawn from many cultures, both high and primitive, his knowledge of Chinese literature and philosophy, of Gnosticism, and of some of the *accoutrements* of religion in various times and places, exerted a strong influence on this attempt by Pound to draw together the threads of his knowledge. Upward was very much present in the final paragraph of 'The Renaissance':

> When a civilization is vivid it preserves and fosters all sorts of artists —painters, poets, sculptors, musicians, architects. When a civilization is dull and anemic it preserves a rabble of priests, sterile instructors, and repeaters of things second-hand. If literature is to reappear in America it must come through, but in spite of, the present commercial system of publication.

And he was present also in a number of articles Pound wrote for the *New Age* during the same year, in which he spoke of the 'modern sense of the value of the "creative, constructive individual" ' and of Upward's constant propaganda on this theme. It was in one of these articles that he quoted Upward's lines:

> I withstood the savages of the Niger with a revolver:
> I withstood the savages of the Thames with a printing press

which thirty years later he worked into the *Pisan Cantos*.

With all Pound's emphasis at this time on other languages and past civilizations in other lands, it is important to note that he was still thinking very largely in terms of English literature and made several attempts to show how his own work at that time was in the English tradition. It was in vindication of *Imagisme* that he wrote:

> Has there been Imagisme in English poetry? Is it part of the insular tradition? It most certainly has existed and been part of the tradition, unconsciously perhaps. That is to say it has been part of the poets' tradition, not part of the critics' tradition, save for that one phrase of Morris ['a good poet makes pictures']. Keats, let us say, exists by virtue of his Imagisme, despite the fact that his language often lacks the directness of prose, and that those who dislike him, dislike him because of a certain lack of hardness . . .
>
> . . . Chaucer is, at any rate, [a standard author] and the figures of the 'Canterbury Tales' stand before us because they speak and move to the life. They, also, are not matter for debate. The wife of Bath was 'some

deal deaf'. She had better cloth on her back than what you'd get at Ypres or Ghent. Her hose were red scarlet, pulled up tight. The merchant had a forked beard. And the goddess Venus is not an abstraction or an allegory, we find her:

> Going in a quaint array,
> As she had been an hunteresse,
> With wind blowing upon her tress.

If Chaucer is the supreme lyrist (and he is the supreme lyrist in such ballads as:

> Hide, Absalon thy gilte tresses clere,

in the legend of 'Good Women,' and whenever he wishes to be), he is also the supreme imagist. Within the limits of his art no one has ever surpassed him.

He continues the article in this vein, pointing to examples of *Imagisme* in Shakespeare ('And with the incorporal air do hold discourse' etc.), in Swinburne, in Browning, and finally in Lionel Johnson's line:

> Clear lie the fields, and fade into blue air.

'Could anything be more Chinese?' he asks of this line, thereby suggesting that his concern with Chinese was not really in opposition to his work as an *Imagist* poet writing in English.

Given Pound's aim, which was to capture emotions, intuitions, 'a moment of song, self-analysis or self-revelation', not to 'explain' them, his work has a consistency all the way from his acceptance and development of his immediate predecessors in *A Lume Spento*, to his use of a far greater variety of past elements—both prosodic and otherwise—in *Propertius* and *Mauberley*. It is wrong to speak of a break in Pound's poetry between *Canzoni* in 1911 and *Ripostes* a year later. The poet is the same, his aim is the same; it is just that he sees things more clearly in 1912, having cleared away those aspects of nineteenth-century prosody and vocabulary which veiled the object of his vision, and replaced them by a clearer language, harder, and closer to the spoken language of the time.

Such an one picking a ragged
Backless copy from the stall,
Too cheap for cataloguing,
Loquitur,

 'Ah-eh! the strange rare name . . .
Ah-eh! He must be rare if even *I* have not . . .'
And lost mid-page
Such age
As his pardons the habit,
He analyses form and thought to see
How I 'scaped immortality.

There is no essential difference between this, which is from
'Famam Librosque Cano' in *A Lume Spento*, and the following
from 'Apparuit' published in June 1912:

 Life died down in the flame and flickered,
   caught at the wonder.

Both present an emotion by means of images; the difference
between them is not, I think, one of kind, but attributable to the
fact that the latter is not only more precise, but, because of its
precision, capable of penetrating further into its emotion and
taking hold of greater complexity. The 'bridge' between the
early poems up to and including *Canzoni*, and 'Apparuit', the
following year, was his translation of the Anglo-Saxon 'Seafarer',
first published in the *New Age* in November 1911. It does not
explain how Pound achieved a more natural language, that was,
at the same time, much more forceful and precise than the earlier
one, but it does illustrate the poet's firm intention to replace vague
images, or images with blurry edges, by those which are hard and
clear; and to join these to a firm clear sound, in order to drive a
sharp image into the reader's mind:

 There I heard naught save the harsh sea
 And ice-cold wave, at whiles the swan cries,
 Did for my games the gannet's clamour,
 Sea-fowls' loudness was for me laughter,

> The mews' singing, all my mead-drink.
> Storms, on the stone-cliffs beaten, fell on the stern
> In icy feathers; full oft the eagle screamed
> With spray on his pinion.

It must not be thought, either, that *Propertius*, composed in 1917 and first published in 1919, was something new, a break with the Pound of *Ripostes* and *Lustra*. It was no more than the poet of these earlier books carrying his discoveries regarding freshness of language and clarity of melody and image, to their logical conclusion, by way of a mask, and upon a subject matter, that gave him for the first time an opportunity to bring all his powers into play. It is no great step from 'Albatre' in *Lustra*:

> This lady in the white bath-robe which she
>   calls a peignoir,
> Is, for the time being, the mistress of my friend,
> And the delicate white feet of her little white dog
> Are not more delicate than she is,
> Nor would Gautier himself have despised their
>   contrasts in whiteness
> As she sits in the great chair
> Between the two indolent candles.

no great step, once you have mastered this kind of verse, to the final page of *Propertius*:

> Like a trained and performing tortoise,
> I would make verse in your fashion, if she should
>   command it,
> With her husband asking a remission of sentence,
>   And even this infamy would not attract
>   numerous readers
> Were there an erudite or violent passion,
> For the nobleness of the populace brooks nothing
>   below its own altitude.
> One must have resonance, resonance and sonority
>   . . . like a goose.

The 'goose' is at least as old as Dante, and the delayed surprise quite common among the Elizabethans. What makes it so effective again in A.D. 1917 is that it is in Pound's voice of the same year, and not that of some earlier poet. The difference between Pound's use of an historical mask in 'Cino', written in 1907, and in *Propertius* ten years later, is, when all said and done, only that the latter is much more accomplished. In 'Cino' Pound tells us (by way of Italy, 1307) a 'truth' or two about the present; in *Propertius* he does the same thing, but it is a bigger 'truth' that he tells, and his language matches perfectly what he is doing, whereas in the earlier poem the telling is in an indifferent language, which in 1907 it was not within Pound's power to alter, even had he been aware of its limitations.

I am in danger here of giving the impression that the progress Pound made in the ten years between 1907 and 1917 was almost automatic; that having started out along a certain path in 1907, he had only to stick at it and in due time *Propertius* would pop out of the slot. This of course is not my intention. The reason I have insisted on the continuity of the process, is that Pound's London years, the most important of all so far as his poetry is concerned, have been sadly distorted by critics who consciously or unconsciously have sought to link Pound's renewal of poetry with some sort of biographical disturbance or change. None of Pound's criticism, none of his poetry, explains this renovation; it is simply there, an accomplished fact. So in the absence of a literary explanation, commentators have sought an answer in biography, even some who perhaps did not realize that it was into biography that they were digging. It was out of this general situation, the search for an explanation, that two inaccurate and related ideas arose: the idea that around 1912 Ezra Pound 'broke with tradition' and started something 'new', and secondly the idea that he did this because he was a wild bohemian American, outspoken and fearless, who was in mortal combat with London, the English, and finally with English literature, which he despised and found out of date and lacking in vitality. If I seem to be pressing this point too far, let me say that I was surprised, looking back through articles and books written about Pound over the past forty years, to find just how often these ideas, or ideas of this kind, were at the bottom of the critic's attitude to Pound's poetry. Much of his best criticism during the London years was written *against* a contemporary current, but there is a great deal of difference between a man working against the current, which is a form of participation in the literary life of the time, and one who is outside the stream altogether and goes his own way.

The truth is that Pound was at home and enjoyed himself immensely in London literary life between 1908 and 1917; certainly he could not have been nearly as much at home anywhere else in the world at that time; and as far as his 'break with tradition' is concerned, it was a renewal and extension of English poetry, upon the basis of the general English tradition, or a part of it, from Chaucer onwards. Even in the *Cantos* where the subject matter is so various and the use of foreign languages so widespread, his attitude to the language he is using is still very much influenced by his feeling for the English tradition. And while the line of five feet or ten syllables is the basis for much of the actual versification of the poem, in several well-known sections of the *Pisan* sequence he is forced, by a certain kind of emotional intensity, to return to a type of cadence he once thought he had left behind. Such was the grip of 'traditional verse' on Pound's sensibility.

CHAPTER XVII

The Cantos

One hasn't any theology to fall back on.
EZRA POUND

I

AT THE age of twenty-seven, writing at a turning-point in English literature, when poetry was springing to life again under the attraction of his genius, Pound said he would like to discover 'what sort of things endure . . . what sort of things are transient . . . what sort of things recur', and further, to understand the workings of the forces of social order, 'both constructive and dispersive'. Since he had set out at an early age—about fifteen— to learn all there was to know about the art of poetry, and had 'learned more or less of nine foreign languages' in this same quest —most likely, I think, with the intention of one day writing a masterwork—it is probable that his concern with the transient, the recurrent and the enduring in 1912 was directly connected with his gropings towards a long poem exploring the nature of civilization.

The abortive first three Cantos were published five years after this statement, and the 'Hell' Cantos and one or two others drafted in London during 1919 and 1920; but the work did not really begin to take shape until a year or two later and the publication of *A Draft of XVI Cantos* in a limited edition in Paris in 1925. This was followed by a limited edition of *A Draft of Cantos* 17–27 in London in 1928, another limited edition of *A Draft of XXX Cantos* in Paris in 1930, and various sections of the poem in normal trade editions in England and the United States, from 1933 until the appearance of *Thrones 96–109 de los cantares* towards the end of 1959.

If we look for an overall plan in the *Cantos*, we look in vain, for there is none. None, in the sense of a scheme based upon a consistent attitude to life and death, that has been worked out in

241

detail, and embraces, even if it does not fully explain, everything that has to do with man. The poem has no formal basis from and through which the poet presents his poetry, with the verse tuned to mount and descend, and mount again, according to the hierarchy of the underlying attitude to existence. The *Cantos* is a post-Renaissance product, the work of one who sees the universe through man's eyes, as something to be mastered and measured: its contents are the things which the poet has seen, heard and read during a lifetime, and its form is the selection, emphasis and groupings made among these things by a lone mind, a present tense, sailing through time in isolation. The poem then is the logbook of a lone voyager: believe what you read there, or not, as you choose; the only way you can ever know whether it is an accurate record is by making the same voyage yourself. Many times of course Pound strikes through to some universal meaning, and when he does the verse sometimes has a touch of that Tennysonian sadness which in his criticism he opposed:

> and from 'Hesperus . . .'
> Hush of the older song: 'Fades light from sea-crest,
> 'And in Lydia walks with pair'd women
> 'Peerless among the pairs, that once in Sardis
> 'In satieties . . .
> Fades the light from the sea, and many things
> 'Are set abroad and brought to mind of thee,'
> And the vinestocks lie untended, new leaves come to the shoots,
> North wind nips on the bough, and seas in heart
> Toss up chill crests,
> And the vine stocks lie untended
> And many things are set abroad and brought to mind
> Of thee, Atthis, unfruitful.

Something which Sappho knew 2,500 years ago lives again in these lines; but most of the matter of the poem is particular, and for its meaning we are entirely dependent on how the poet presents it to us and what he tells us about it. If it has a meaning in the poem as a whole—as distinct from a narrow and local meaning—it is because the poet manages to convey to the reader the meaning it has for him. Where he fails to do this, it is meaningless.

I do not mean to suggest that the author of the *Cantos* would necessarily agree that man is the measure of all things; he has, in several places, said that he is not; but the fact remains that the poem, the whole direction of it, was born of this conception. If, at one of his ports of call, the voyager selects from traditional wisdom it is not because the traditional has any special value over and above the knowledge we acquire by our sciences and disciplines, but because for him it is just one more aspect of ordinary knowledge, to be sifted through, accepted here, rejected there, and used, according to the judgement of the isolated individual, without reference to any higher system of measurement. Only one sort of knowledge exists for Pound: knowledge that fits together with other knowledge like the parts of a machine. He has no sense of tradition, no sense of a wisdom that is older and deeper than the mind of any one man and is able to travel by a process that is not at all 'mechanical'.

Pound has seen this process and noted it; he has at times paid tribute to it; but he has never submitted to it, as one must if one wishes to make use of it in such a way as not to destroy its essential meaning. Pound's 'tradition' is of another sort altogether. It is the knowledge handed down by one creative individual to another, sometimes over a wide span of time. Sometimes this knowledge is real, and is passed on without corruption; but as I have pointed out in discussing the pagan mystery religions, it is often turned inside out in the handing-down, or even changed essentially so that there is no relation between the seed and the tree. The result sometimes is a long tradition which preserves nothing except the name tradition. Nor is it at all certain that a Pound or a Botticelli, when he does create some beauty apparently by way of the pagan mysteries, is in fact tapping this source, even though he may think he is doing so at the time. Great artists are more sensitive than other people; they also, some of them, have an enormous capacity for self-deception.

Had Pound been content to regard the *Cantos* as a record of his own voyage through time and history, the voyage of a lone man attempting to discover law and order among the transient, the recurring and the enduring, he might have been able to impress some definite and self-contained form upon the work as a whole. He was not so content however, and doomed the work to remain forever fragmentary, by introducing history—not history as part of the poem, but history as history, a record of facts. He undertook to discover the true factual history of civilization, in competition with historians, not realizing, apparently, that this left a large part of the poem at the mercy of historical studies, to be judged according to the normal standards of historical writing, and at the same time prevented him from giving the work a major form. His blunder in introducing history in this way can be appreciated better if we compare the *Cantos*, on this point, with Dante's *Divine Comedy*.

Dante was content to work within a system. Unlike Pound he was not burdened by the desire to consume all knowledge, and, simultaneously, to correct it; singlehandedly to set the world once and for all upon its right course. He was content to write a poem, the purpose of which, he said, was to 'remove those who are living in this life from the state of wretchedness, and to lead them to the state of blessedness'. But as far as Dante was concerned, the terms 'wretchedness' and 'blessedness', and the means for achieving the latter, had long since been defined and settled. He did not think it was his duty, or within his province as a poet, to establish a new set of credentials for the saints—those already canonized—or to refurnish Paradise. He concentrated on writing a long poem, and the history in it, as well as the condemnations and the praise of well-known figures, is subservient to the poem as a whole. When Dante makes an historical error, it does not affect the poem. When, for instance, he confuses one Moslem ruler with another who lived some time earlier, it is hardly even a minor blemish, since we know from the poem what the man stands for, and why Dante mentions him. And it is the same with most errors of fact in the *Comedy*.

But the place of history in the *Cantos* is another matter altogether. There, it is history plain and simple; and it is not subject to the poem as a whole, for there is no overall form of which history is merely a part. Pound undertakes to give a 'true' history, and even to correct historians. The result is that when he commits an error of fact, it dislocates what he has set out to do in that section of the poem. If you set out to tell a particular history in its particularity; if through the words of Senator Thomas Hart Benton you tell how Andrew Jackson fought for 'the people' against the Second Bank of the United States, and it turns out later that the 'true history' of the period is neither the story as told by Benton, nor even as related by Benton's opponents and the Second Bank, but something else again, some third arrangement of facts of which you had absolutely no knowledge, then your story crumbles and is lost. If you base your point upon a particular history, instead of on the great accumulation and sifting of traditional wisdom, then your point lives or dies with your narration. A great part of the work of great poets is not individual, but due to their ability to tap the reservoir of traditional wisdom. What they produce is new; nobody had thought of it before in quite that way; and yet readers of many different views are able to assent to it as something they feel in their whole being. But Pound, by adopting a peculiar method which depends upon the particularity of events, denied himself the possibility of access to this wisdom—except of course when he discarded his own theory, as he did in moments of poetic intensity. Traditional wisdom is much more than the sum of the various histories. Pound's individual wisdom, on the other hand, is limited to a knowledge of particular occurrences in which certain features seem to recur. When he was forced along certain lines, as in the case of prosody, where he had to submit to tradition in the shape of the language, or not do the job he had set out to do, then he was able to make use of tradition and do so with great success. But given his freedom, with no power to inform the *Cantos* beyond the power of his own mind, he undertook a work which was beyond his capacity, beyond, I should think, the capacity of any man, and was unable to prevent it from dispersing.

II

We gain a better insight into Pound's method, and the errors into which it led him in the *Cantos*, if we consider a typical incident

R

in his association with an English poet whose work he favoured. During the 1930's Pound in a letter to this poet attacked a well-known English economist, then of the London School of Economics, for refusing to face up to the facts of contemporary history. The implication was that a person who did not agree with certain economic theories, or Pound's interpretation of certain economic events, was out of touch with the whole cultural history of the time. In other words he was inclined to jump automatically from one's refusal to accept Douglas to the assumption that there was no place for you in the great stream of modern culture. However, as the recipient of the letter pointed out in reply, the economist in question was by no means a fool; he was in fact well-informed, with a good knowledge of at least some aspects of modern literature, and had introduced him to the early poetry of Eliot, before Eliot was well known. Transfer this method of thought to the *Cantos*, and we have:

> War, one war after another,
> Men start 'em who couldn't put up a good hen-roost.

This would be wonderful, if it were true; but it is not. Quite apart from the assumption that it is possible to lay the blame for wars on just the right shoulders, there is a gratuitous leap to the conclusion that these men are incompetents who lack the virtues of the American handyman. Pound did not draw his conclusion from a survey of the facts. No; he assumed his facts from his conclusion. And, in this case, the conclusion is all the more pernicious in that it is one we would all like to be true, all like to take refuge in, away from our responsibility for what goes on in the world around us.

One of the means used by Pound to bind the *Cantos* together is the repetition of an idea or nugget in various places through the poem. This is made possible by the fact that much of the basic material was gathered between 1900 and 1910, long before he had started on the actual writing of the work. Sometimes the repetition is of a person, as for instance Eleanor of Aquitaine, mentioned first in Canto 6 (written in 1921) and repeated several times in the later cantos, including Canto 94 (written about 1953). There are

numerous repetitions of this sort, some of them obvious and easy
to place, as for instance these references to the armaments vendor,
Sir Basil Zaharoff:

> I said 'I am interested.' And he went putty colour
> And said: 'He don't advertise. No, I don't think
> You will learn much.'
>
> (Canto 18)

> Taffy went putty-colour when I mentioned Zaharoff (1914)
> And General Whoosis, when he read the name, Aquarone,
> 30 years later
>
> (Canto 93)

At other times this device is not so effective and the allusions more
difficult to interpret:

> a little flame for a little
> conserved in the Imperial ballet, never danced in a theatre
> Kept as Justinian left it
>
> (Canto 77)

> Or Astafieva inside the street doors of the Wigmore
>
> . . .
>
> So Astafieva had conserved the tradition
> From Byzance and before then
>
> (Canto 79)

Astafieva was a Russian ballet dancer and teacher whom Pound
knew in London about 1918. It would appear that these passages
are meant to recall the same thing—a dance tradition preserved
since the time of Justinian or before, but one cannot be certain.
In some cases the solution lies in a good reference library, but there
are times when the facts accurately uncovered are no guide whatever to the poet's highly personal interpretation of them.

Some of the more important ideas in the poem are not only
repeated at intervals but also developed or widened as the poem
goes along. The suggestion in the *Spirit of Romance* (the chapter
'Poeti Latini') that probably 'the Renaissance brought in rhetoric

and all the attendant horrors', appears again twenty-five years later in Canto 46, but in a wider context:

> look about you, look, if you can, at St Peters
> Look at the Manchester slums, look at Brazilian coffee . . .

The rhetoric of Renaissance architecture is seen within the context of a world undermined by usury, a world in which 'the groggy church is gone toothless' (Canto 52) and no longer holds against the power of the usurers. About twenty years further on, in the *Rock-Drill* section, this idea is developed still further:

> so the arcivescovo fumbled round under his
>   ample overcloaks as to what might have been
> a left-hand back pocket of civil clothing
> and produced a cornucopia from 'La Tour'
> or as Augustine said, or as the Pope wrote to Augustine
>   'easier to convert after you feed 'em'
> but this was before St Peter's
>   in move towards a carrozza
> from the internal horrors (mosaic)
>   en route to Santa Sabina
>   & San Domenico
> where the spirit is clear in the stone
>   as against
> Filth of the Hyksos, butchers of lesser cattle.
>
>   (Canto 93)

There was a time, according to Pound, when the Church was blessed with the idea of plenty and fecundity, and architecture with a corresponding clearness of line, as opposed to the 'horrors' of the Renaissance. The earlier tendency was born of the 'agricultural' type of mind (stemming from the Greek grain goddess Demeter and her Sumerian counterpart, Ashnan), which, about the time of St. Peter's, was forced out of power by the shepherd or 'butchers of lesser cattle' mentality—those who think in terms of feeding their animals for what they can get out of them later. The Hyksos, an alien people who ruled ancient Egypt for a time, are included in this passage because they were known as 'the Shepherd Kings'. This same idea is mentioned again in various ways in the *Thrones* Cantos:

> Ambrose:
> 'First treason: shepherd to flock.'
> and they want it apochryphal.

The quotation 'First treason: shepherd to flock' is really a loose paraphrase from the latin work *De Moribus Brachmanorum*, sometimes attributed to St. Ambrose.[1] Pound's comment 'and they want it apocryphal' is his way of saying that the work is definitely by St. Ambrose, but that churchmen of the 'butchers of lesser cattle' variety have managed to question its authenticity and throw doubt upon its importance.

Many of the errors in the *Cantos* are errors of fact, rather than of method, but there are other occasions when Pound enlarges his ideas beyond what we might call their factual basis. When he says that everything beneath the moon is under the pagan goddess Fortuna, he does not seem to realize that for many pagans this was not so. Much of the popularity of Isis was due to the fact that she could cancel Fortune, even on earth: 'I am victorious over Destiny; Destiny obeyeth me.' Oversimplifications of this kind are unavoidable in a work like the *Cantos*: no man, no ten men, could ever know enough to keep all the threads tight in a work of such magnitude. There are other faults, however, which stem directly from Pound's method. The approach which he derived from Fenollosa, when applied to the *Cantos*, caused him to arrange, at first, blocks of history, mythology and anecdote in such a way that one is able to see what the arrangement suggests; but more and more as the work progressed he introduced particular examples which are noted with extreme brevity, remaining isolated and beyond the power of the reader to connect with anything else in the poem. In Canto 97 the lines:

> And out of Scanda in Colchis,
> Getes had been in Cythera
> (vide Pausanias, the Laconics)

have no meaning by themselves. Obviously, if they do have a meaning within the poem, it is because they connect up with some

---

[1] A new edition of this work (latin text only) was published at Pound's instigation in Milan in 1956.

other part of it. Unable to discover this link we are driven, finally, to look up Pound's source, Del Mar's *History of Monetary Systems*, chapter XII of the Chicago edition of 1896, where we read that in the eighth century the Goths were destroyed or dispersed by Charlemagne, and escaped to countries now known as Denmark, Sweden and Norway, and collectively as Scandinavia. Attached to this information is a footnote: 'Scanda was the name of a Getic city in Colchis, and Scandea that of a Getic seaport at the extremity of Cythera, a large island off the southern coast of Greece. Pausanias in *Laconics*.' Out of this slender evidence Pound may be implying that there was some connection between the Goths and the goddess of love, Aphrodite of Cythera; the matter hardly seems worth pursuing; it is a leftover from the superficial tracing of tribal and racial origins so popular among anthropologists and historians in the nineteenth century. Sometimes the brevity of Pound's examples is beyond even the patient reader's endurance, for instance when he copies the name 'Andoleon of Paeonia' from a passing reference to his coinage in Del Mar's *Monetary Systems*. This is probably the same king who is listed in the British Museum's *Guide to the Principal Coins of the Greeks* as Audoleon: 'Patraus and Audoleon reigned over Paeonia between 340 and 286 B.C.' But why Pound mentions him in Canto 97 remains a matter for speculation. Elsewhere in the same Canto we are told that 'Upsala, was the golden fane', in a context which suggests that this Gothic temple was somehow connected with a holy pagan tradition which did not allow blood sacrifices. Turning to Pound's source, *Monetary Systems* (p. 273), we read in a footnote that 'Adam of Bremen described the temple of Upsala as being roofed with gold and filled with the greatest riches'. So far so good. But when we turn the page and see that 'pagan sacrifices smoked upon the polluted altars of Upsala', it is difficult to know what Pound means or why he included such a reference.

It may be argued that these faults occur only towards the end of the work, in the *Thrones* section, where the poem no longer holds together; but other weaknesses of method, such as his tendency to convert what are, or may be, social politenesses into definite statements of conviction or principle bearing the stamp of a lifetime's hard thinking, can be found in the earlier sections of the work. In Canto 19, first published in 1925, he quotes the Sinn Fein leader, Arthur Griffith, as saying: 'Can't move 'em,' meaning people in the political mass, 'with a cold thing like economics'. This statement, according to Pound, was the Irishman's reply to his own attempt to interest him in economics, but instead of treating it in this light, as an interesting statement, but one uttered nevertheless in circumstances which suggest polite evasion, he gradually turns it, in the course of the poem, into a nugget of wisdom. But this is not the only example, by any means, of this procedure, although it is to be found more often towards the end of the poem than in the earlier Cantos. I will mention two more cases so that the reader may gain some idea of the extent to which this fault weakens the texture of the work. In Canto 95, in the *Rock-Drill* series, where the actual writing is sharp and clear evincing no decline in power, he quotes the Spanish philosopher George Santayana:

> 'Something *there*.'
> sd/ Santayana.

in support of his own idea about 'the intelligence working in nature' which enables the cherry-stone to grow cherry trees rather than oaks. But when we turn to the *Letters of George Santayana* we find that the letter from which this is taken (Santayana to Pound, Rome, 7 February 1950) does not warrant the interpretation given to it by Pound; the finality and assertiveness have been put there by Pound, not by the man who wrote the letter; Santayana simply says: 'somehow it possesses a capacity to develop other cherries under favourable circumstances, without getting anything vital wrong. That is "intelligence" of an unconscious sort. I agree in "respecting it". (It would be fussy to object to your word intelligence to describe that potentiality in the cherrystone).' Santayana gives Pound the hint in the word 'potentiality' that the matter had already been dealt with in some detail by certain philosophers in the past, but Pound does not heed him. As usual, he cannot see beyond the message he is trying to drum into his correspondent's head. In the same Canto we are informed, very briefly, that Van Buren had been engaged in 'unsmearing Talleyrand'. Since the name Talleyrand is a synonym for deviousness (Pound expressed disgust at his scheming in the middle Cantos) we assume, on reading this line, that Van Buren had gone into the subject and produced material which shows Talleyrand in a new light. The passage in Van Buren's Autobiography, from which Pound composed this line, turns out, however, to be a few lines on the pleasantness of the aged Talleyrand's company when Van Buren met him in London as United States ambassador during the 1830's.

The Cantos composed before the Second World War, and the *Pisan* sequence, are carried along, despite flaws, by the force of Pound's artistry, which not only produces great writing, but also the general directions to enable the reader to negotiate the maze. The flaws begin to have a more serious effect in the *Rock-Drill* Cantos, starting with the first page of Canto 85, where a subject as difficult as the Galileo story is summarized in the words: 'Galileo index'd 1616'—not, let me say, after a study of the evidence (which is quite different in some ways from the popular notion of the case) but by way of an inconsequential reference in the late Russell Grenfell's *Unconditional Hatred*, a book about the Second World War. Grenfell was an important naval historian, but hardly to be taken as an authority on Galileo. By the time Pound wrote the *Thrones* section, between about 1954 and 1959, he was no longer able to hold the work together; not so much because of any deterioration in the writing, but for the reason that the meaning which he had hoped would emerge as the poem moved towards its end, did not in fact appear. As a result he was driven to impose a patently false 'theology' and 'meaning' upon some of the *Rock-Drill* Cantos and the whole of *Thrones*, a 'theology' and 'meaning' made up of shreds derived from Catholic theology, Chinese philosophers, pagan writers like Philostratus, the works of Del Mar and L. A. Waddell, and fragments remembered from his early reading. Under this pressure to find some way of making the poem into a whole he returned to his earlier view of the pagan gods and miracles—or perhaps I should say, to his earlier way of presenting these gods and miracles—which he had abandoned after the false start to the Cantos in 1917; he returned to this method or convention, and began to treat them as realities in the actual world. One can sympathize with Pound in his predicament, but not with the result.

III

Surveying the eight hundred pages of the poem as it now stands, from 'And then went down to the ship' in Canto 1, to 'You in the dinghey (piccioletta) astern there!' in Canto 109, we are able to draw out certain general ideas, not by chance, but because the poet, by his selection of material and groupings, has put them there: they are the form of the poem, in so far as it has a form. There is the voyage back into the past, and the achievements of Pound's heroes, the creators; recurrences and parallels in history; glimpses of a world which endures, over and above its incarnations in the churning sea of matter and movement; a detailed account of John Adams, the wise and temperate leader, in action; and in the Chinese Cantos Pound's record of Confucianism in history—'the only process that has repeatedly proved its efficiency as a social coordinate'. Most of the Cantos up to the end of *Rock-Drill* appear to fit somewhere within these categories. It is not until we get to *Thrones*, where these general ideas should be drawn into a single category which has more meaning than the sum of its parts, that the hopelessness of Pound's endeavour becomes obvious.[1] Actually, the panic which is clear in *Thrones*, was already present in parts of *Rock-Drill*; in his need, for example, to bring in new heroes like Apollonius of Tyana, and new heroines, not because he really needed them, but to keep the work in progress in the hope that something would turn up that would enable him to bring it to a just conclusion. Note also that in Canto 91, where he praises virgins and women who have had dealings with divinity, he refuses to include Mary, the implications of whose presence, were it more than a passing reference,

---

[1] Sections from later Cantos which have appeared in magazine form since the publication of *Thrones* do not add anything to what is already there—they are just more of the same thing.

might force the work towards a conclusion which the main bulk of it could not possibly sustain. The Confucian individual must be self-sustaining; there is no place in Confucianism for a 'Refuge of Sinners', a saint in heaven to whom man may apply for strength and comfort. The final collapse of the work in *Thrones* is nowhere more evident than in the poet's frantic efforts to pin together an age-old religious tradition that will not clash with Confucius or the determination to exclude Original Sin (the 'hex-hoax'). In order to show the extent of this collapse and of Pound's recourse to questionable materials, it is essential, if I am to make my meaning clear, that I supply a detailed examination of two separate parts of the *Thrones* section.

Towards the end of Canto 97, he begins to trace his religious 'tradition' back to the *Rig-Veda* of ancient India. This is stated rather briefly in the words: 'Aswins drawing the rain-cloud', the Aswins being some sort of Aryan spirit. Several lines further on we find the words:

> From Sargon of Agade
> > a thousand years before T'ang

accompanied by a rough sketch of an ancient seal and a name written in cuneiform script. Then follows this passage:

> gothic art out of India,
> > from Multan 700 *li*,
> > torchlight, at Multan, offer perfume,
> Son of Herakles, Napat son of Waters,
> > Panch, that is Phoenician, Tyanu
> > > lion head
> Came then autumn in April and
> > 'By Knoch Many now King Minos lies',
> From Sargon to Tyana
> > > no blood on the altar stone.

The words 'lion head' are accompanied by the sketch of a lion's head. The general idea behind this section is that there is some common religion binding all these elements into one, a religion stretching from the *Rig-Veda* of India, and Sargon of Mesopotamia, down through Minos of Crete and the Phoenicians, to the kingdom of Tyana, whence sprung Apollonius, one of Pound's heroes in *Rock-Drill*. Now Pound did not derive this idea of a long tradition from any study of the many texts and works of reference on these subjects, which have been available for some years, but from the works of L. A. Waddell, a nineteenth-century explorer, historian and philologist, who lived on into the present century and propagated the theory that the inhabitants of England are the true descendants of the ancient Aryans—these latter being the creators of all civilization. The works used by Pound for most of his information were: *Indo-Sumerian Seals Deciphered, Egyptian Civilization and Its Sumerian Origin, Makers of Civilization*, and the *British Edda*. *Indo-Sumerian Seals* was published in London in 1925, the other works about the same time. The line about Aswins drawing the rain-cloud has its origin in a passage from the *Rig-Veda*, quoted by Waddell on page 42 of *Indo-Sumerian Seals*: 'Bountiful Aswins, by whose aid the cloud shed sweet rain.' The information on the gothic arch (Pound had already noted 'the correspondences of Indian to Gothic Art' in *Spirit of Romance*) is from a footnote on page 103 of the same work by Waddell:

See my report on Mission for collecting Indo-Scythic Sculptures, Beng. Govt. Press, 1895; and in Trans. Internat. Orient. Cong., Paris, 1897, sec. I, 245 f., which disclosed the Gothic arch there in sculptures of second to third centuries A.D., i.e., about a thousand years before its supposed origin.

The references to the holy place Multan are from the writings of the Buddhist pilgrim and geographer Hiuen Tsiang, quoted by Waddell on page 108:

There is a temple dedicated to the Sun, very magnificent and profusely decorated . . . Women play their music, light their torches, offer their flowers and perfumes . . . They have founded a house of mercy . . .

while the references to Herakles and the son of Herakles which follow, are from statements by Waddell:

Assias, 'one of the most famous ancient Aryan Vedic Fire-priests . . . he is styled as we shall see, "the far-famed merchant"; and he nearly always associates himself, and is associated, with the Panch (-ala), i.e., the Phoenicians . . .' (p. 9). '. . . the Vedic Sanskrit *Napat*, or "son of the Waters" . . .' (p. 127). '. . . son of Herakles . . .' (p. 130).

Herakles ('Izzax of Erek') has a lion head, according to Waddell's reading of the ancient seals (p. 134).

The line ' "By Knoch Many now King Minos lies" ' (a reminder of Pound's prosodic skill) stems from Waddell's theory (*Egyptian Civilization*) that King Menes of pre-dynastic Egypt was the same as Manis of Mesopotamia and Minos of Crete. According to this explanation, the Ebony Labels at Abydos in Egypt are written in Sumerian script and tell how Menes died in Ireland. Engravings on prehistoric stones at New Grange on the Boyne River, near Drogheda, are essentially replicas of Sumerian and Hittite sacred seals, Waddell says, and engravings found at Knoch-Many ('The Hill of Many') near Clogher on the southern border of County Tyrone practically identical with the Ebony Labels at Abydos. Whether anybody is in a position to disprove what Waddell says, I do not know; certainly some of his dating does not agree with more recent findings; but what concerns us here is the manner in which Pound published this material. This was not something he had read about from many different angles and pondered until it had become a part of him; he used the first thing that came his way which seemed to offer a way out of his dead-end. Nor is his use of Waddell an isolated instance: almost the whole of *Thrones* is put together in this way. When Pound tells us in Canto 100 that half the land and slaves in the Roman Empire belonged to the pagan temples, implying that the struggle over this wealth was somehow connected with the attaching of the label 'Apostate' to the Emperor Julian, we have a right to expect that he has based his statement upon a study of at least some of the documents and is acquainted with the general trend of such studies in his own time. The wealth of the pagan temples played an important part in the history of the Empire in the fourth century, as we see in a general way from Gibbon's twentieth chapter; but Pound is far more definite than Gibbon, and we might be led to suppose that this was due to his having gone into the matter more thoroughly than the learned historian of Rome's decline and fall. This is not so, however: Pound's hunch is based upon a number of vaguely documented passages in two books by Del Mar: *The Middle Ages Revisited* and *Ancient Britain Revisited*, both published in 1900. On page 60 of *Ancient Britain* Del Mar says, in dealing with religious unrest at the time of Gratian: 'As the established (pagan) church owned half the lands and slaves of Europe, avidity may have also had something to do with it.' I have not been able to discover how he arrived at his estimate of 'half'. He continues:

Gratian's measure was no less than the confiscation of all the lands, slaves, treasures, benefices, revenues, privileges, and livings of the Roman church throughout the Western Empire, which he declared to be of right the property of the imperial fisc, and which he withdrew from its pagan, to bestow upon Christian incumbents, many of whom, like Ambrose and Augustine, had been recently converted from the polytheistic, the Julian or Augustan, the Bacchic, the Manichaean, and other idolatrous or mythological worships.

There are several similar statements in *The Middle Ages Revisited*. Working from this evidence, Pound took it upon himself to correct the history of Rome and to hint at the influence of the ever-present usurers at a turning-point in the history of the Christian Church, without specifying what part they might have played. It may be that Pound's intuition about the corrosive effect of usury is right; but what truth, if any, he has seen, has been lost again beneath the rubble and waste dredged up by his false method. There is no virtue in using language that is hard and clear, if it is merely to disguise the trickiness of your material and method; nor any achievement to use cryptic phrases, with a ring of profundity about them, if it is only to veil what you dare not say clearly and in language that will enable the reader to test your depth.

There could be little quarrel if the poet exercised the right now and again to disagree with academic and accepted history and back his own fancies, or if he had soaked himself in these ideas drawn from many cultures, so that they had become a part of his outlook; but in *Thrones* we are faced with a poem that is almost entirely made up of questionable material disguised as profundity—material drawn together, not because believed in, as Yeats believed in his magic, but desperately because the poet wanted to give his work the semblance of depth and design as it neared its conclusion. There may be something to be said for the single assumption in history, which fills a gap between facts, but a series of assumptions supporting each other, if turned into a method, does away with the whole concept of history as we agree to accept it. If Pound's method were less arbitrary than the one we already use, then it would be an advance and we should have to adopt it, slowly perhaps, but eventually; but in reality it is something of a parody of the present method, with all the checks and safeguards removed.

There is another objection to Pound's use of material in *Thrones*, which I will mention very briefly. In the case of a number of items (the Muan Bpö ceremony, for instance, in Cantos 98, 101, 104), he uses material which appears to have a reasonable source, but he does not get his meaning into the poem. In several cases, even the source, when consulted, tells us nothing of what the poet intends, so that the meaning, if it exists at all, remains in the poet's head. A few of the lines in *Thrones* are simply isolated phrases taken from stories which Pound has in mind but has not committed to writing, either in poetry or prose. So unless you have had the story direct from Pound, or an accurate version of it secondhand, there is no way that you can possibly know what the phrase in question means.

By adopting, after a fashion, the methods of legitimate history Pound forfeited the possibility of being able to put his history forward in the form of poetic intuitions; and then, by falsifying the methods of legitimate history, lost what claim he might have had upon our attention as a legitimate historian.

IV

The *Cantos* is a tragedy: it mirrors the tragedy of man in the twentieth century in a way that is unique. The very materials gathered there by the master craftsman who is its creator testify to the hollowness of his conception of man, and the terrible hollowness of the men he would honour by this conception. We live in an age in which men can only think in terms of quantity and measurement. They are unable to conceive of a universe that is not simply the sum of its mechanical parts, however complex. A universe transformed by the presence of another world, the world of spirit, is quite foreign to them. Nor can they comprehend the idea of there being a mysterious and non-measurable thing called moral evil, the introduction of which brought about, and is still bringing about, a chain of events which completely eludes the mind obsessed with matter. Pound's world is not really very different from that of the prosperous commercial classes of the past century and a half, for whom dishonesty and cheating are almost the worst possible offences a man may commit. For the Confucian, as for the Victorian husband of comfortable means, the sly thief is not a sinner whose act of perfect contrition may place him among the blessed, but an unmentionable cad who has polluted the social workings and is best put out of mind just as soon as the administrative details can be settled. The Confucian idea of society, like the best secular ideas of our own time, is one in which a certain type of social honesty and frankness rank far above charity and chastity. Charity is tolerable, so long as it doesn't hurt, and chastity is nobody's business, so long as it doesn't get into the newspapers; if it does it becomes an occasion for lust and polite regret, and perhaps for a certain amount of social manœuvring.

Pound saw past this narrow view of the world, into a world that is very different, but he was forced by something in his temperament and character to remain an onlooker, who could never really share the thoughts and beliefs which excited his intelligence. He appreciated the mild satire of Ford's poem 'Süssmund's Address to an Unknown God', with its assault upon those who have

> Perjured themselves in courts, and sworn false oaths
> With all the skill of Protestant British tradesmen
> Plundering a Papist and a foreigner
> With God on their lips
>
> . . .

> —Adultery, foul murder, pleasant things,
> A touch of incest, theft, but no Reformers.
>
>   .   .   .
>
>   in such a heaven
> Where there's no feeling of the moral pulse,
> I think I'd find some peace—with treachery
> Of the Sword and Dagger kind to keep it sweet.

but he could not understand it, as Ford did, in his whole being. Pound appreciated this other world and did much to illustrate it, but always he remained outside it, never taking part in it, from within, because such a course would have required submission of a kind he was not disposed to accept.

The mind of man is so constituted that it acts properly only when under a certain kind of pressure or discipline. Pound belonged to an age which had thrown this discipline aside and plunged into the 'absolute' in search of All-Knowledge. The result was to reduce knowledge to quantity and measurement, so that in the end no knowledge existed that was not quantitative and measurable; and the men who had thrown off all 'chains', with the intention of sailing beyond the beyond, settled finally for a world of inane gadgetry. Pound opposed this world, sometimes with all his might and with memorable skill; but he was a part of it in a way that drove him to create a long poem that mirrors the mind of man freed from restraint. The mind that is 'free' has nothing to rest on, it is incomplete; only through discipline, devotion and submission can it find the support which supplies its integrity.

Select Bibliography

I

EZRA POUND

A Lume Spento	A. Antonini, Venice, 1908.
A Quinzaine for This Yule	Pollock and Co., London, 1908.
Personae	Elkin Mathews, London, 1909.
Exultations	Elkin Mathews, London, 1909.
The Spirit of Romance	J. M. Dent and Co., London, 1910 (Peter Owen, London, 1952).
Canzoni	Elkin Mathews, London, 1911.
Gaudier-Brzeska: A Memoir	John Lane, The Bodley Head, London, 1916 (The Marvell Press, Hessle, Yorkshire, 1960).
Quia Pauper Amavi	The Egoist Ltd, London, 1919.
Poems 1918–21	Boni and Liveright, New York, 1921.
The Natural Philosophy of Love	by Remy de Gourmont, translated with a postscript by Ezra Pound, Boni and Liveright, New York, 1922 (Neville Spearman, London, 1957).
Antheil and the Treatise on Harmony	Three Mountains Press, Paris, 1924. (The *Treatise on Harmony* was published with *Patria Mia*, under the title *Patria Mia and the Treatise on Harmony*, Peter Owen, London, 1962.)
Personae: The Collected Poems of Ezra Pound	Boni and Liveright, New York, 1926 (Faber and Faber, London, 1952; contains a few poems not in the 1926 edition).
ABC of Economics	Faber and Faber, London, 1933 (Peter Russell, Tunbridge Wells, 1953).
ABC of Reading	G. Routledge and Sons, Ltd, London, 1934 (Faber and Faber, London, 1951).
Make it New	Faber and Faber, London, 1934.
Jefferson and/or Mussolini	Stanley Nott, London, 1935.
The Chinese Written Character as a Medium for Poetry	by Ernest Fenollosa, foreword and notes by Ezra Pound. Stanley Nott, London, 1936 (Square Dollar Series, Washington, D.C., 1951).
Polite Essays	Faber and Faber, London, 1937.
Guide to Kulchur	Faber and Faber, London, 1938 (Peter Owen, London, 1952).
The Unwobbling Pivot and The Great Digest	by Confucius, translated by Ezra Pound. With Chinese text. Peter Owen, London, 1952. (First published New Directions, Norfolk, Connecticut, 1947, but without Chinese text.)

S

The Cantos	Nos. 1–84, including the *Pisan Cantos*. New Directions, Norfolk, Connecticut, 1948 (Faber and Faber, London, 1954).
The Letters of Ezra Pound	Edited by D. D. Paige, Harcourt, Brace & Co., New York, 1950 (Faber and Faber, London, 1951).
The Confucian Analects	Translated by Ezra Pound, Square Dollar Series, New York, 1951 (Peter Owen, London, 1956; with an additional note called 'Procedure').
The Translations of Ezra Pound	Faber and Faber, London, 1953.
The Classic Anthology Defined by Confucius	Translated by Ezra Pound, Harvard University Press, 1954 (Faber and Faber, London, 1955) (usually referred to as 'The Confucian Odes').
The Literary Essays of Ezra Pound	Edited with an Introduction by T. S. Eliot, Faber and Faber, London, 1954.
Section: Rock-Drill	Cantos 85–95. Scheiwiller, Milan, 1955 (Faber and Faber, London, 1957).
The Women of Trachis	by Sophocles, translated by Ezra Pound, Neville Spearman, London, 1956.
Rimbaud	Scheiwiller, Milan, 1957. Although called simply 'Rimbaud by Ezra Pound' this small book consists of four pieces by Rimbaud and one by Laurent Tailhade, translated by Ezra Pound.
Pavannes and Divagations	New Directions, Norfolk, Connecticut, 1958 (Peter Owen, London, 1960). Drawn largely from *Pavannes and Divisions*, 1918, and *Instigations*, 1920.
Thrones	Cantos 96–109. Scheiwiller, Milan, 1959 (Faber and Faber, London, 1960).
Impact	Edited by Noel Stock, Henry Regnery, Chicago, 1960. Previously uncollected writings on economics, politics, history and the arts.
Love Poems of Ancient Egypt	Translated by Ezra Pound and Noel Stock, New Directions, Norfolk, Connecticut, 1962.

Some of the more important uncollected writings of Ezra Pound quoted from or referred to in this book (with their page references)

II

LITERATURE, THE CANTOS

BRIDSON, D. G., 'An Interview with Ezra Pound', *New Directions 17*, New Directions, Norfolk, Connecticut, 1961. Edited from BBC Third Programme broadcasts of July 1959.

CORY, DANIEL (editor), *The Letters of George Santayana*, New York, 1955.

DEL MAR, ALEXANDER, *History of Monetary Systems*, Charles H. Kerr and Company, Chicago, 1896. Contains material not in the English edition of 1895.

—— *Barbara Villiers, A History of Monetary Crimes*, The Cambridge Encyclopedia Co., New York, 1899. Also, Square Dollar Series, Washington, D.C., 1951.

—— *The Middle Ages Revisited*, Cambridge Encyclopedia Company, New York, 1900.

—— *Ancient Britain Revisited. Ancient Britain in the Light of Modern Archaeological Discoveries*, Cambridge Encyclopedia Company, New York, 1900.

ELIOT, T. S., 'The Method of Mr. Pound', *Athenaeum*, London, 24 October 1919.

—— 'Isolated Superiority', *Dial*, New York, January 1928.

FORD, *see* Hueffer.

GRENFELL, RUSSELL, *Unconditional Hatred*, The Devin-Adair Company, New York, 1954.

HUEFFER (FORD), FORD MADOX, *Collected Poems*, Max Goschen Ltd, London, 1914.

HULME, T. E., *Speculations*, Routledge and Kegan Paul, London, new ed. 1960.

—— *Further Speculations*, edited by S. Hynes, Oxford, 1955.

WADDELL, L. A., *Indo-Sumerian Seals Deciphered*, Luzac and Co., London, 1925.

—— *Egyptian Civilization and Its Sumerian Origin and Real Chronology*, Luzac and Co., London, 1930.

—— *The British Edda*, Luzac and Co., London, 1930.

III

Religion, Philosophy

CROMBIE, A. C., *Augustine to Galileo*, 2 vols., Mercury Books, London, 1961.

CUMONT, FRANZ, *Oriental Religions in Roman Paganism*, Dover Publications, New York, 1956.

—— *The Mysteries of Mithra*, Dover Publications, New York, 1956.

FESTUGIÈRE, ANDRÉ-JEAN, O.P., *Personal Religion Among the Greeks*, University of California Press, Berkeley and Los Angeles, 1960.

HARRISON, JANE, *Prolegomena to the Study of the Greek Religion*, Cambridge University Press, 1922.

LANG, ANDREW, *Custom and Myth*, London, 1885.

TURGOT, A. R. J., *Oeuvres*, t. 1, Paris, 1913.

TYLOR, E. B., *Researches into the Early History of Mankind and the Development of Civilization*, London, edition of 1870.

KIRCHBERGER, CLARE (trans. and ed.), *Richard of St-Victor, Selected Writings on Contemplation*, Faber and Faber, London, 1957.

UPWARD, ALLEN, *The Divine Mystery*, Garden City Press, Letchworth, 1913.

WESTON, JESSIE L., *From Ritual to Romance*, Doubleday Anchor Books, New York, 1957.

WIND, EDGAR, *Pagan Mysteries in the Renaissance*, Faber and Faber, London, 1958.

IV

American History

ARRINGTON, LEONARD, J., 'The Mormon Tithing House', *Business History Review*, Vol. XXVIII, No. 1, Harvard, March 1954.

BEHRENS, KATHRYN, L., *Paper Money in Maryland, 1727–1789*, The Johns Hopkins Press, Baltimore, 1923.

DAVIS, L. E., AND HUGHES, J. R. T., 'A Dollar-Sterling Exchange, 1803–1895', *Economic History Review*, Second Series, Vol. XIII, No. 1, Utrecht, August 1960.

FERGUSON, E. JAMES, 'Business, Government, and Congressional Investigation in the Revolution', *William and Mary Quarterly*, Third Series, Vol. XVI, No. 3, Williamsburg, Virginia, July 1959.

GRAS, N. S. B., AND LARSON, H. M., *A Casebook in American Business History*, Appleton, New York, 1939.

HAMMOND, BRAY, *Banks and Politics in America from the Revolution to the Civil War*, Princeton University Press, 1957.

HANDLIN, OSCAR AND MARY F., 'Revolutionary Economic Policy in Massachusetts', *William and Mary Quarterly*, Third Series, Vol. IV, No. 1, Williamsburg, January 1947.

HIDY, RALPH W., *The House of Baring in American Trade and Finance*, Harvard University Press, 1949.

JENKS, LELAND HAMILTON, *The Migration of British Capital to 1875*, Alfred A. Knopf, New York and London, 1927.

KEMMERER, DONALD L., 'Financing Illinois Industry, 1830–1890', *Bulletin of the Business Historical Society*, Vol. XXVII, No. 2, Harvard, June 1953.

MITCHELL, BROADUS, *Alexander Hamilton, Youth to Maturity, 1755–1788,* The Macmillan Company, New York, 1957.

MORGAN, H. WAYNE, 'The Origins and Establishment of the First Bank of the United States', *Business History Review,* Vol. XXX, No. 4, Harvard, December 1956.

SHAFER, ANITA, 'The Williams Brothers, Merchants and Shippers', *Bulletin of the Business Historical Society,* Vol. XXVI, No. 2, Harvard, June 1952.

SOLTOW, J. H., 'Scottish Traders in Virginia, 1750–1775', *Economic History Review,* Vol. XII, No. 1, Utrecht, August 1959.

Presidential Messages and State Papers, Review of Reviews Company, New York, 1917.

V

BANKING IN THE MIDDLE AGES, THE JUST PRICE

BALDWIN, JOHN W., 'The Medieval Theories of the Just Price', *Transactions of the American Philosophical Society,* New Series, Vol. 49, Part 4, Philadelphia, 1959.

BARATH, DÉSIRÉ, 'The Just Price and the Cost of Production according to St Thomas Aquinas', *The New Scholasticism,* XXXIV, 1960.

CASTELLI, ENRICO, *I Banchi Feneratizi Ebraici nel Mantovano, 1386–1808,* Banca Agricola Mantovana, Mantova, 1959.

CIPOLLA, CARLO M., *Money, Prices and Civilization in the Mediterranean World, Fifth to Seventeenth Century,* Princeton University Press, for University of Cincinnati, 1956.

GRICE-HUTCHINSON, M., *The School of Salamanca: Readings in Spanish Monetary Theory 1544–1605,* Oxford, 1952.

HOLMES, G. A., 'Florentine Merchants in England, 1346–1436', *Economic History Review,* Second Series, Vol. XIII, No. 2, Utrecht, December 1960.

LOPEZ, R. S., AND MISKIMIN, H. A., 'The Economic Depression of the Renaissance', *Economic History Review,* Second Series, Vol. XIV, No. 3, Utrecht, April 1962.

NELSON, BENJAMIN, *The Idea of Usury,* Princeton University Press, 1949.

NOONAN, JOHN T., JR., *The Scholastic Analysis of Usury,* Harvard University Press, 1957.

ROOVER, RAYMOND DE, *Money, Banking, and Credit in Mediaeval Bruges: Italian Merchant-Bankers, Lombards, and Money-Changers,* The Mediaeval Academy of America, Cambridge, Mass., 1948.

—— *The Medici Bank,* New York University Press and Oxford, 1948. A greatly enlarged version, *The Rise and Decline of the Medici Bank, 1397–1494,* Harvard University Press, 1963.

—— 'New Perspectives on the History of Accounting', *The Accounting Review,* Vol. XXX, No. 3, July 1955.

—— 'Cambium Ad Venetias: Contribution to the History of Foreign Exchange', *Studi in Onore di Armando Sapori,* Instituto Editoriale Cisalpino, Milano-Varese, 1957.

—— 'The Story of the Alberti Company of Florence, 1302–1348, As Revealed in Its Account Books', *Business History Review,* Vol. XXXII, No. 1, Harvard, Spring 1958.

ROOVER, RAYMOND DE, 'The Concept of the Just Price: Theory and Economic Policy, *Journal of Economic History*, Vol. XVIII, December 1958.

—— 'La Balance Commerciale entre les Pays-Bas et l'Italie au quinzième siècle', *Revue belge de Philologie et d'Histoire*, t. XXXVII, No. 2, Bruxelles, 1959.

VI

MONETARY HISTORY

BLOOMFIELD, ARTHUR I., *Monetary Policy under the International Gold Standard: 1880–1914*, Federal Reserve Bank of New York, New York, 1959.

BOLIN, STURE, *State and Currency in the Roman Empire*, Almquist and Wiksell, Stockholm, 1958.

BOYCE, LEIGHTON J. A. S. L., *Smiths the Bankers 1658–1958*, National Provincial Bank, London, 1958.

BROWN, DELMER M., *Money Economy in Medieval Japan*, the Institute of Far Eastern Languages, Yale University, for the Far Eastern Association, 1951.

CARSON, R. A. G., AND SUTHERLAND, C. H. V. (editors), *Essays in Roman Coinage presented to Harold Mattingly*, Oxford, 1956.

DUNNING, JOHN H., 'The Present Role of U.S. Investment in British Industry', *Moorgate and Wall Street*, a review issued by Philip Hill, Higginson, Erlangers Ltd (London), and Harriman Ripley and Co. (New York), Spring 1961.

—— 'British Investment in U.S. Industry', *Moorgate and Wall Street*, Philip Hill, Higginson, Erlangers Ltd (London), and Harriman Ripley and Co. (New York), Autumn 1961.

—— 'U.K. Capital Exports and Canadian Economic Development', *Moorgate and Wall Street*, Philip Hill, Higginson, Erlangers Ltd (London), and Harriman Ripley and Co. (New York), Spring 1962.

EMDEN, PAUL H., *Money Powers of Europe in the Nineteenth and Twentieth Centuries*, Sampson Low, Marston and Co., London, n.d., but apparently issued sometime between 1939 and 1945.

INTERNATIONAL MONETARY FUND, *International Reserves and Liquidity*, I.M.F., Washington, D.C., 1958.

LANDES, DAVID S., *Bankers and Pashas. International Finance and Economic Imperialism in Egypt*, Heinemann, London, 1958.

PONTECORVO, GIULIO, 'Investment Banking and Security Speculation in the Late 1920's', *Business History Review*, Vol. XXXII, No. 2, Harvard, Summer 1958.

ROOSA, ROBERT V., *Federal Reserve Operations in the Money and Government Securities Markets*, Federal Reserve Bank of New York, New York, 1956.

SCHLOSS, H. H., *The Bank for International Settlements*, North-Holland Publishing Company, Amsterdam, 1958.

Index